Mapping the Pitch

UCFB

Dedicated to Jimmy Hogan

Coaching Visionary

'HE USED TO SAY FOOTBALL WAS LIKE A VIENNESE WALTZ, A RHAPSODY. ONE-TWO-THREE, ONE-TWO-THREE, PASS-MOVE-PASS, PASS-MOVE-PASS. WE WERE SAT THERE, GLUED TO OUR SEATS, BECAUSE WE WERE SO KEEN TO LEARN.'

Tommy Docherty

Edward Couzens-Lake

MAPPING
THE PITCH

Football Formations Through the Ages

Meyer & Meyer Sport

British Library Cataloguing in Publication Data
A catalogue record for this book is available from the British Library

Mapping the Pitch – Football Formations Through the Ages
Maidenhead: Meyer & Meyer Sport (UK) Ltd., 2015
ISBN: 978-1-78255-060-0

796.334

© 2015 by Meyer & Meyer Sport (UK) Ltd.
Aachen, Auckland, Beirut, Cairo, Cape Town, Dubai, Hägendorf, Hong Kong,
Indianapolis, Manila, New Delhi, Singapore, Sydney, Tehran, Vienna
🕮 Member of the World Sport Publishers' Association (WSPA)
Printed & Binded: CPI – Clausen & Bosse, Leck, Germany
ISBN: 978-1-78255-060-0
E-Mail: info@m-m-sports.com
www.m-m-sports.com

TABLE OF CONTENTS

PROLOGUE

*The Romans were, of course, famous for the military formation
known as the Testudo, or Tortoise, one that Giovanni Trapattoni,
a master of organisation and discipline, would have been proud
to call his own.*

Football, like so many things in life, beloved or not, was invented by the English.

Alas, also like so many things in life, it almost certainly wasn't. What they did do for the game was burden it with its very first set of rules and regulations, applying bureaucracy to a game in much the same way they had done to the countries in their Empire.

Countries, cultures and societies that exercise a claim to *inventing* the world's greatest game (probably) and its second greatest obsession (possibly) are numerous. A game that involved using the feet in kicking, and propelling an object of sorts has certainly been recorded in both Ancient Greek and Roman history, with the Roman version, known as *hapastum* thought to have been a bastardised variant of the even earlier Greek version. Who knows, perhaps the Romans, style and form ever to the forefront even on the battlefield, included the first on-field *trequartista* in their noble ranks – an early Andrea Pirlo, resplendent in toga and sandals?

The Romans were, of course, famous for the military formation known as the *Testudo*, or Tortoise, one that Giovanni Trapattoni, a master of organisation and discipline, would have been proud to call his own. Testudo involved a group of around 36 Roman legionaries advancing into battle in such a manner that they were completely protected by their shields. The soldiers at the front held their shields in front of them whilst those at the sides held them outwards and those in the middle of the advancing rectangle would hold their shields over their heads. The result of this was effectively a mobile metal box that contained all of the men safely within its protective confines.

Not particularly pretty, not particularly fast or exciting, but very effective. Italian pragmatism in the mould of some of their national football teams. Nobody can say they weren't forewarned. And, as far as any and all opposing armies were concerned, they couldn't say they weren't warned. Because it's what the Romans did. In every battle. Time and time again. Predictable? Yes. Effective? Certainly. They had a battle plan, and by Mars, they were going to use it.

After all, once you've found a battle plan that works, you're hardly going to deviate for as long as remains the case.

Thus, on rather more literal fields of physical combat, the leaders of fighting men continue to redefine warfare. Rome had, with its highly trained soldiers and tightly disciplined *Testudo,* turned the art of battle into a science. Long gone were the days when hordes of fighting men and women would simply form into two large and unorganised groups and simply run into one another, pell-mell, a blur of axes, swords and assorted blunt instruments with no one really sure of what they are doing or who they are bludgeoning to death. It was bloody anarchy.

Rome helped change all that.

People raved about Testudo. It was the tiki-taka of its day, reliant on close movement and finding space in the most effective manner. Cassius Dio, a 1st century Roman consul, historian and forerunner of the modern day studio pundit ('Well Cassius, the ancient Britons are getting a mauling in this battle, can you see any way back into it for them?') followed the campaign of Roman general Marc Antony, a very fond advocate of Testudo and, whilst observing Antony's disciplined soldiers in combat, described both its formation and effectiveness with no little excitement:

'This Testudo and the way in which it is formed are as follows. The Baggage animals, the light-armed troops and the cavalry are placed in the centre of the army. The heavy-armed troops who use the oblong, curved and cylindrical shields are drawn up around the outside, making a rectangular figure, and, facing outward and holding their arms at the ready, they enclose the rest.

The others who have flat shields, form a compact body in the centre and raise their shields over the heads of all the others, so that nothing but shields can be seen in every part of the phalanx alike and all the men by the density of the formation are under shelter from missiles. Indeed, it is so marvellously strong that men can walk upon it and whenever they come to a narrow ravine, even horses and vehicles can be driven over it.'[1]

Few opponents could live with Testudo when the Romans were fighting to the very best of their abilities. It was a remarkably successful, effective and, as far as the enemy was concerned, psychologically frightening sight to come across. And no wonder. If your best defence was nothing more than a few layers of animal skins and a pointed stick, you're really not going to fancy your chances when you come up against it. In many ways, the battle was lost even before it had really begun.

What Testudo was, of course, and its relevance to our story here is a very early example of pre-battle tactics being planned and passed on to the proverbial foot soldiers just before battle. It was an action plan that was devised and passed on by the watching generals, which ensured that, if followed correctly and the orders of the battalion captain obeyed to the letter, they and their armies had the very best chance possible of departing that field of battle as the victorious army.

The Testudo action plan is rather like pre-match tactics being planned and passed on to the professional footballers just before a match – an action plan devised and passed on by the watching managers and coaches,

---

1   *Plutarch. 2008.* Roman Lives: A Selection of Eight Lives. *Ed. P. Stadter. Translated by R. Water-field. Oxford Paperbacks.*

which ensures that, if followed correctly and the orders of the team captain obeyed to the letter, they and their team have the very best chance possible of departing that football field as the victorious team.

Bloody battle and sporting battle. United in their use of pre-battle and pre-match tactics and on-field formations.

The word *tactics* is said to have originated from the 17th century Latin *tactica*, meaning the 'science of arranging military forces for combat, which is exactly what Marc Antony and his legionaries were doing with their established, trusted and much feared Testudo.

And eaxctly what Joachim Löw and his formidable and much feared Germany side were doing with their very own version of Testudo two thousand years later as they swept up a world conquest all of their own in winning the 2014 World Cup. Löw's 4-2-3-1 formation was based on the same basic principles as Testudo was: a solid defensive foundation at its most vulnerable point allied with an attacking zeal that swiftly switched from defence to offense, designed to catch opposing teams when they have over exposed themselves.

The Germans may not have had the benefit of curved wooden shields to help repel attacking forces, yet, with a world-class goalkeeper in Manuel Neuer supported by the likes of Philipp Lahm, Jerome Boateng, Mats Hummels and Benedikt Howedes, they didn't need them. After all, a defence that concedes just four goals in seven games hardly needs any additional assistance, shields included.

Marc Antony and Joachim Löw. Brothers-in-arms separated by two millennia yet united in their mastery of effective on-field formation and tactics.

I'm sure they'd find they had a lot in common were they ever to get together over a bottle of the finest Sassicaia. Or Riesling, come to that. They'd both be lost in a world of their own: dining implements, glasses and condiments moving in an ever-quickening blur over the brilliant white tablecloth as they swapped ideas and theories on formations and tactics regarding the battles they'd have fought in heart and mind. Antony, no doubt, would be pleased – yet hardly surprised – to learn that Rome, in the guise of modern-day Italy has conquered the world a further four times, even if it had been in football rather than war and conquest.

The old and the new. Both tactical masters.

It may have come to pass, therefore, that the great Barcelona side that was coached so ably by Pep Guardiola from 2008 to 2012 was the one that, in footballing terms, waked many of the sports devotees up to the science and appreciation of football tactics and on-field formations with their perceived application (since rubbished by Guardiola himself) of the now famous tiki-taka style of play. The phrase itself sounds almost as sexy as the type of football it portrays: short passing and movement whilst constantly maintaining possession. Everyone loved it, the world fell in love with Pep and his team and, with it, both the footballing cognescenti and its rank and file became enamoured, enraptured by football tactics.

It was as if no one had ever considered, talked about or even applied tactics to football before. Yet here we were, eulogising Guardiola, fawning over Barca, Messi and tiki-taka.

Coaching became the new playing.

Yet of course, as far as football is concerned, the application of formations and tactics in the game has always been part of it, and as integral to the successes of Blackburn Olympic, the winners of the FA Cup in 1883 as they were to Löw's all-conquering German side 131 years later.

Plus any and all points in between.

Like the great Austrian side of the 1930s and the work of Englishman Jimmy Hogan who coached with some success and no little distinction on the continent at that time, including in Austria, but also in Hungary, Switzerland and Germany.

And Vittorio Pozzo who coached the Italian national side to victory in the 1934 and 1938 World Cups, the man credited with creating the Metodo tactical formation, and, to this day, still the only person to have won two World Cups as a coach.

The great Hungarian side of the 1950s, Sir Alf Ramsay's 'wingless wonders' who won a World Cup for England in 1966, and the great, possibly the greatest of all time, the magical, mercurial Brazil of 1958 who redefined the way the game was played, setting a benchmark as they did so, which people still look to today as one that has rarely been matched and certainly never surpassed.

Mapping the Pitch explores the history and development of the game and some of its most influential and successful teams, players and coaches but with specific reference to and exploration of the way in which they played the game and how they were coached and set up; the on-field formations they established and championed as well as the tactics introduced and practiced by their coaches.

The strategic placing of salt and pepper pots throughout the footballing ages, in fact.

Let us play.

INTRODUCTION

Be yourselves. You need to dig into your own DNA. I hate tiki-taka. Tiki-taka means passing the ball for the sake of it, with no clear intention. And it's pointless.

Pep Guardiola is held in the same venerated esteem amongst football players, supporters and his fellow coaches that Michelangelo is amidst the throngs of self-appointed experts and devotees of Renaissance art.

The urbane man from Santpedor enjoyed a highly respectable playing career, one that peaked with around 300 games for Barcelona from 1990 to 2001. His role as a defensive midfielder in Johan Cruyff's revitalised side resulted in La Liga and European Cup winners medals by the time he was 20.

A prodigy no less.

Yet it is for his coaching skills and the reputation that Guardiola earnt for himself as a master of the tiki-taka style of play rather than any of the accomplishments he achieved as a player that raised him into the footballing stratosphere. Guardiola is not the creator of the tiki-taka, nor is, or was he ever, the sole advocate of its method on planet football. Yet he has been lauded as a man whose work as Barcelona coach gave football its very own renaissance and introduced its finer arts to an audience whose hitherto understanding of the game might have been as basic as the tactics of the teams they were watching.

Tiki-taka is not, it is worth repeating, a footballing philosophy that was developed and implemented by Guardiola during his time as Barcelona coach. Yet its place in the footballing lexicon is a fairly contemporary one; its use, if not all of the theory behind it, being widely credited to the respected Spanish sportswriter and commentator Andrés González. As football commentators go, he was a flamboyant and extrovert antidote to many of his anodyne peers throughout the game, particularly in Europe where excitement and passion is demanded on the pitch but not so in the TV gantry. González was different. His liberal and occasionally florid style of commentary saw him beget to the phrase tiki-taka, it's onomatopoeic quality perfectly reflecting the sounds of a football being repeatedly and swiftly passed from one player to another and henceforth to another and another.

Short, sharp and swift. Tiki-taka-tiki-taka-tiki-taka. And repeat.

The BBC's Kenneth Wolstenholme and his breathless conclusion of the 1966 World Cup Final ('...and here comes Hurst, he's got... some people are on the pitch, they think it's all over...it is now, it's four') went into sporting commentary folklore[2] – at least in England. With tiki-taka, Andrés González coined a phrase that reverberates around the footballing world, one that has been lovingly applied to the Barcelona side coached by Guardiola from 2008 to 2012. But the man himself would be the last to say that he was only committed to one type of football, that his coaching manual started and finished with the phrase tiki-taka. It could be argued that the Barca side coached by Guardiola's predecessor, Frank Rijkaard was a more entertaining, even more flamboyant, side to watch. Built around the extraordinary abilities of Ronaldinho, Rijkaard preferred a 4-3-3 formation with the Brazilian talisman acting as a hub for the entire team, every attacking move and declaration of intent going through and by him as the entire team swept forward as an offensive force, the verve and joy in their play being rewarded with two consecutive La Liga titles and a Champions League.

But no one spoke of Rijkaard and a specific game plan or formation; no critic or sportswriter mentioned him and his preferred 4-4-3 formation in the same sentence. He was simply identified as a good coach who had a great time and played, more often than not, some exquisite football.

---

2   *Hurst's goal, his third and the fourth in England's 4-2 win over West Germany, was about as far removed, footballing style-wise, from tiki-taka as it is possible to be, the ball travelling from the England penalty area into the West German goal in around three seconds and two kicks later!*

So why can't the name of his successor be spoken with relation to his time at the Camp Nou without someone, somewhere, inserting the, presumably tiresome, reference to tiki-taka?

Guardiola did, of course, receive a lot of praise for the manner and spirit in which his side played. But the credit all too often seemed to go to the perceived system of play his team adhered to rather than to the versatility and capability of the coach alone.

Imagine a road race between two Ferrari cars. One has a V12 engine, the other a V6.

If the V12 won, everyone would nod knowingly and heap praise upon the car. Yet if the V6 triumphed, all of the praise and adulation would be on the drivers.

Guardiola had the V12. Yes, they were good, they were great. Unbeatable at times. But, well, you know. They were Barcelona. They had the system, the players; they had the tiki-taka. Rijkaard, on the contrary, had fine-tuned the V6. They were good; he made them better. With added Ronaldinho.

No wonder Guardiola eventually snapped when he was asked about tiki-taka. Wouldn't, couldn't, someone, for once, credit him for his capabilities as a coach rather than a system coined by a pundit and adopted by the watching masses? Guardiola claims he left Barcelona because he could no longer motivate his players or himself. But you also have to speculate as to whether he was also weary of how he and his team had been labelled and that he wanted to get away from all of that and redefine himself as a coach with a brand new team in a different country, which he has done, very successfully, at Bayern Munich where no one mentions tiki-taka. Except in passing reference to the Spaniard and his former club. For his part, Guardiola did his best to shatter the myth about it with a quote he is attributed to have made to a group of journalists following defeat for his new team at the hands of local rivals Nürnberg, saying:

'I loathe all that passing for the sake of it, all that tiki-taka. It's so much rubbish and has no purpose. You have to pass the ball with a clear intention, with the aim of making it into the opposition's goal. It's not about passing for the sake of it.

Be yourselves. You need to dig into your own DNA. I hate tiki-taka. Tiki-taka means passing the ball for the sake of it, with no clear intention. And it's pointless.'[3]

The man shatters the myth. Barca were not all about tiki-taka and neither, by definition, was Guardiola. It was a strong statement, a surprising one. But it came from a man desperate to be identified for more than one way of playing, a way that, Guardiola added, was 'pointless'.

No redeeming features at all then?

His point made, Guardiola moved on. He speaks of a future, post-Bayern where, perhaps one day, he coaches Manchester United. And if that were to ever happen, then his connection with tiki-taka would surely be at an end, dead, buried and gone forever. Think about it. Tiki-taka in the Premier League?

---

3   *From the* Daily Telegraph *(online article)*, Oct 16th 2014; Peranau, Marti. 2014. Pep Confidential: Inside Guardiola's First Season at Bayern Munich. *Arena Sport.*

Impossible.

Which just might be why Guardiola hopes to have the chance to coach there one day, so he can escape the system and the association once and for all.

But Guardiola's association with tiki-taka is hardly new, at least not in terms of teams, coaches and even individual players being eagerly and, in some cases, complacently identified as either the originator of or a sworn disciple of a specific manner of play, formation or position.

Indeed, it's something that has been happening since the earliest days of the professional game.

Everyone, of course, has heard of Guardiola and tiki-taka and made the assumption that you can't have one without the other.

But how many judges of the game are aware of the Danubian School of football from the 1920s? Or the Metodo, a derivation of the Danubian School that evolved around a decade later?

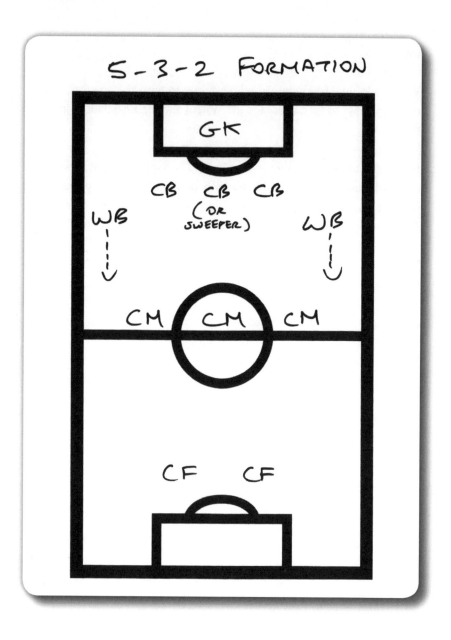

The 5-3-2 formation, also known as the Pyramid, was favoured by England manager Glenn Hoddle from 1996 to 1999. Five defenders, two attacking full-backs behind three central midfielders and two attackers. There were lots of options with three central defenders, one who could play as a sweeper, allowing the full-backs to maraud forward as members of the team's attack. These roles were perfected by Brazilians Cafu and Roberto Carlos and adopted for England during Hoddle's time in charge by, amongst others, David Beckham on the right side of the pitch and Graeme La Saux on the left. As far as one of the Brazilians was concerned, his attacking role in the Brazilian side that played with that formation in the 2002 World Cup finals has now gone down into footballing folklore, and any full-back since with an attacking bent to his game now is compared, style-wise, to him. For example, the Norwich City right back Russell Martin, a competent but hardly stellar member of the English side from 2010 onwards, is affectionately referred to as the 'Norfolk Cafu', because he liked to abandon staid defensive duties in order to make an attacking run down the right side of the pitch.

Hoddle's adoption of 5-3-2 was, and still is, regarded in English footballing circles as revolutionary, brave, daring. Even a little crazy. Yet there is nothing that is really new under the footballing sun, and the method that Hoddle had chosen to follow was a mirror image of the original Pyramid formation, a 2-3-5 line-up which was in vogue throughout Great Britain from the latter decades of the 19th century.

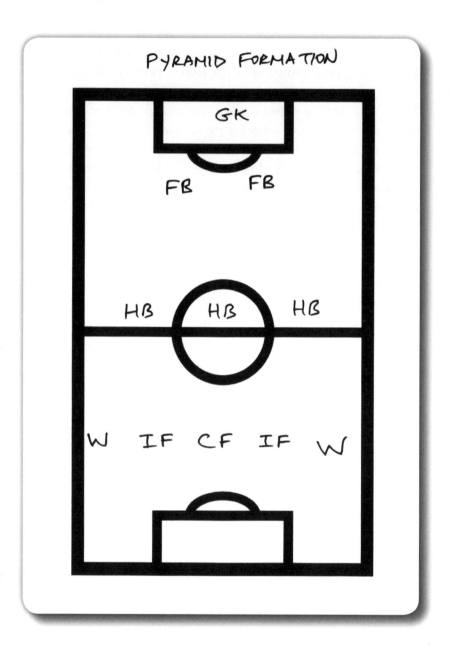

Same shape, differing priorities. In 1890 both Cafu and Russell Martin would have been wingers who occasionally defended rather than defenders who occasionally attacked. That 2-3-5 formation, the original footballing pyramid, is seen as a progenitor of much that was to follow in the game as we know it today – contrasts and departures, modifications, variations and return visits.

Yet it was positively negative compared to some of the earliest formations of the modern game which were best exemplified by the very first international games to be played, specifically those between the greatest and most bitter rivals in the sport: England and Scotland.

It's November 1872. And everyone wants to be the centre forward.

CHAPTER ONE:
MOB FOOTBALL

Whenever a player from either side got the ball, he had but one objective in mind: put his head down, take on an expression of grim countenance and attempt, at all costs, to dribble both himself and the ball up the field and into the opponent's goal.

1872. Let's set the scene in a general, historical sense before we focus on the football to get a sense of perspective.

In the US, Republican Ulysses S. Grant is the incumbent president. The country's flag, not yet the venerable Stars and Stripes, has just 37 stars, 13 short of its current total, a sign of a young and growing nation. But the nation is already making its fair share of world headlines, one of which was the discovery by the British ship *Dei Gratia* of the deserted and seemingly abandoned US vessel *Mary Celeste* that December.

In what is now the Federal Democratic Republic of Ethiopia, Yohannes IV has been crowned as Emperor whilst in Australia, the Australian Overland Telegraph Line has been completed, the two separate lines having been joined at Frew Ponds in South Australia.

The Great War, that terrible conflagration that claimed 37 million casualties, was still 42 years into the future, a generation away.

Samuel Morse, the inventor of the electric telegraph dies. As does the man considered one of Mexico's greatest heroes, Benito Juárez.

Amongst those historical figures who were born in 1872 are future US president Calvin Coolidge, the mathematician and philosopher Bertrand Russell and the first man to reach the South Pole, Roald Amundsen.

Another significant birth that occurred that year was that of international football.

It was contested between Scotland and England in Partick close to the north bank of the River Clyde in Glasgow and took place at, of all places, the West of Scotland Cricket Club's ground in front of just 4,000 curious, yet, you suspect, suitably fervent supporters demanding a drop or two of English blood, just as rather more had been dropped, nay, poured at Bannockburn in the 14th century.

It wasn't the first time the two nations had met in a football match, though. They'd already played a series of unofficial games, all arranged at the behest of the top hats and toffs at the Football Association who saw the Scots as malleable opponents there for the proverbial taking. It could also be, of course, that no one else wanted to play England or have anything to do with the FA who, a little under a decade earlier, had devised and introduced the first formalised rules of the game, one advantage of that of course being (and don't let anyone convince you otherwise) that if you make up the rules then you own the game.

It was, after all, what the English had already been doing for several centuries, a combination of fighting spirit and an altogether rather too fond love of rules, regulation and bureaucracy, making them, in their eyes, the perfect nation to own and regulate a game that looked set to conquer the world just as they had set out to do.

Thus both the rules of the game and the manner in which it was first played reflected the nation that had taken ownership of the same with both on-field formations and tactics reflecting the zeal of the soldiers and sailors that had set out with orders to take over the world.

In other words: attack, attack, attack.

Anyone who was at that first Scotland versus England game would therefore have witnessed the spectacle of 22 men repeatedly running, en masse, at each other, carrying the ball with them as if it was a battle standard with the mission objective very clear and simple: plant that standard (the ball) behind enemy lines as swiftly and effectively as possible. And if someone gets in the way, take them out.

It was, for all intents and purposes, a small outbreak of war on the banks of the Clyde, albeit one that was played out in a spirit of good sportsmanship allied with a reportedly 'firm but fair' performance from the Scottish referee (this was in Great Britain after all).

Formations, such as they were, typified the 'up and at 'em' approach of both sides with England opting for a 1-1-8 formation – that is, with eight forwards in their side, or, in contemporary parlance, two inside and outside rights, two inside and outside lefts and four centre forwards. Scotland, on the other hand, opted for the relatively more cautious 2-2-6 formation, a decision that, no doubt, provoked howls of protest from the Scottish support, aghast at their sides decision to offer such a negative response to the front eight of the opposition.

Twenty-two players, 14 of which were attackers – that's nearly 65% of all the players on show. Compare that, say, to today's game where the away side might choose to counter the home teams tried and trusted 4-4-2 formation with a 5-4-1, opting for that little extra security at the back. It's still 22 players, but only three of that 22 are now attacking players, or just 14% of all the players on show. Put it another way, nine of them are defenders; that's nine in total from *both* teams, just one more than all of the attacking players who represented England alone on that dim and distant day in 1872.

Twenty-two players, 14 attackers. It sounds like footballing heaven. All either side could do was attack. And attack they both did. For 90 minutes. There were no back passes; in fact, there were hardly any passes that went backwards at all. Whenever a player from either side got the ball, he had but one objective in mind: put his head down, take on an expression of grim countenance and attempt, at all costs, to dribble both himself and the ball up the field and into the opponent's goal. Whilst he was attempting to do this, his nine outfield teammates would be in close proximity to him, all eager to have a chance of their own to get their head down and run like hell whilst the opposition did everything they could, including body checks, in order to dispossess him and regain possession.

And then one of their own players would get his head down, take on that same determined expression and...well, you get the picture. And that's how it was for the entire game. First one group of players collectively swept forward. Then the other. And repeat. It really was end-to-end stuff; in fact, it was the very definition of that oft expressed footballing quotation.

In his book *Don't Mention The Score*,[4] Simon Briggs imagines viewing the game from above, observing that, to the aerial observer, the '...shapeless bustle must have resembled particles in Brownian motion.'[5] With such a commitment to attacking football from both sides, there could, of course, only be one consequence as far as the final score was concerned.

A 0-0 draw.

Quite how both sides managed to throw so many of their players into attacking mode only for the game to end as a 0-0 draw defies footballing logic. You could perhaps understand it if the game had been played in a mirror universe with England's sterile 8-1-1 coming up against the similarly dank 6-2-2 of the Scots. But not this way, not the way the teams had been set up to play the game – in other words, to get as many goals as they could. But 0-0? To even the casual observer, it would have

---

4   *Briggs, Simon. 2007.* Don't Mention the Score. *Quereus. 13.*

5   *An apt description of the frantic, frenetic movement of the players in question, Brownian motion describes the highly random motion of particles suspended in a fluid which results from their collision with rapidly moving atoms or molecules in that gas or liquid-in other words, lots and lots of tiny little objects all randomly scurrying around with no perceived plan or purpose.*

seemed, with the teams set up as they were with the emphasis on attack, to be more difficult not to score a goal than it would have been to score at least one or even the proverbial hatful. So how on earth did two such trigger happy teams manage to play out a goalless draw?

The answer to that is simple – they were two very good teams who managed to cancel each other out on the day. They may well have been set up to play offensively and most certainly would have gone into the game with that intent in mind. But this was England versus Scotland, and neither side wanted to lose. Indeed, it was quite likely that the players of each side saw not losing to their greatest foes as more of a priority than beating them. That rivalry has endeared ever since with the two sides meeting in a full international a further 111 times between then and 2014. With both players and fans from both sides going into the game with thoughts of 'we mustn't lose this' rather than 'we must win this' – a mentality perhaps reflected in 1872 just as it would have been in the days leading up to the two teams most recent meeting – a comfortable 3-1 win for England at Celtic Park in 2014 that saw the Scotland side play just one man, Chris Martin of Derby County, in an attacking role at home, in front of a fired up crowd and against their most hated rivals.

Going all out to win? Or going all out not to lose? Scotland's 4-5-1 formation on the night seems as overtly negative now as their 2-2-6 seemed rather too carefree for their first ever game.

Unlike that contemporary meeting, the two teams that met in 1872 were very evenly matched. The Scotland side, for example, was made up of 11 players, all of whom played for the same club team, Queens Park, then the leading side in Scotland. They therefore knew each other and the way they played the game as well as any international team has ever done, and this would have translated onto the pitch where England, the marginal favourites on the day, would have found the combination of team spirit (there was a rallying cry prior to one early clash between the teams that implored '...any Scotch players who may be desirous of assisting their country... may communicate with Messrs A F Kinnaird') plus the heavy pitch two significant obstacles towards their expected victory.

Another point worthy of consideration is that the overtly attacking nature and line-ups of both teams were more of a hindrance than an asset to the match as far as goals were concerned. Briggs referred to the match as taking on the appearance of a 'shapeless bustle', and he is spot on. Yes, whenever one of the two sides found itself in possession, the man with the ball at his feet would have set out for goal with up to seven of his teammates all closely gathered around him. They would have had to contend with all of their opponents standing, running, punching, barging and even kicking them as they attempted to retain possession for themselves, the whole game resembling a scrum of players slowly moving up and down the pitch but never really getting anywhere. Players seeking space or a pass, players even doing something as ordinary as making a pass to one of their teammates was largely anathema to them; it was all about getting the ball at your feet and running with it until such time as someone took it off you. The whole process would then start again in the opposite direction, the defending posse became the attacking one and vice versa.

Run and jostle forwards, lose the ball, run and jostle backwards. And repeat.

No wonder it ended in a goalless draw. It was football Jim, but not as we know it. And perhaps that's not too surprising as the game was, in many ways, still evolving from one of its forerunners, an early version that they would more like have been aware of, even if none of the England and Scotland players had played it themselves. As, too, would have their fathers and grandfathers, both of whom would almost certainly have played the game themselves. That version of the game could be up to 200 a side or more and rarely, if ever, see a 'goal' scored.[6]

It was called mob football.

Mob football by name and mob football by nature. It was a game that was exactly as its name implies – one that was played by a mob.

A loose definition of mob is that it is a large crowd of people, especially one that is unruly, disorderly and intent on causing trouble or even violence. So, how about getting two opposing mobs together, throwing them a football and letting them get on with it?

There you have it. Mob football. A primitive, yet genuine forerunner of the game we all know and (mostly) love today. It was an occasionally violent and disorganised form of the game that was usually contested between two neighbouring villages, but was nothing like the conventional eleven-a-side. In fact, around 200-a-side would be regarded more as the norm. Those 200 men would comprise the strongest and most athletic working men from the village as well as a sprinkling of the landed gentry; each, no doubt keen to give their social opposites a good kicking in the process regardless of whether they were on their own side or not.

---

6   *Ball games where the objective is to score a goal yet hardly ever seeing one being scored are hardly unique. Take the Eton Wall Game, for example, played annually at the world-famous school between Collegers and Oppidans up against a 110-metre-long wall and on a pitch just five-metres wide. The sole objective, by just about any non-violent means possible, is to get the ball down to one end of the pitch to score a goal. It sounds simple enough, and it isn't for the want of trying. However, the last time a goal was recorded as being scored in one of the matches was in 1909!*

LVDVS QVEM ITALI APPELLANT IL CALCIO

An early form of football played in 17th-century Florence.

Picture the scene. A typical English market town at around the turn of the 13th century. Two large groups of people have gathered at the market cross; one has been gathered from the north and eastern side of the town, the other from the south and the western edges. The two groups are comprised entirely of men (though it would not be unknown for some women to disguise their appearance so they could take part), and all are now focused on the figure standing at the market cross, holding aloft in his hand an inflated animal bladder of some kind that will act as the ball and the focus of the game. As the town clock begins to strike 10, he throws the ball into the melee where a great and near uncontrollable scrum breaks out between all of the competitors. Their objective? Those from the north and eastern parts of the town have to get the ball to a pre-ordained spot in the southwest part of the town, those from the south and west have to get it to a point in the northeast of the town. That is their group's prime aim and sole objective, that site more than likely marked by two posts stuck in the ground with a piece of netting hung between them.

Their goal.

The rules are fairly straightforward and easy to follow. Admittedly, yes, one of the great strengths of the modern game is its simplicity, the fact that it remains a game easy to understand and play. Yet the rules of today's game are in no way as user friendly as those of mob football, rule one of which was, pretty much, there are no rules.

Now that's maybe a slight exaggeration. Although kicking, punching, head-butting and even a little light gouging were all considered as much a part of the game then as a clearance into row Z or perfectly executed slide tackle is now, there was one possible consequence of the game that was regarded as being unacceptable and contrary to the spirit of the occasion.

Killing someone. Intentionally, at least.

Such was the rough and violent nature of mob football. There would certainly have been instances where players-cum-combatants died as a result of their taking part in the game. After all, if you're part of a surging group of a hundred-plus men, all with their testosterone raised to unheard of levels and the scent of opposition blood in their nostrils, it would be advisable not to stumble or fall over as part of that group because, rather than collectively stop to pick you up and dust you down, they would have carried on regardless, leaving the unfortunate faller at the very real risk of being trampled to death. There were myriad other ways in which you might have an inclination to expire during the game; they seemed limitless. One historical account, for example, tells of a game in Northumberland where a player was killed as a result of running against the dagger of his opponent, whilst another tells of a player taking part in a game in Cornwall who was struck and killed by a stone that was thrown at him by an opposing member.

Such was the popularity of the game and the zeal in which it was played that complaints about both it and the conduct of its players were soon being raised and noted. Early 14th-century London saw complaints by wealthy and influential merchants to King Edward II that led to the game being banned in the confines of the city due to the fact that it created '... great noise in the city, caused by hustling over large balls from which many evils may arise.'

Football in England was later banned by both King Edward III and King Edward IV, the reason given at the time was that it was preventing archers from practicing their art, an art considered, like themselves, a valuable asset in the many battles the country was actively taking part in at the time. Various illustrations that reference the ban often show a somewhat genteel group passing a ball from one to the other on what looks like a verdant village green whilst their bows lie, discarded, on the ground. This is fanciful at best as it would have been the mob form of the game that those monarchs were so keen to ban rather than the romantic and somewhat fragrant (as well as non-existent) form pictured. One reason was that the archers weren't missing their practice sessions because they were playing football but because they had incurred assorted injuries playing football, including broken or permanently disfigured bow fingers.

No wonder the two Edwards were anti-football if it meant their most important soldiers were missing due to incapacitations earnt whilst playing what was still, after all, a mere game.

One of the most famous and endearing examples of mob football to be played in England was one of the many annual Shrove Tuesday games that took place around the country. One of these happened in Alnwick, the Northumberland town where one unfortunate had to, if you remember, retire (dead) from the game after running into an opponent's dagger. It became an annual event in the town in 1762 and like earlier forms of the game had also been played, took place in the town and its streets, continuing to do so after street football was finally banned in 1818. That is, until nine years later when the Duke of Northumberland provided the players a field on which they could, finally and legitimately, play the game, one that is played to this day between the two rival parishes in the town of St Michael's and St Paul's. The game is no longer played with anything like 200 people turning out on each side, and, mercifully, there are few injuries other than the occasional bruise and various aches and pains that might slow the participants down for a couple of days after the event, meaning that no one will need to be excused from either archery practice or another day at the office.

So perhaps it's not too surprising, therefore, that the very first international football match played under something resembling the rules of the game today ended in a 0-0 draw. Sheer weight of numbers in both mob football and the Eton Wall Game meant that goalscoring opportunities were, to say the least, running at a minimum, which makes sense. Because it didn't really matter if the playing area was the size of a small town or one closer to a modern pitch size, if the game's active participants, whether they be 400 in total or 20 are all huddled around the man with the ball, that proverbial 'shapeless bustle' then the time, opportunity, and, most importantly of all, space for someone on that pitch to conceive and put into practice that split-second act that results in goal was severely muted. This, of course, was later reflected in that drab 0-0 draw between England and Scotland back in 1872. The English players, in particular, were all so focused on both the mob and the ball that the notion of scoring a goal hardly came into it at all.

To be fair to the Scottish team, there had at least been a little more planning and thought put into their approach to the game. With the English side by far the more physical in terms of both size and weight, the Scottish players, drawn exclusively from the venerable Queen's Park Football Club, swiftly realised that if they attempted to match their English counterparts in a trial of strength, they would likely come off second best. This had certainly been the case in three of the five previous 'unofficial' games between the nations that had ended in victories for England, with the other two ending in draws. A different approach was therefore needed if Scotland were to avoid defeat in this first official game, one that, if at all possible, veered away from the seemingly tired and tested plan of getting the ball, putting your head down and running with it as fast as you can.

That approach, one that raised more than a few bushy English eyebrows in response as time went on, was to ensure that whenever one of their players was in possession of the ball, he would look to maintain that possession, but not by running with it and hoping for the best, but by making sure that a member of his team would, in turn, receive it.

Win the ball before looking to give it to someone else in the same coloured shirt as yourself. And repeat.

In other words, the Scottish players were introducing the concept of passing to the game of football, of outwitting and outplaying their opponents by ensuring that they had as little time with the ball as possible.

It's 1872. And Queen's Park FC, founded five years earlier and one of the oldest football clubs in the world, have invented tiki-taka.

Pep who?

Their bold and imaginative approach certainly saw them end the match and the day as the moral victors. They had not only played a full part in the first competitive international football game, but had also, in taking part, started to draw the game away from the mentality of mob football which was still attached to it with its emphasis on strength and physicality, as demonstrated by the England side on that day. The Scots had spawned, by design rather than accident, a way of playing football that suggested that it needn't be all about physicality and strength alone and that, with players being primed to keep their heads up and to think about running into space rather than one another, the fledgling offshoot of mob football might just have a future. It was, even at this early stage of the organised game, a stellar step forward in its development, the belief that running with the ball could be combined with passing it from one player to the other

It was very much destined to be dominated, as far as the English FA was concerned, by the dribbling rather than the passing game. They seemed to have little time for any variations of the game that took it away from its humble origins, the core belief being that football was exactly that – a game played with the feet and a ball, the former still being quite free and able to kick an opponent as much as they could the ball, if necessary.

A future which was exported south of the border and away to England by two Scotland players who, rather than being tied to the Queen's Park FC as had exclusively been the case for both that initial 0-0 draw in Glasgow as well as the follow up match three months later, a 4-2 win for England in London. One of them was Henry Renny-Tailyour, and, in a game where visionaries have always been either celebrated or regarded with great suspicion (and we'll be looking at some of them throughout this book), Renny-Tailyour, or RT as we will refer to him from now on, was one of the game's great originals.

For a proud Scot, RT's upbringing was very English upper class. He was born in India whilst his father was serving in the army before heading home to Argus and growing up on the family estate, going through his education at the elite (and English) Cheltenham College before joining the British Army and being commissioned into the Royal Engineers as a lieutenant. RT was a consummate, all-round sportsman who relished the opportunities to 'play up, play up and play the game' whilst he was serving in the British Army and went on to represent the Royal Engineers football team, one that was good enough to reach the very first FA Cup Final where they met the Wanderers at The Oval in March 1872, eight months before that first international game between Scotland and England. He had, however, already played in an international game between the two sides before then, an unofficial meeting between the two sides in November 1871. RT had, during this game, noted how the Scots tended to mix it up in combining that traditional hard running (and dribbling) method with a passing game, such was, again, the greater physical presence of the somewhat more industrial England team.

And he was impressed, so much so that he spoke of the Scots' 'combination football' in such glowing terms upon his return to his regiment that the Royal Engineers, a very English regiment and football team, felt compelled to try this type of game for themselves – with more than favourable results.

The foundation of that Scotland international side, Queen's Park FC had also entered that inaugural FA Cup competition, reaching the semi-finals. A laudable achievement you might think? You'd be wrong. They'd reached that late stage by virtue of not even playing a game, their progress made easy by a combination of byes and their potential opponents' reluctance to play them in the first place (their form of the game was regarded with some suspicion by many of their English peers). To their credit, they played, and drew, with Wanderers in that semi-final but, unable to raise the required finance to travel to London for the final, then withdraw from the competition – much, you would think, to the collective relief of the newly-formed Football Association based, naturally, in one of the more exclusive parts of London.

Which is a pity, because had they won, RT would have found his loyalties deeply divided, playing for his regimental side against the team made up of his countrymen and international colleagues. Instead of that, he lined up for the Royal Engineers against Wanderers, the latter winning the game by a single goal.

Despite that disappointment, RT and the Royal Engineers made another two finals of the competition, losing 2-0 to Oxford University two years later before finally winning the competition in 1875, beating Old Etonians 3-0 in a replay after a 1-1 draw, with RT scoring in both games. He'd secured, forever his place in the long and distinguished history of the world's oldest knockout football competition. But not only that, he'd also sealed his place in the history of the British game as a whole, for, as well as being the first Scottish player to score in game against England,[7] RT's realisation that the way the Queen's Park/Scotland side adapted their game to play against England illustrated the way the game *should* be progressing; that is, away from the mob mentality of kick and

---

7   *England 4, Scotland 2 at The Oval in March 1873.*

rush and towards a game where passing the ball and moving into space superceded the old ways.

The game didn't exactly change overnight. English football is famously resistant to anything new or different, after all. But it certainly caught on for, within a decade, football club formations had already changed enough to illustrate how the game was steadily evolving.

And all due to a Scot born in India who served with the Royal Engineers in London.

It wasn't as if two sides lining up with 1-1-8 formations guaranteed a glut of goals and feast of attacking football, for reasons that we have already explored. Indeed, the somewhat romantic notion that the early days of organised football were ones of free-scoring, goal-laden festivals can be given a further, and perhaps terminal, dent when the results from some more of the earliest games played are taken into consideration. Examples include the finals of both the FA Cup in England and its Scottish counterpart, the first of which were played in 1872 and 1874, respectively. Despite more attacking emphasis placed on formations and the game in its early years, the first 10 FA Cup Finals in England (excluding replays) from the competition's inception in 1872 resulted in 21 goals being scored – an average of 2.1 a game. The 10 FA Cup finals played up until May 2014, games in which teams would often play with just one out-and-out forward player, saw a total of 22 goals being scored – 2.2 per game. It's a similar story in Scotland, with 26 goals (2.6 per game) scored in the first 10 finals (excluding replays) since 1874, and 27 (2.7) scored in the 10 finals up to 2014.

Eight forwards per team then, or just the one, it would seem that the end result was, and remains, more often than not, the same.

An early watershed moment for the English game could be regarded as another FA Cup Final, the one that took place in 1883 between Blackburn Olympic and Old Etonians.

The Old Etonians were, as their name suggests, a team whose players were made up of former pupils from the elite Eton College, near Windsor in Royal Berkshire. The club had been founded by Lord Kinnaird, one of the principle members of the early Football Association in England and, by all accounts, a man who was, despite his privileged upbringing, a bit of a rascal and one who subscribed to the physical aspects of the game and it's old school 'mob football' mentality. That's not to say he wasn't a fine and effective footballer. He was most certainly that, taking part in nine separate FA Cup Finals as a player; his place in footballing history doubly assured when, in the 1877 final between his side Wanderers against Oxford University, Kinnaird, playing as goalkeeper, inadvertently stepped backwards over his own line after catching a speculative long range shot from an opposing player. This ended up being the first significant own goal recorded in any football match, one that, you can be sure, he tried to use his influential position within the game to have expunged from the records, such was the shame he felt at the time and one that contradicted the long-held belief that he and his peers were all exponents of fair play and good sportsmanship, that proverbial Corinthian spirit.

Not Kinnaird. He just wanted to win and wasn't particularly bothered how either he or his team went about doing so. He was, in effect, a prototype footballing hard man, a 19th-century Patrick Viera or Claudio Gentile. Indeed, such was his reputation for ferocity within the game that his wife was once alleged to have commented that she feared he would '...come home one day with a broken leg', only for a family friend to reassure her by saying that, 'You must not worry. If he does, it will not be his own.'

Arthur Kinnaird

Kinnaird was a big supporter of the traditional games between his old school fellows and those from their greatest rivals at Harrow, the old Harrovians. These games could be feisty enough without Kinnaird's own brand of physical enthusiasm, one that was marked out by an opponent in one such clash who, fed up with the not-so-sporting Lord's continued assaults on both his and his teammates' limbs, exclaimed aloud and with Kinnaird in earshot, 'Are we going to play the game, or are we going to have hacking?' to which Kinnaird's replay was, 'Oh let us have hacking!'

Hardly surprising, therefore, that Kinnaird and his Old Etonians team were nothing like the paragons of sporting virtue that you might have expected from those with such a background. It wasn't so much a case of play up, play up and play the game with them as turn up, have a punch up and win the game. And that is exactly how they went about things, a team that continued to espouse the virtues of the scrimmage, the spirit of mob football and its inclination for opposing players to get as much attention during the game as the ball. Indeed, it may well have been with the Old Etonians and Kinnaird in mind that the oft quoted line 'Football is a game for gentlemen played by hooligans' came about in the first place.

It was hardly surprising, therefore, that the Old Etonians were becoming a regular fixture in the FA Cup Final during its formative years. Their appearance in the 1883 Final was their seventh in 11 years, their route to that final tie typified, as it had been previously, by a succession of physical battles against teams who, whilst they might have been their equals as far as football was concerned, were either unable or unwilling to match them in the physical aspect of the game. Two otherwise notable footballing sides of the time, Rochester and Hendon, found themselves brushed aside (7-0 and 4-2, respectively) by Kinnaird and company as they progressed to the final where they would have discovered, much to their delight, that their opponents would be a gathering of working-class lads from a working-class town; it was an opportunity for them, therefore, to not only put the northern rogues and rascals in their place, but also to give them a jolly good kicking in the process.

The contrast between Kinnaird's Old Etonians and Blackburn Olympic was as wide as the miles that divided the sides geographically. Even a casual look at the team line-ups for the day shows the vast social and cultural difference between the two sides.

For a nation that is, and has always been, obsessed with class barriers, this could have been as good as it ever got with the solid, no-nonsense Northern side, including in their starting line-up a Warburton, Dewhurst and Hunter as opposed to Lord Kinnaird and his contemporaries, gentleman all with titles as well as names with one of Kinnaird's teammates on the day being the wonderfully named Percy de Paravicini, the son of Baron James Prior de Paravicini of Windsor.

Both teams elected to line up for the final in what was now the conventional 2-3-5, or Pyramid, formation, that is with a goalkeeper, two full-backs, three half-backs and five forwards. Compared to the cavalier and somewhat anarchic 1-1-8 formation that had typified English football in its earliest years, this new approach sounds very cautious, but it wasn't really that much different, in appearance at least, to those origins. It did mean, of course, that the previously solitary defender left at the back had now been joined by a teammate. The centre half still played in a very advanced position, one that today might have been called the playmaker whilst the two half-backs tucked in on either side of him, slightly behind the attacking five which was, in essence, two early versions of conventional wingers and three centre forwards. The introduction and development of the outside right and left positions, those prototype early wingers, was a nod to the earlier forms and habits of the game, the time honoured tradition of players getting the ball at their feet and running with it. In other, and welcomed, respects, though, the steady spacing out of players all around the pitch was, slowly but surely, starting to allow for clubs and players who wanted to pass the ball rather than run en masse with and around it in that ill-defined and occasionally anarchic scrimmage of old.

Blackburn Olympic were an example of a team that wanted to do just that, and, if their meeting with the Old Etonians back in 1883 was a clash of social standing, then it was also one of football's two styles of the time. It would be the tried and tested rumbustious one preferred by the Old Etonians against the new, revolutionary combination game favoured by Olympic. It was clear that the winners of the game would not only take the trophy home with them but, in doing so, have the type of football they played vindicated and, no doubt, copied by more clubs, eager to latch onto a proven winning formula.

The Blackburn Olympic team from 1882

A rich and privileged team of the upper classes set to take on the working class, cloth-capped men of the town who relied upon the cotton industry to house and feed its poor against the top-hatted and tailed men of the aristocracy. There's a big budget movie in there somewhere, one with, as it turns out, a happy ending.

One of the myriad reasons that the players and supporters of the Old Etonians would have had for actively despising their opponents in the final was the professional approach they were bringing to the game. They'd seen, admired and imitated the passing game that had been practiced by Scotland's international side (something which might have been regarded as near heresy alone) and had also, under Jack Hunter, their player-coach, began to look into ways to supplement their players diets as well as develop training regimens to improve both their speed and fitness. This was a necessity. The Olympic players, like the Scotland ones before them, were at a considerable physical disadvantage to their well-heeled opponents who could also, remember, count on easy living and a relatively healthy and regular diet. They didn't have to worry about going hungry unlike the Olympic players whose diet would have been, at best, of a frugal and rather spartan nature.

Hunter, therefore, joins RT as an early footballing revolutionary in terms of his approach not only to the game, but also to it's very design. Before Olympic's semi-final tie against Old Carthusians, another team made up of ex-public school boys, he took his players away from their homes and places of work to Blackpool for a week's hard running on the town's famous sands as well as a regular diet of oysters, and, very strictly, no beer. A modern approach developed by a man who was as advanced in his way of thinking with regard to how the game should be played then as Arsène Wenger was when he was appointed Arsenal manager 113 years later. Who knows, maybe Wenger was as much an advocate of oysters at the time of his appointment as Hunter had been during that very first mid-season break he took with his players?

Olympic's week at the seaside certainly seemed to benefit them on the day of the semi-final, a game that was initially delayed as no one had thought to bring along a ball. However, once it did get under way, Olympic took an early lead and, from then on, never looked remotely like they were in danger of losing to their well-heeled opponents. Indeed, such was their overall superior fitness and pace, one that left the Carthusian players confused, outwitted and, eventually exhausted, Olympic's winning margin of 4-0 was a more than fair reflection of how the game had gone.

Thus, Blackburn Olympic had reached the FA Cup Final, becoming only the third team (and one of those had been from Oxford University) from outside of London and England's prosperous Home Counties to do so. But not only that, they were from the north, a working men's team from a working town, one who had successfully replicated the achievement of their neighbours, Blackburn Rovers who had reached the final the previous year only to lose to, yes, you've guessed it, the Old Etonians. On that occasion, the rugged approach of the Old Etonians had, quite simply, bullied their opponents out of the game, and most people expected the same thing to happen again. But Olympic were different. Their players were fit, they were fast and they had a plan. They were going to beat the Eton old boys in exactly the same way as they'd seen off the challenge of Harrow's old boys.

By playing football. By passing the ball into space and using the whole pitch. It was, like those training methods employed by Hunter prior to the semi-final, revolutionary. Whether that approach became the fashion in the game or not very much depended on the result of the final. Had Olympic lost, it is quite likely that the mob football approach favoured by the Old Etonians and all the other southern-based teams in England would have prevailed long into the game's future; there might even have been the risk of a split in both the rules and format of the game as there had been in Rugby Union and League, with two versions of the game played with the round ball eventually accompanying the two played with the oval one.

Old Etonians started the game as strong favourites. And little wonder. Their team was, by some margin, bigger and stronger than Olympic's; the final was being played on virtual home territory for them in London whilst the very great majority of the 8,000 people who attended the final were their supporters. Olympic, in contrast, had gone to the considerable time and expense in travelling to London for the final, a near 500-mile round trip as well as having to find accommodation that provided adequate and suitable sustenance as well as a bed for the night. The odds were stacked against them whichever way you looked – not would that have bothered, you suspect, the London-centric FA (of whom Kinnaird was a prominent figure) which had insisted that this and every final be played in London despite Olympic's success in getting that far.

You might, with all of this in mind, have been excused for thinking that no one in football, let alone the Old Etonians side, wanted Olympic to have even the slightest chance of winning. And you might be right for thinking that.

Typically, the Old Etonians players tried to get stuck in, literally, to their opponents as soon as the game commenced. Tackles were hard and not particularly fair with it whilst Kinnaird proceeded to hone his skills of kicking opponents shins with the same lusty vigour that he might have reserved for the ball. And yet Olympic refused to yield to their opponent's near violent approach to both the game and themselves, despite the fact that they went a goal behind when Harry Goodheart scored to put the Old Etonians ahead.

Instead of capitulating, as many there might have expected, Olympic continued with their game plan, finding space, passing the ball and looking to outwit their opponent in the process. And, slowly, almost imperceptivity, it began to pay off with both the match and the future of the game beginning to swing their way. Their equaliser came from

Arthur Matthews, one that eventually saw the game go into extra time, and, with the Etonian side now fading fast, they made their overall fitness count in that additional 30 minutes with Jimmy Costley volleying the ball past the opposing goalkeeper after a run and cross from Thomas Dewhurst.

A goal that not only decided the game but also gave a casting vote to the way the game would be played in the future, not only in England but all over the world, especially in mainland Europe where it was already hugely popular if not quite as organised, regarding administration and competition, as it was in England. Olympic had not outfought their opponent and their brutal approach to the game, they had out thought them, the winning goal coming as the result of a passing movement involving several members of the team, one that, no doubt, Hunter would have instilled into them time and time again during that trip to Blackpool. And if scoring that goal and the victory it gave Olympic wasn't so significant that it actually saved the game of football in England *per se*, then it certainly saved it from itself and offered it a singularly more pleasant path to head down.

Unsurprisingly, there were post-match repercussions. Blackburn Olympic had become the first northern side to win the FA's showpiece trophy, something which had virtually become the private property of the 'chosen few' in its short history. Wanderers, for example, the stiff upper lip and quivering moustaches galore club that was comprised solely of the ex-pupils from a number of different English public schools, had already won it five times since 1872. Blackburn Olympic had now committed the cardinal sin of upsetting the establishment and the way of things with it, with the Old Etonian team swiftly lodging complaints about Olympic's new-fangled and deeply, in their view, vulgar approach of not only preparing for matches by practicing but by refusing to play the same sort of game they employed. They subsequently followed those criticisms up with what probably remains the biggest display of collective pique in the history of the game by claiming, an accusation that was backed up by *The Times* newspaper, that Olympic had only won the game because they resorted to foul play – this, if you recall, from a team whose captain and lynchpin was reckoned to be so aggressive that the only broken leg he would ever encounter as long as he played the game would be someone else's.

Needless to say, the FA didn't like it either. But they had to accept it. The FA Cup was heading north and, with it, the destiny of the game, *their* game, was all set to change. Olympic had seized their ball and were now taking it home with them. The horror.

The fates of both competing clubs changed after that final as well. The Old Etonians stuck ruggedly to their all for one and one for all sulk and refused to enter or have anything to do with the competition ever again whereas Blackburn Olympic returned home in the manner of conquering heroes. This they did to the accompaniment of not one, not even two, but three brass bands. Not unnaturally, both the club and their supporters wanted to build on their success and look to win the trophy again and again and again if it continued to put southern noses out of joint. Admittedly, full-time professional football as an occupation was still a few years off, but there were ways and means a player could be retained by a club, especially if his employer could be persuaded to step in. Players were told not only would it be good for them but it would also be for the good of the company they worked for as well as the town itself. How could they resist?

As things turned out, they didn't need to. The Olympic players had a wide variety of working backgrounds to their name, none of which paid particularly well, especially if you were a 'conquering hero'. The players' trades included three weavers, two pub landlords, a picture framer and a dental assistant. And they were open to offers from anyone, anywhere, including, just down the road, the hungry eyes of the bigger and wealthier Blackburn Rovers.

A pity really, as it is intriguing to speculate what might have happened if that side and Hunter, their remarkable coach, might have achieved had they stayed together. There was soon, and perhaps inevitably, talks of splits in the camp. Petty jealousies perhaps, or some players let their newly-won fame go to their heads, but, whatever it was, the club proceeded to fall apart with goalkeeper Hacking (the dental assistant) becoming the first departure as he duly left to sign for Rovers. Others soon followed, and Olympic ultimately went out of business at the end of that decade, leaving Rovers as the sole football side in the town.

Rovers certainly benefitted from Olympic's swift fall from grace, putting together a team that was good enough to win the FA Cup for themselves for the next four years. As a club they have stayed the footballing course ever since, even winning the Premier League title in England in 1995, well over a century since Hacking had symbolised both their rise and Olympic's fall with his cross-town move soon after Olympic's FA Cup success in 1883. They survived and thrived whilst Blackburn Olympic, English football's great visionaries, died, quite simply because they couldn't keep up with the fast-changing nature of the game for which, ironically, they had done so much to initiate.

Yet as a fledgling chapter in footballs story drew to a close, Blackburn Olympic's legacy is clear and there for all to see – even if few, if anyone, would give them the credit for it today. They were the cause of many of the game's innovations, under the watchful eye of Jack Hunter, that 19th-century Wenger whose superb marshalling of his defence in that final against the Old Etonians had given his forwards the time and space to come back from 1-0 down and win the game; Hunter who had taken his squad for a hitherto unknown and virtually scandalous mid-season break in Blackpool; Hunter, the man who introduced training sessions that focused on fitness and agility; and Hunter, the man and coach who was amongst the first in the game to truly map a football pitch and make use of its wide, open opportunities to his team's advantage.

As far as the English game in general was concerned, Olympic's success had lit the blue touch paper for further progress and innovation with those clubs that took up the 'combination' game being the ones to prosper. Those first 11 FA Cup finals from 1872 through to 1882 had all been won, without exception, by clubs that came from London, playing the game as true as they could to its 'mob' origins. Following Olympic's success in 1883, 18 consecutive finals were won by sides playing combination football, clubs that all hailed from northern England. Tottenham Hotspur eventually ended that run in 1901, becoming, as they did, the first and only non-league club to win the competition and by playing combination football. With that success, and, no doubt to the massive relief of all at the FA, London had finally fallen back in love with the game, the reality of that evidenced by the crowd of 110,820 who saw them and Sheffield United play out a 2-2 draw in the first game before Tottenham won 3-1 in the replay. Hunter eventually joined the exodus from Olympic to Rovers, playing for them for a short while before becoming the club's assistant manager and groundsman. He combined this with working as a licensee in Blackburn, ending his footballing adventures as coach to Cheshire side New Brighton Town that he managed to take, albeit briefly, to the Football League from the depths of the Lancashire League. He could still weave his managerial magic, that was abundantly clear, his success at New Brighton Town clearly illustrating that all he had done with Olympic had been anything but a fluke or fortuitous one-off.

Yet, for all that, none of the major clubs in the English game at that time saw fit to employ him as their manager, not one of the 12 founding members of the Football League, the first of its type anywhere in the world, would give Hunter a job, many of them household names in both the English and world game to this day, a distinguished list that included Aston Villa, Bolton Wanderers, Everton and Wolverhampton Wanderers. Was Hunter seen as being a little bit too left field? Were the clubs and their owners frightened of him, his techniques and his reputation? Did they somehow think he might have had something to do with Blackburn Olympic's sad demise?

If that was the case then, sadly for the game in England, it was, and remained typical of the attitude English football has always reserved for its pioneers, coaches and players alike with many of the former, in particular, left no choice but to ply their trade overseas. This remains evident in the English game today at the very highest level with Roy Hodgson, England's national team manager having to commence, at just 29, his coaching career in Sweden before going on to work with 16 different teams in eight countries as well as working as a coach for the Switzerland and Finland national teams, his success at the latter including guiding the Finns to their highest ever position of 33rd in FIFA's world rankings.

In many ways, Hodgson defies the traditional image of the English football coach. He has served as a member of UEFA's technical study group at European Championships as well as being part of a similar set up with FIFA at the 2006 World Cup. He speaks five languages fluently,[8] meaning he has been able to work as a television pundit, as well as a coach in many of the countries in which he has coached. Hodgson, remarkably, finally found himself appointed as coach to a major English

---

8   *Despite this and his other qualities as both an individual and a football coach of the very high-est calibre, the English press constantly choose to malign Hodgson for a perceived lisp whilst he talks, poor judgement indeed when you consider many of them cannot even grasp the fundamentals of their own language, let alone a further four.*

club in 1997 when, over two decades after he began his coaching career, he took over at Blackburn Rovers,[9] although it is uncertain that they would have even considered him had he not spent the previous two years at Italian giants Inter Milan, his legacy at the San Siro being this ringing endorsement from club president Massimo Moratti: 'Roy Hodgson was an important person in the development of Inter Milan to the point we have reached today. He saved us at the right time. When he came we were in trouble and things appeared dark. He didn't panic, he was calm and made us calm. Disaster was averted at the most important time. Everyone at Inter will remember him for that and his contribution. He is considered by us all as an important person in our history. He left an endowment to this club that's important in our history.'

Perhaps Jack Hunter would have enjoyed both success and the recognition he clearly deserved as one of football's earliest pioneering coaches had he been given the opportunity to do so away from the all too often blinkered confines of English football. Football's growth and popularity in mainland Europe was increasing with, ironically, many English expats responsible, one way or another. Hunter would perhaps have been the most knowledgeable and experienced of them all had the chance come his way, as, perhaps it would eventually have done. Sadly for football, Jack Hunter died of tuberculosis in 1903 when he was just 51, his legacy short but, nonetheless significant as one of the pioneering men of the game, a man who mapped the pitch and truly started to realise its, and football's, potential.

---

9   *Hodgson had a spell as assistant manager and an even shorter one in charge of English side Bristol City from1980 to 1982, ending up being sacked as their manager after just four months in charge. Bristol City ended up being relegated to the lowest tier of full-time English league football whilst Hodgson returned to club football in Sweden.*

CHAPTER TWO:
THE AGE OF THE PYRAMID

A non-league side winning the FA Cup? There must, the old traditionalists would have mused, be something in this. Their win in the competition that year put the final nail into the already cold coffin of mob football, of the scrimmage.

Football was catching on. But it hadn't taken the growth and success of the organised game in England, with its national cup competition and organised national league both established and running by 1888, for the rest of Europe to sit up and take notice of the way the game was changing from its mob football roots, a pursuit that had, perhaps been more popular in some parts of mainland Europe than it had ever been in Great Britain.[10]

The first football club to be formed outside of Great Britain is widely believed to have been the Dresden Club in Germany—or, to give it its full name, The Dresden English Football Club. No false modesty shown by its founders maybe, but, at the same time, the fact the club was founded in 1874, only two years after the first FA Cup Final in England serves notice of the game's pending lift-off throughout the continent. Their formation was seen as notable enough to merit coverage in the local press with a Leipzig-based newspaper observing that football was '...a game in which the ball is catapulted away with the foot', another comparison of the game to ancient battle and conflict. Yet the comparisons with the modern game are there. The article goes on to note that the players were clad in '...costume of a woollen or silken under-jacket, with, or without sleeves, tight short pants which display the knees, long socks and very comfortable shoes or boots.' Their first game attracted a crowd of around 100 people with reports adding that the impression that those watching got of the game and the players was 'exotic'. That must have been because their knees were showing. But, exotic or not, Dresden were, from the start, a very good football team. So good that, if there had have been a late 19th-century version of the Champions League, they would almost certainly have won it. They convincingly won their first six matches, recording a goal difference of +34 in the process, and that's 34 goals scored without conceding one.

---

10   A form of mob football known as La soule was recorded as having been played in Paris as long ago as the late 14th century.

Formidable, to say the least. After one match they had played, a 7-0 victory over a Berlin-based side that had also been formed by some keen Englishmen, Philipp Heineken, the founding president of the German Football Association (remarkably, the surplus of football-loving Englishmen in Germany at the time had agreed that the role had best go to a German, rather than one of them!), Dresden's type of play was described as *nonplus ultra* – a Latin term but also one used in colloquial German that means, quite simply 'unsurpassable'. In other words, their performance on the day could never be improved upon.

Illustration of the Dresden English Football Club

In terms of their setup and the way they approached the game, Dresden were considerably ahead of their British counterparts in a number of ways. For a start, the ways of kick and rush, the scrimmage, that roughhouse football so beloved of Kinnaird, the Old Etonians and the London-centric clubs in England, was not for them. Their players were young, fit, fast and very athletic, preferring a swift and offensive attacking game not unlike that practiced by Hunter and Blackburn Olympic a few years later. They were also ahead of the times when it came to some of the smaller details of the still-developing game. One example is the kit they wore. English clubs and players, in yet another nod to the dreaded mob football, tended to dress for a match as if they were about to go into battle with thick, heavy wool jerseys, long and equally thick shorts and socks, together with boots that doubled as those they wore for work, so they would be tipped with steel toe caps as well as metal studs or tacks that were hammered into the sole, giving players some stability on the muddy pitches they played on. It's football apparel at its earliest and most basic, and, in terms of the boots they wore, positively prehistoric. Little wonder Kinnaird was as likely to break other people's legs as he was his own when he was playing. In contrast, Dresden's players wore coloured kits, of which the tops were as likely to be made out of silk as they were wool and relatively light and, according to one player at the time, 'very comfortable shoes or boots'. And, whilst they weren't exactly Adidas Copa Mundial boots, they were infinitely superior to the hob-nailed, steel-toed variety that found its way into the formative years of the British game.

The modern version of the game reached Italy at around the same time with the first Italian football club widely believed to have been the Genoa Cricket and Football Club were formed in 1893. Their origins lie in their name; does anyone think a group of red-blooded Italian men would have longed for the sound of leather on willow during infinitesimally long summer afternoons in Liguria? Of course not. Its formation was, once again, down to the exploits of bored Englishmen abroad.

The club was originally founded with athletics in mind and football a secondary consideration, eventually becoming the prime focus of the club in 1897 under the watchful eye of one James Richardson Spensley. He was London born and a bit of an all-rounder in life, being not only a doctor by trade but combining that with a lot of football (he was a goalkeeper, albeit not a very good one) as well as being a boxer, linguist, journalist and scout leader. He'd travelled to Genoa principally to treat English sailors who had docked there but soon found himself being distracted by the lure of football, eventually becoming the club's first manager and, no doubt to a few concerned cries of 'I say old chap', going as far as allowing a few Italian men to join the club.

One distinction that he and Genoa had to call their own was the fact that the club was amongst the very first to play in international friendly matches, their opponents of choice being the crewmen of some of the British naval ships docked in the harbour. They duly recorded a notable victory over the crew of *HMS Clementine* but lost in a follow-up game to the sailors of the famous dreadnought *HMS Revenge* who, you would imagine, were under the strictest of instructions to win by just about any means possible, fair or foul. For the good of the Empire, you understand.

Further recognition of the influence of the English as football spread throughout Europe is evident in Spain where, for example, Seville FC, founded in 1890, still retain the 'FC' part of their name (short for football club as opposed to CF, *club de futbol* in Spanish), and in France where Le Havre AC were formed in 1872 by a group of British residents. Back to Italy now where, to this day, AC Milan have retained the English spelling of their city name rather than the Italian *Milano* in tribute to their English founders, two men from Nottingham, Alfred Edwards and Herbert Kilpin. And the influence of the English on the spread of the game doesn't stop there, not by a long shot. Grasshoppers in Switzerland, Athletic Bilbao in Spain, Newell's Old Boys in Argentina and Everton de Vina del Mar (Everton for short) founded in Chile in 1909 by a group of Anglo-Chilean teenagers are amongst the myriad and often noteworthy clubs throughout world football whose origins derive from the determination of English expats to do something with their time rather than just sit around and complain about this damned hot weather and how perfectly intolerable foreign food was.

A game of football, after all, was not only healthy and suitable vigorous in nature, but it also had the added benefit of giving you an opportunity to beat the locals at something!

As the 19th century drew to a close, the dominant formation in the game remained that of 'combination' football, the Pyramid – that is, two defenders, three midfielders and five attacking players, named as such because when viewed from above the team's shape roughly resembles that of a pyramid with the goalkeeper the lone figure at the very top. Jack Hunter's success with that formation and manner of play, the one that had originally been developed in Scotland by the players of Queen's Park FC had drifted over the border into England and was now being exported into Europe and championed as the 'right way' to play by progressive clubs. Genoa were just one example, a forward-thinking club that preferred the balance between attacking and defending to that of the scrimmages of old; the two defenders in the side were encouraged to zonally mark the advanced central trio of attackers in the opposing side whilst the three midfielders would mark their opposite numbers.

From that shapeless bustle of up to 20 players, all kicking, elbowing and pushing each other in the process, to zonal marking and strict lines denoting defence, midfield and attack in a little over two decades. Football was growing up whilst at the same time interest in the sport was going through the roof. A little over 4,000 fans had bothered to attend the 1884 English FA Cup Final between Blackburn Rovers and Queen's Park in 1884 yet, for the last final of that century, 73,833 had crammed into the Crystal Palace stadium in London to watch Sheffield United beat Derby County 4-1. This was a match between two sides that were nowhere near London; indeed, in the case of Sheffield, at that time the steel-making centre of England, the city was nearly 200 miles away.

It was a case of put on a game, and they will come.

For that final, both clubs utilised the Pyramid formation; the reporter dispatched by London-based newspaper *The Observer* duly observing that, even though Derby were without two of their key players for the game, they still played with 'splendid dash and skill' throughout the first half. Splendid dash AND skill? Whatever would Lord Kinnaird have had to say about that? More to the point, what might he have done to stop the Derby players exhibiting such wanton footballing habits? No prizes for guessing the steel toe-capped boots of old might have gotten some even greater than usual practice at making contact with skin and bone. One of Derby's forwards in the match has the distinction to this day of being one of the game's first superstars, an epithet that is perhaps bandied around too easily and at the promptings of only a half-decent season or two in the modern game. This was not the case with Steve Bloomer, who at 25 was nearing his peak as a player and sportsman of the highest order, being extraordinarily proficient in cricket and baseball as well as football. Over the course of his Derby County career, he scored 332 goals in 525 appearances, adding a further 28 goals in just 23 appearances for England. He was a player able to excel because of the Pyramid formation; quick of both thought and movement, he was also extraordinarily strong, despite not being the most physical imposing of men. But he was fit, an athlete par excellence as his prowess in those two other sports illustrate, compelling evidence of the 'new professionalism' which was sweeping through the game throughout Europe, one which had seen the evolution of the flexible and tactically savvy Pyramid formation; emerge from the dark chaos of mob football. Players were fitter, they were tactically aware, they wanted to improve and they wanted to play as part of a team where each and every one of them had a specific role to play and responsibilities to follow.

Steve Bloomer in the national jersey

Bloomer's job was simple. Score goals. No need to worry about anything or anyone else. But he would be the first to acknowledge the role that those teammates had to play with regard to his feats, including, at international level, his fellow forward Gilbert Smith. Smith was respected enough as a player to get an obituary in *The Times* after his death in 1943, noting that he was 'a maker, rather than a scorer of goals.'

Now stop for a moment. Take a breath and read that again. *He was a* **maker**, *rather than a scorer of goals*.

This is a piece referring to a footballer who was born in 1872. It's a well-used phrase in the modern game, an easy reference to give a modern striker who, whilst he may wear the number 9 on his shirt or play in the traditional centre forward role, may not always be there for the goals he scores but for the opportunities he creates, one way or another, for his teammates, and not always in and around the penalty area. Most of the great international sides have had this type of player, many of them have gone to World Cups. They are informally referred to today as 'false number 9s'– a perfect description of someone who isn't what he appears to be. In recent years, England have played Emile Heskey[11] in that role – a physically dominating forward with a licence to roam, to draw his marker away from danger areas or a target for the high or long ball, someone for the smaller forwards or advancing midfield players to feed off.

The equally imposing Luca Toni has played a similar role in the Italian national side whilst Roy Makaay, six goals in 43 appearances, did much the same for the Netherlands. Makaay was greatly valued for his ability in the air as well as for his sheer presence, a player who the likes of Patrick Kluivert and Ruud Van Nistelrooy (35 goals in 70 appearances for the Netherlands) would have enjoyed playing alongside because of the unselfish manner in which he contributed to both their game and the team in general. And that is what Gilbert Smith was, an early prototype of the false number 9 – selfless and able to carry out his role to such a high level that, in doing so, he made the players around him stand out so much that they got the plaudits and the headlines rather than Smith. Not that Bloomer was unaware or unwilling to show his gratitude to his England teammate, commenting that Smith '...transformed the role of the centre-forward from that of an individual striker to a unifier of the forward line, indeed, the whole team' – a statement that Michael Owen could easily have said about Heskey or Kluivert of Makaay, such was the similarity of the roles they played.

---

11   *Heskey made 62 appearances for England from 1999 to 2010, rated and respected enough by five different full-time England managers including Glenn Hoddle and Fabio Capello. His goal return of just 7 from those games emphasises just how much he was valued for all the work he did on the pitch that didn't involve scoring goals.*

That begs the question, therefore, of whether Smith could have played in the game today. Could he have lined up in the current England team alongside Wayne Rooney or Danny Welbeck; could he, at club level, slotted in alongside someone like Ezequiel Lavezzi at Paris Saint-Germain, or, and here's a delicious thought, could he have complemented Cristiano Ronaldo at Real Madrid?

You'd like to think he could. Contemporary reports describe Smith, like Bloomer, as being a complete athlete, noted for his exceptional balance and timing as well as his ability when on the ball to either run with it or make a pass, short or long. He certainly didn't fit the description of the late 19th-century centre forward. He was of slight build, didn't like heading the ball if he could help it (one report suggested he wanted heading the ball banned from the game) and suffered from asthma. Quite what Kinnaird might have done to him is not worth thinking about; indeed, it's true to say that, whilst Smith could probably have played at the highest level of the game at any point of the 20th century and into the following one, he wouldn't have lasted five minutes had he been born just two decades earlier. Kinnaird would have seen to that.

Bloomer would also have prospered in the modern game. He was, for a sport that was still finding its way, the complete player, one who was ahead of both his and the game's time. Sir Frederick Wall, a former FA secretary, recalls how Bloomer would, in the manner of any great goalscorer, look for any chance to score, commenting that he always '...tried to take every chance, every half chance from any angle that presented itself. There was no hesitation, [no] desire to trap the ball or steady it[12]...[he] wanted the ball near the goal, [he] lived to shoot...the keepers would say it was difficult to tell which foot he would use for a shot.'

---

12   *And little wonder, that would have been Smith's responsibility!*

Jesse Pennington, another England teammate of Bloomer's, commented that Bloomer was very much a two-footed player, able to pass or shoot equally well with either his right or left foot, adding that he '...never had a swing at the ball, his shot was quick, like a boxers short punch. He was also quite a good header of the ball and he was a quick mover over short distances.'[13]

The great player he was, one who is deservedly recognised as the game's first footballing superstar,[14] he, like Smith, would seem to be as easily able to play in the modern game as he did over a century ago, even if the famous Pyramid formation, the 2-3-5 that he and Gilbert Smith were familiar with, has now been turned on its head to a 5-3-2. But no matter, Smith and Bloomer would have played in attack on their own and excelled at that.

The scrimmage had expired and gone to meet its maker.

The Pyramid formation now dominated the British game; it was one that was played by all of the leading clubs as well as the national side. Even the once reticent London clubs, previously almost hostile to their northern equivalents and all things 'professional', had adopted it. The success of Tottenham in the 1901 FA Cup Final (London's first success in the tournament since 1882) illustrated how they, then a non-league club, had successfully adopted that formation and style of play. A non-league side winning the FA Cup? There must, the old traditionalists would have mused, be something in this. Their win in the competition that year put the final nail into the already cold coffin of mob football, of

---

13   Referenced from www.cradleylinks.com.

14   As befitting any footballing superstar, Steve's wife, Sarah has now been described as the 'game's first WAG'! Mind you, the media attention she received in comparison to a certain Mrs Beckham, for example, was minimal. When Steve and Sarah married in 1896, it got the merest footnote in the Derby Daily Telegraph which observed, 'By the way, Steve Bloomer was married this Wednesday afternoon'.

the scrimmage. It had, to paraphrase a future West Ham fan, passed on, it was no more, it had ceased to be.

The Pyramid was now seen as being the way ahead. Except that it wasn't, at least, not everywhere or by everyone. Because as the game continued to spread throughout Europe and South America where, once both the presence and interest of the British expats began to both physically and mentally wane, not a little bit of scepticism and self-assertion began to creep into the minds of those they had left behind. Shape was, they agreed, important, but so was style, flair and panache even. Despite the advances it had made in only a few decades, football was hardly the 'beautiful game' in any way or form. Efficient, yes. Effective, yes. Disciplined, most certainly. But where was the movement, the fluidity? Players knew what their roles were, and they stuck to them resolutely and without question. Steve Bloomer was a magnificent player, of that there was no doubt. But he'd never been encouraged or felt inclined to widen his understanding of the game, to become more than a mere goal scorer. What if he was able to fashion, to create goals as well as score them himself? But not just Bloomer, what if the thinking behind the game encouraged *every* player to think for himself a little bit more rather than simply adhere to the plan? The importance of sheer physicality and strength in the British game had remained devoutly in place (and has, arguably, never gone away), and it was this aspect of it that European and South American club coaches and players started to shy away from, taking ownership of the game and the way they felt it should be played away from their British founders and influence.

One such club were Barcelona, currently, and rightly, revered as one of the biggest, most popular and attractive to watch football clubs on the planet. Their first president had been an Englishman, one Walter Wild, who combined playing duties with that of leading the club from 1899 to 1901. The club itself, founded by Swiss businessman Joan Gamper, held its first club meeting in 1899 following an appeal for players, a meeting that saw 11 interested individuals attend, three of whom were English. Wild, in a moment of marketing ingenuity, adopted the Catalan name Gualteri, plus brothers John and William Parsons. Surprisingly (or perhaps not) Wild was elected as club president, with another Englishman, Arthur Witty, becoming president of the club two years later.

This is *the* Barcelona we're referring to here, by the way. The Barcelona of Johan, Txiki, Diego, Andres, Lionel and Pep. Continental names, continental spirit, players whom, at the very mention of their names, conjure up an image of sophisticated football with flair in abundance. Style rather than shape. But not back then. That was the Barcelona of John, William and Arthur. Witty was particularly committed to establishing a code of conduct at the club which every player was expected to adhere to without question. This included never talking, discussing or arguing any action or decision made by the referee; accepting that, if they lost a game, it was because the other side were better than they were, a fact they had to acknowledge by shaking their victors hands and, no matter what, to always act as a gentleman, both on and off the pitch. Being something of an rugby aficionado as well, Witty also insisted that his players were never hurt, even if they were, and should always pick themselves up and keep going.

Admirable, of course. But rather staid, even boring. And very British in outlook. It was never going to last. And it didn't. Witty was succeeded by the Catalan musician Josep Soler in 1905, and, from that moment, the British influence at the club, both in its culture and ideology as well as its style of play, began to fade. Soler, for a start, was a bit of a rebel, an avowed Catalan who wanted his football club to represent his city and Catalonia. Great Britain was, like Spain itself, too 'establishment'. And

Barcelona was never going to be a club of the establishment. They would be free spirits, doing things their way with that flair and style that was missing from the efficient yet limited ways of the Pyramid.

They wouldn't, of course, hesitate, just as they do not today, to recruit the very best in both playing and coaching talent to the club. Yet it was made very clear to both the rest of Spain as well as the growing football world that supporting and being part of Barcelona was not about the establishment but about a connection with the ever-present historical struggle for the club to retain its Catalonian culture and identity. They were throwing off the shackles and looking to do things their own way, just as many of the other clubs around the world with British roots and origins were beginning to do exactly the same.

And this spelt trouble for the conventional, and very English, Pyramid, now regarded as ancient a monument as the physical examples that stand in Egypt. Only not as revered or treasured.

The Pyramid formation remained the standard in England. Once revolutionary and daring, it was now, in that country at least, becoming rather a rigid and predictable type of play. Admittedly, you couldn't knock it or the approach. It was effective, and it worked. It had certainly served Preston North End very well during the very first English league season as they cantered to First Division Championship success without losing a game in 1889. They played the Pyramid formation just as the 11 other teams in the league did. But there was nothing different about the way they played, no revolutionary tactics or coaches like Jack Hunter leading the way with more of his own unique way of doing things. What Preston had ensured was that they played the system better than anyone else could or did. Yes, everyone was playing the same game, adopting the same shape, doing the same things. But Preston did it better than anyone else. Not least because their manager, William Sudell, recruited specialists for his team, making sure it contained as many Scottish players as possible, something he got around by giving those he wanted at the club jobs in the cotton mill he managed.

Was he 'buying' the Championship? It's an all too common accusation driven at the biggest and best clubs in the world today, that their success is solely down to the fact that they can afford to buy and play the best players in the world. It's a criticism that has long been levelled at Chelsea and Manchester City in England, Real Madrid in Spain, Bayern Munich in Germany and, in more recent years, Paris Saint-Germain in France. Though a big club, PSG had struggled financially for much of their brief history (they were only formed in 1970); the poor balance at the bank meaning they often had a team that didn't, and couldn't, live up to the expectations of their support. In the 10 seasons from 2002 to 2011, their final League placing in France's Ligue One was 4th, 11th, 2nd, 9th, 9th, 15th, 16th and 6th. Not particularly bad but not very good either if you aspire, as they did, to being successful club worthy of the city you represent. Imagine, if you will, Arsenal and Chelsea in England or PSV Eindhoven in the Netherlands, River Plate and Boca Juniors finishing 15th and 16th over two consecutive seasons in their respective leagues. Intolerable! Yet that was how it was for Paris Saint-Germain, hamstrung by debt and seemingly destined to always be bit part players to the long established giants of French domestic football, especially Lyon with seven consecutive Ligue One titles from 2002 to 2008 to their name. The same in England applied to Manchester City, who, since their Division One title success (now the Premier League) in 1968 had seen their city rivals Manchester United win the top honours in England in 12 different occasions with their other closest rivals, Liverpool, winning it 11 times.

For Manchester City and for Paris Saint-Germain, the only way to be dominant again was to be able to afford to buy the very best players, something which, for both clubs, became a reality when they were bought by wealthy owners. Had that not happened, it is very likely that both clubs would have remained trophyless rather than going on to win major honours with the world's greatest players suddenly happy to play for them. Manchester City won the Premier League title in 2012 and 2014; Paris Saint-Germain won Ligue One, for the first time in 19 years, in 2013, following that up with a second consecutive victory the following season. But neither team had done it because their coaching operations had improved or because they had introduced new formations and ways to play.

They'd 'bought' their respective honours just as a lottery winner living in a one-bedroom flat can suddenly afford a twenty-bedroom mansion. It's not down to their actions or endeavours that they've bought that property, it's because of the money. Even an economics professor writing for Wall Street publication *Forbes* knew what Manchester City had done. Stefan Szymanski observed, 'Money buys success—it's not a very exciting observation, but one that I have always believed to be the fundamental truth about football.' Szymanski is correct. But nothing is new under the sun, and it is exactly what Preston North End had done in 1889, and he could just as easily have been referring to events in Lancashire, England 127 years ago when he said it as he could about Chelsea, Manchester City and Paris Saint-Germain, to name but three examples of today.

This 'new professionalism', of devising any and all means possible of winning games without necessarily playing better than your opponents, was not universally popular. There is little doubt that, by looking to get the very best players in their team, in such a spurious manner (a job was always found for them by Sudell and both the working hours and conditions experienced by his players never seemed to be as long or arduous as they did for the regular employees), would certainly have been frowned upon by both other clubs and the FA. Even Corinthians, the London based club formed in 1882 with the objective of doing for England's national team what Queen's Park had done for the Scottish team, refused to have anything to do with anything that might have been regarded as overtly professional – in other words, going against the spirit of the game. Most of their players were affiliated to southern Universities whilst, upon the formation of the Football League, Corinthians refused to participate as one of the club rules strictly forbade them to 'compete for any challenge cup or prizes of any description.' Which is a pity, because they were a good side, indeed, potentially a great one, another Dresden or Barcelona in the making. Or a Preston. They would have certainly ran Preston very close for that first ever English league title in 1889, and, had they won it, the fact that they had done so from a dedication to sportsmanship and fair play rather than, as Preston had, signing all the best players, might have set the future of the game on an entirely different path. They eventually entered the FA Cup for the first time in 1923 (by now most of their starched collar and very traditionalist founders had either moved on or passed away), having made the momentous internal decision to '...depart from their usual rules and to take part in a contest which did not have charity as its primary object.'

The ideals of the Corinthians Club were so anti-professionalism and the path the game was treading that they even refused to take penalties if awarded (within the game, the penalty was originally called the 'kick of death' – perhaps that is why Corinthians refused to take them?), the reason being that they believed that no player would ever deliberately trip or foul an opponent. They also chose, when one of the opposing players had to leave the field hurt (substitutes were not introduced into the game in England until 1965), to remove one of their own players from the pitch in return so that the numbers on both sides remained even.

Thus, you had the two extremes in the game. On one side there was Preston North End, all conquering, professional, doing whatever it took to win. And doing it very well indeed, remaining unbeaten throughout the entire 1888/89 season, winning a League and FA Cup double and doing so with six prominent Scottish players in their ranks, one of whom, James Ross is said to have scored 250 goals in just 220 games for Preston. They were the game's first behemoths, strong, unyielding, win at all costs, a team from a working-class town made up of working-class players, but one which, as far as preparation, planning and professionalism was concerned, was top of the class, a football club with no equal.

Then there was Corinthians, a throwback to the (even then) 'olde world' ethos of play up, play up and play the game, of good sportsmanship and endeavour, of wanting to see the other chap do his best more than you wanted it for yourself, of desiring glorious defeat rather than a questionable or ill-deserved victory. Of being gentlemen above all else.

Attitudes that might have been all very well on the playing fields of Eton or in and around other elite British educational or military establishments. But which were, as far as the game of football was concerned, as archaic and out of touch with the way the game was expanding as the dinosaurs. Professionalism was now everything. And it was embodied by Preston North End. Proud Preston, the 'Invincibles', had swept aside those old-fashioned values within the game with their single-minded drive for success, their determination to have the best players and to acquire them in any way possible.

An approach that opened up new ideas as to how the game could be played or, to put it more succinctly, how to play to win. It was time for the first of a new breed of footballing men to shape the game in their image so that clubs could now look to do just that.

The time of the modern football coach had arrived. With that came some of the football formations we know today.

CHAPTER THREE:
A NEW APPROACH

Hogan had certainly been noticed, and he had been noticed by the FA. Not the English FA, of course. They were too busy trying to pretend he didn't exist.

So, in summary:

Football *was* changing.

It was no longer a pursuit followed by the wealthy and privileged, those lords and sundry other titled gentlemen who played for the clubs that dominated the early game. Teams like Wanderers, Old Etonians, Oxford University, Royal Engineers and Old Carthusians. They'd dominated the early years of the game. Privileged and wealthy young men who could afford to play the game for a bit of a laugh. It was a sideline, a pastime, a rich man's plaything, one that was stolen, in a move akin to the street urchin making off with the lord of the manor's best silver, by Blackburn Olympic, a team of working men from a working town who, with their FA Cup triumph of 1883, had opened up the game to a whole new host of possibilities.

The English football league, the very first of its type anywhere in the world, commenced its inaugural season just five years after the Olympic's FA Cup triumph. Of the 12 founder member clubs, not one came from London, the London area or even southern England. Indeed, the club that was placed, geographically, closest to London from that historic dozen was Birmingham-based Aston Villa, a 'mere' 118 miles or so from the nation's capital.

Football had been mugged. The North had come, seen and conquered – in England at least.

How had they done this, how had one part of the country, systematically and emphatically, come to dominate the English game?

The answer is, as we have seen in the previous chapter with Preston North End, the growing influence and role of professionalism, one that was swiftly being adopted by clubs overseas keen to go their own way and, in doing so, reflect local and national characteristics rather than the rigid ways set down by their English founders, whether players or bureaucrats.

Blackburn Olympic's Jack Hunter was one of the first renowned football coaches to work in the game. He was, as we have seen, a visionary, a man way, way ahead of both his time and that of the sport. He'd seen the obstacles that his players had needed to overcome in order to compete with their southern rivals and had acted upon it accordingly, developing training routines that focused on their health and well-being. This included fitness, diet and an emphasis on team spirit; all revolutionary ideas at the time, ones that the FA[15] collectively tut-tutted at (with even the occasional harrumph) but felt powerless to do anything about. Yet, for all his genius, Hunter was never really trusted with a 'top' job and drifted out of the game, a victim more of the ongoing suspicion of coaching than of his own reputation as a maverick.

And that might have been that had another top coach, one as left field in his ideas as Hunter had been, not come onto the footballing scene in the early years of the 20th century.

His name was Jimmy Hogan. And he should be as much of a legend in the game today as Pelé.

---

15   *The English FA never really accepted the fact that good football teams needed a dedicated and suitably qualified coach to lead them, denying it to such an extent that England's national side, which played its first international game in 1872, did not have a coach solely in charge of team affairs until 1946.*

Jimmy Hogan in 1936.

As a player, Hogan could best be described as a journeyman, starting his playing career with Rochdale Town in 1902 before subsequent moves to Burnley, Nelson, Fulham, Swindon Town and Bolton Wanderers. It's fair to say he didn't make much of an impact as a player – a Steve Bloomer he was not, or even a Gilbert Smith.

He was, however, a student of the game, one who realised throughout his career that poorly executed passes, bad shots and any and all mistakes that a player might make in the course of a game were not, as one of his managers had suggested, down to bad luck but due to bad technique on the part of the player. This, Hogan mused, could be something that he or any other player could eliminate from their game through devotion to one thing: practicing their technique.

Such thoughts amongst players might have been regarded as near to heresy at the time. Training was, by now, a mildly accepted part of the game. That is, as long as it dealt with the virtues of physical fitness and strength, a notion that the culture of the time deemed essential and a sign of 'clean living' to all men. Not surprisingly, some football clubs promoted the benefits of physical fitness with so much zeal that some of their sessions would have closely resembled military fitness drills with the only evidence of a ball in these sessions being a heavy medicine ball rather than an actual football. The dominant logic at the time dictated that if you kept the players and the ball apart in between games then, rather like starving dogs denied meat, by the time they saw one again in match, their desire to possess it would have made them unbeatable.

Hogan went as far as developing and building an exercise cycle for his personal use, avowing that its daily use would help improve his pace, only to find out that its only real 'benefit' was in tightening his calf muscles. But that was not the point; he had, to paraphrase Thomas Edison, not failed but merely found a way of doing something that didn't work. From then on, he was hooked on improving himself and his game by means of technique and the practise and study of same. He was all set to become of THE first great *coaches* (rather than 'trainers') in the sport.

The tragedy for the English game was that it was amongst the far more progressive and eager to learn clubs and associations within continental Europe that he found his place rather than the clubs and games in northern England where he had spent much of his playing career. Hogan's impact in countries such as Hungary, Switzerland and Germany was enormous, his influence on tactics and formations significant enough for the legendary Gusztav Sebes, the coach of that great Hungary side of the 1950s (we will be looking at the impact they had on the game later on in this book) to proclaim that, 'When our football history is told, his name should be written in gold letters.'

Praise indeed for a man who was, and remains, disgracefully, a virtual unknown in his country of birth.

Hogan's time at Fulham as a player acted as fuel for his coaching ambitions. He had been asked to join the London club by their manager, one Harry Bradshaw who, although a more than competent administrator and businessman, knew absolutely nothing about football and wasn't, to his credit, afraid to admit it.[16] He made up for that by employing people who did, players like Hogan as well as a few players from Scotland, players steeped in the passing game that had originated in that country and who were still exporting those skills south of the border, as they continued to do so a century later. That combination saw Fulham win Southern League championships, gain promotion to the Football League as a consequence and even reach the semi-finals of the FA Cup. This was

---

16   *If only some of the present-day club owners would admit to the same failings rather than trying to do the coaches' job for them.*

a truly extraordinary achievement for a club who were, prior to Hogan joining, heartily content at going absolutely nowhere and making a very good job of it.

You might reasonably think that this record of achievement and ongoing success might make Bradshaw rather keen to tie Hogan down to his club for as long as he possibly could. That did not prove to be the case. Hogan sustained a knee injury during his time with the club, one that cast doubt over him being able to continue as a player. Bradshaw's business mind was set from then on. No matter what Hogan's knowledge of the game might have been or his undoubted leadership and coaching qualities were, he was, first and foremost, a player.

Thus Bradshaw, unable to even begin to conceive the idea of retaining Hogan simply as a coach, chose not to renew his contract. Hogan had, by now, decided that his priorities lay in coaching anyway, his 'Damascus moment' coming during a pre-season tour with Bolton Wanderers, the club he joined after leaving Fulham. During the course of the tour, Bolton had beaten a team based in southern Holland called Dordrecht 10-0. Emphatic as the victory had been, Hogan mused afterwards that he would like one day 'to go back and teach those fellows properly.' Throwaway remark or not, in its saying he had set the wheels in motion for his remarkable career in the game to well and truly take off.

The spark to all of this came as a result of a meeting Hogan had with James Howcroft, a friend who worked as a referee; the games Howcroft took charge of included many on continental Europe. Howcroft mentioned during the course of the conversation that he had refereed in Holland and knew of a club that was looking for a new coach, but not only that, a coach who had core experience within the British game. That club was Dordrecht.

To Hogan this must have seemed like fate served up on a plate alongside an appetising garnish. He'd played against the club, knew it and their players, players who, yes, had been outclassed in their outing against Bolton. Yet to Hogan these players looked to play the game in the right way. They'd largely been physically outfought against Bolton, a side with more than one player in their line-up able to look after himself, and, despite the battering they inevitably got at the hands of the English side, Hogan had admired how they had stuck to their beliefs and game, trying to the end to out-pass and out-think their illustrious opponents. He simply could not resist the opportunity, nor the way it had presented itself to him, a year after he had made that seemingly throwaway comment about wanting to teach those 'fellows' how to play the game properly.

It is important to remember at this point that Hogan was not the product of any coaching course at the time. There weren't any; in fact, there were barely any coaches in the traditional sense. Clubs were run in a fairly autocratic manner by managers, men who were skilled administrators and orators able to run the club on behalf of the owners who appointed them, as was the case with Harry Bradshaw at Fulham. They invariably lacked any football knowledge. Bradshaw's limited comprehension of the game as a sport meant that the thought of employing Hogan solely as a coach had never entered his mind. It wasn't, in other words, something he even considered as an option before rejecting it. He just never knew it was an option in the first place. The concept of coaching, briefly brought into the spotlight by Hunter at Blackburn Olympic, was still anathema within the game, a game that believed that as long as the players were fit then everything else could look after itself. Hunter, unable to stay in the game, had drifted out of it and into obscurity before an early death. It is more than likely that had Hogan tried to follow in his footsteps in England the same might have happened to him: the obscurity and exit from the game, at least. Yet if he was to try to launch his career in

Europe, surrounded by more progressive clubs and people that ran them, maybe, just maybe, he could return to England and take a high-profile coaching job in his home country.

Which didn't seem at all an unreasonable thought.

Hogan duly got the job and began it as he meant to go on. The attaining of physical fitness was, for him, something that his players could pretty much address in their own time. He took it as read that professional sportsmen would look after themselves, so instead of spending time watching his new players run, run, and then run some more followed by a little bit more running, he introduced to their training sessions an object that had rarely, if ever, been seen as part of them in England. It was called a football.

English football fans might, at this point, like to look back to 1996 and the appointment of Arsène Wenger as manager of Arsenal. Wenger immediately raised eyebrows, not to mention a few hackles in his early days at Highbury, banning his players from eating anything other than those items he believed (and there weren't many!) made up a healthy diet. He was also behind the introduction in their coaching of sessions of disciplines like yoga and Pilates, much to the disdain of the footballing traditionalists who had questioned his appointment anyway, not least because Wenger arrived in England after a spell coaching the game in Japan.

'What on earth', mused his critics, 'can a Frenchman, who's hardly played the game and has been coaching in Japan, teach us about football?'

Arsène Wenger

A great deal it would seem. As was also the case with Hogan at Dordrecht. Luckily for Hogan, many of his young charges were students. They, therefore, had an aptitude for learning; they wanted to hear his ideas and were open enough to listen to them. And listen they did. The values that Hogan wanted them to most appreciate were those that had been introduced into the English game from Scotland, notably the Queen's Park Club. These were those notions of playing the game in a 'thoughtful' manner, of finding space on the pitch to run into when the players didn't have the ball as well as when they did have it, of a passing game with plenty of movement and imagination. It was one where each player in the team was able to contribute a special quality rather than all of them simply being able to knock an opponent over with one swing of a mighty steel-capped boot.

Scotland had exported its game to England where, like many things that originated north of Hadrian's Wall, it was met with a measure of suspicion and distrust. In Europe, though, they were hooked from the off. This type of game encouraged thinking and creativity; it was also less rigid than the previous model of the game that had been brought over to Europe, one typified by a 2-3-5 formation which ensured that every player knew his place as well as the place of his teammates. Woe betide anyone who tried to shift their game away from that sort of thinking and where it might have left them.

Hogan liked 2-3-5. It did work, and it did provide the necessary balance between attack and defence. However, like those Europeans who had started to regard its rigidity with scepticism, he believed that it needed to be pepped up with a little more movement, on and off the ball – that and passes that were deliberate and played to the feet of a teammate rather than long, hopeful punts into space. For Hogan, keeping hold of the ball was King (is this beginning to sound like tiki-taka to you?); nothing else mattered. It is such a simple belief as far as the game is concerned, a belief that says as long as we have the ball, the other team cannot hurt us. Yet no one had taken it to heart as a basic principle of how the game could be played, no one, at least, until now. Hogan would have recognised that Barcelona side of Pep Guardiola; he might even have called them one of his own.

Barcelona FC training in Hamburg in 1963.

In football, as we discover time and time again, nothing is new under the sun.

As a result of Hogan's philosophy and deep thinking, the Pyramid formation, something which had been the core of all football for nearly three decades, was about to get a makeover, and the game was, again, about to take a giant leap forward. Not that it hadn't already at Dordrecht where Hogan had introduced theory and tactics through the now tried and tested method of a blackboard, one that he filled with Xs, Os and arrows, illustrating where he expected his players to be, where opponents would be (easy enough to deduce, given they'd all be playing pretty much the same variant of the original 2-3-5 formation) and what movement and positions his players should take up.

Technical team talks using blackboards remained de rigeur in the game for over a century following their introduction to the game by coaches like Hogan; they were an essential part of any club's day-to-day life and a ubiquitous sight in every changing room at every club, from the smallest in the game to the mightiest of behemoths. Back in 1910, it was as revolutionary a step then as the advent of iPads and Prozone has been in the modern game in the last decade or so.

Hogan had certainly been noticed, including by the FA. Not the English FA, of course. They were too busy trying to pretend he didn't exist. No, on this occasion, his admirers were the Dutch FA who, based on the impact he'd made at Dordrecht, asked him to take over their national team for a one-off match against Germany, which, against expectations, they won. That win and the reputation he was now building for himself in the Netherlands should have been the catalyst for bigger and better things for Hogan, but he was a pragmatic man who, despite his now burgeoning coaching career, still felt he had something to offer the game as a player. He returned to Bolton to do just that, the club wisely having retained his registration, and, with Hogan in the playing ranks, they finished second in English football's Division Two at the end of the 1910/11 season, winning an immediate promotion back to Division One in the process. A year later, having played his part in helping the team finish in a highly respectable 4th place, he decided to spend the summer of 1912 looking for, and working in, another coaching role, one that came to him through a meeting, again arranged by his friend Howcroft, with another of the games early pioneering coaches, the Bohemian-born Hugo Meisl.

Meisl remains, arguably, the first truly great coach in European football. His interest in the game was not immediate; indeed, he began his professional life in banking, but, after moving on and into an administrative role with the Austrian FA, he developed a healthy appetite for all things football, swiftly rising to the position of general secretary as well as training to be a match referee. His reward for that particular endeavour was a game in the 1912 Olympic Games, which were held in Sweden. Previous to that, Meisl had taken charge of the first-ever international match between Hungary and England in June 1908. England won, and convincingly, to the tune of 7-0, due in large part to Chelsea's George Hilsdon, a player with the nickname of 'Gatling gun', the reason being, as if further explanation were necessary, that his shots were '...simply unstoppable and which travel like shots from a *gun*.'

Hilsdon was following in the powerful footsteps of his illustrious predecessor in England's attack, the aforementioned Steve Bloomer. He, like Bloomer, was fast, strong and direct, with an eye for goal and a tendency to shoot at every opportunity. His presence and role in the England team neatly summed up the way that team, one that was still picked by an FA committee (which had its collective eye on the good old days of the scrimmage and had little time for coaching and tactics), played, the style of the team mirroring Hilsdon's own approach to the game.

In other words, uncomplicated.

Yes, English football had, reluctantly, accepted the 2-3-5 formation as the way ahead for the game, one that, at least, distinguished football as both a playing and spectating event, distinguishing it from rugby, as well as the brawling ruckus that had been mob football. But that was as far as they were prepared to go. There was certainly no room in the game for visionaries, individuals who wanted to see the game grow and progress. Jack Hunter, the forward-thinking coach of Blackburn Olympic had followed up his remarkable success with that club by combining working as a licensee with coaching a non-league side, whilst the man he would have been proud to have been a mentor to, Jimmy Hogan, was forced to work outside of England in order to find the kind of tolerance for new ways of thinking and playing the game that was far more readily embraced in Europe than it was in England.

So, despite being aware of England's predictable triumph in 1908, Hogan's sympathies and support would, again, have been for the 'underdogs', in this case, the beleaguered Hungarians. They had at least tried, in vain, to mimic the way their opponents played and paid the price. But at least, he would have mused, the same thoughts that would have been coursing through Meisl's mind as he refereed that game, the Hungary players played with a little more flair and imagination. Yes, their playing formation may have been the same at the start of the game, yet they were far from being as rigid as the England players were. They were always seeking out space and opportunity in ways which defied current football convention and which, in part, contributed to their eventual heavy defeat.

Because England had, quite simply, brushed them aside. There was little finesse or imagination in England's play. Power and pace, yes; adherence to a game plan, most certainly yes. But it was predictable stuff, and, seven goal margin of victory or not, Meisl realised that it had been done at the expense of any aesthetic values: the 'beautiful game'[17] it was most certainly not. Both Meisl and Hogan thought that it should, and could be just that, or, at least something that was played and coached far, far differently to how it had been in England and, by default, in the rest of the world. Europe was already tiring of the English influence on the game, so it is wonderfully ironic that one of the men who went down in the game's history as working to help them escape it was an Englishman. Hogan's mantra of pass-and-move football, made in England but applied in the Netherlands with Dordrecht, was a philosophy that Meisl readily accepted and agreed to as being the way to play, to move forward. England had shown in their demolition of Hungary that if two sides played in broadly the same manner and with a similar formation and game plan, then the team that had the faster, stronger, more physical players would prevail. Every time and without exception. If Jack Hunter had attempted to match up the sheer physicality and brute strength of the Old Etonians by playing them at their own game, then yes, he might have gotten a 'well played old chap' at the end of the game – after his side had been well beaten. He'd decided not to play his illustrious opponents at their own game but to take his idea of how it should be played to them. The result was success, swift infamy and even swifter obscurity. But the foundation stone had been laid, and now people like Meisl and Hogan were busy building the walls of a new footballing age. The antipathy that the English FA had towards Hogan was so acute that, at one point, they actually accused him of being a 'traitor'; a reference to his working in Hungary throughout World War I. Little wonder that he chose to develop his friendship and professional relationship with Meisl in an environment that, like the Europe he worked

---

17   *That phrase had yet to come into existence – certainly as far as football is concerned where its origins are widely attributed to Pelé, a man who knew a thing or two about beauty and football. Interestingly, however, the term had already been coined and used twice in the 19th century, once in relation to an early form of lacrosse played by the native Ojibwe in North America and in 1890 to describe a game of tennis played in London. Sport and beauty were, as far as many people were concerned, two things that could, and should, go together, a desire that wasn't shared by the English FA.*

for the first three decades of the 20th century, was also affected by huge cultural and ideological change. The two of them went out of their way to share their ideas as well as absorb new ones from other coaches and nations throughout the continent with Meisl, in particular, a fanatical networker. As well as his friendship and work alongside Hogan, he also contacted and visited the Italian coach Vittorio Pozzo as well as Herbert Chapman, another with an, at best, modest record as a player but massive reputation as a coach. He was noted for his creation of the WM formation, the introduction and development of which we will explore in the next chapter.

The Austrian "Wunderteam" 1931

Meisl's influence on Austrian football could not go unnoticed. He took full control of their national side for a second time[18] in 1919, and, over the next decade, he masterminded their rise to footballing prominence as they became one of the most feared and accomplished international sides in the game. Amongst their impressive wins during the early years under Meisl was a 3-2 win over Germany, wins of 2-1 and 4-1 over Hungary, a 7-1 demolition of Switzerland and a 6-0 victory over Bulgaria.

---

18   *He also had a brief spell in charge of their national side from December 1912 to October 1914, a period that encompassed six games of which three ended in a win with one draw.*

On each of these occasions, the Austrian victory wasn't down to their steamrolling their opponents aside in a demonstration of overwhelming physical strength and power, as England's humiliation over Hungary had been in 1908, but by playing football as Meisl and, later, Hogan decreed. This put the emphasis on technique rather than that tried, tested and predictable formula of stamina and physicality. There can be little doubt that Meisl would have longed to have sent his team out to play against England, a game that would have been a real acid test of his methodology which, although it imitated the 2-3-5 formation in terms of how the teams lined up at kick-off, centered on his centre forward, Matthias Sindelar, who played in a slightly withdrawn position, one which was new to the game and extremely effective.

As centre forwards of the time went, Sindelar was, in many ways, everything that Steve Bloomer and George Hilsdon were not. For a start, he probably would not even have been considered for a starting place in any half-decent club team in England, let alone their international side. One of his nicknames was 'Der Papierene' which translates as 'the Paperman'. This was a cutting reference to his slight frame; Sindelar looked like a man who might be blown over in a slight breeze, never mind one who would battle it out as the leader of a line of five attacking players where the going would get rough. Meisl, therefore, drew him slightly back from the front line, allowing Sindelar a little more time and space to operate and best utilise his phenomenal ability on the ball, that special creative role and place for him in the side meaning the Austrians tended to play in 2-3-1-4 formation. As they did, Sindelar became a forerunner of the traditional number 10 so revered in the game today. He was a pioneering playmaker, the *trequartista*, a treasured role today, particularly in the Italian and Spanish game, but one long regarded as a 'luxury'[19] in English football.

---

19   *Perhaps the finest exponent of a trequartista in English football was, or could have been, Paul Scholes of Manchester United and England, a player of whom Zinedine Zidane said, 'You rarely come*

Austria did have a footballing history against England, albeit long before Meisl was involved with the squad. The two teams had met twice in 1908 and again the following year with England recording victories of 6-1, 11-1 and 8-1. The middle of those three games had been a particular embarrassment to the Austrian side as it had been played in Vienna, the intention being to showcase the national side to a population whose interest in the game was growing. They also wanted to see the England team 'in the flesh' in much the same way that people will turn out today to see any all-conquering sports side from another part of the world, either out of sheer curiousity or just to be able to say 'I was there'. England were light on visiting courtesies with one of their players, Tottenham's Vivian Woodward scoring four of the eleven goals scored against them. Woodward was the archetypal English footballing 'gentleman', cutting quite a dash in his immaculate kit and manner, 6-feet-2-inches of finely honed athlete who, unsurprisingly, was able to win every physical battle during the match, so much greater was his strength and stamina than that of his opponents. Austria were, like Hungary, torn apart by the massed ranks of English muscle and sinew, just as they were the following year when England recorded the 8-1 win.

Strangely enough, as the Austrian team found its own way of playing and began to win their games in as effective and overwhelming manner as England had long been used to, the English FA found various reasons to avoid playing them again. This state of affairs continued until 1930 when the two sides met again in Vienna for the second of two games in what was essentially regarded as an end-of-season 'gentlemen on tour' jolly for the England side and the accompanying FA bigwigs. England,

---

across the complete footballer but Scholes is as close to it as you can get.' Scholes would have fitted into that withdrawn forward role with England with consummate ease yet was hardly played there with some England managers choosing to play him on the left side of midfield instead. There can be little doubt that Meisl would have appreciated Scholes a lot more as a player and played him in his best position, a very sorry indication of the failings of English football when you consider the best international manager Scholes could have played under died 37 years before he was born.

then still managed and ran by an FA committee fortified on brandy and cigars rather than any coaching acumen, had only played four matches that season, beating Ireland (3-0), Wales (6-0) and Scotland (5-2) before a 3-3 draw against Germany four days before the Austria game.

The 0-0 draw that followed was the first game in which an England side had failed to score against an opposing international side from outside of Great Britain, a tribute to the way Meisl had organised his team, in particular the defence to keep out a formidable England attack that had scored 18 goals in its previous four outings. Confirmation, not that it was needed, that despite wide held belief to the contrary, size really didn't matter anymore. At least as far as football was concerned.

Meisl went on to guide Austria to a 14-match unbeaten run from April 1931 through to December 1932, putting him and his side right at the forefront of international football and making them, in the process, one of the clear favourites for the 1934 World Cup, deserved billing which made them pre-tournament favourites that February when they travelled to Turin and proceeded to put four goals past Italy, winning the game 4-2 in the end. The performance, result and shockwaves it sent around the game were right on cue with that World Cup due to start in Italy three months later.

The World Cup is now, for all the ongoing controversy that surrounds FIFA, as big and prestigious a sporting event you could wish to see, the biggest event of any type dedicated to a single sport. Back in its early days, it was still treated with some disdain by many nations, not least Uruguay who declined to enter, primarily in retaliation for the refusal of some European nations to attend the tournament that they had hosted four years previously. Another notable absentee was the England national team, the xenophobic actions of their FA at the time meaning that they were not even members of FIFA. They didn't seem keen to put that right in the future either, with FA committee member Charles Sutcliffe sniffily announcing that '...the national associations of England, Scotland, Wales and Ireland have quite enough to do in their *own International Championship* which seems to me a far better World Championship than the one to be staged in Rome'.

When in Rome, it would seem, the message from England was that they would rather not do what the Romans as well as the footballing elite of 15 other nations wanted to do. That arrogance and self-imposed exile meant that the development of the game in that country was set further back with its continuing adherence to the rigid Pyramid formation set to typify the football played in that year's domestic British Championship whilst the rest of the footballing world, led by the likes of Meisl and Hogan, continued to adapt, make progress and to revolutionise the ways teams set themselves up to play the game. This aloof attitude was something that would, inevitably, come back to haunt the England team and their FA in years to come.

With the tournament having a straight knock-out format, there was no room for error for any of the teams taking part. Austria duly won their first round match against France 3-2, but it had been a close run thing that they only sealed with two extra-time goals, the reliable Sindelar having put them ahead. Hosts Italy meanwhile, having engineered for themselves a relatively easy first round match against the United States, won that 7-1, and it became clear that the two sides, now joint favourites for the trophy were seeded to play against each other in the semi-finals. This is exactly what happened, Austria, having beaten Hungary in the second round, whilst Italy beat Spain after a replay meaning the hosts had now played three games in five days. Surely the initiative was now with Meisl and Austria in that semi-final due to be played in Milan on June 3rd?

Meisl and Austria had certainly laid down a marker with that win before the tournament and the manner in which they had dispatched both France and Hungary. Yet both had been difficult fixtures against good teams, and you can't help but speculate as to how much the draw was 'engineered' to ensure that, if Italy did meet Austria in the semi-finals, they'd have as a good a chance of winning as possible? Their wins in the opening two rounds merely strengthened their position as joint tournament favourites, but the quarter-final win over Hungary was disappointing. It should have been a match that was a wonderful advert for the short passing game that Meisl preached and that Hogan had taken to both countries, but it ended up being an ill-tempered encounter that more resembled the type of mob football both countries were so desperate to distance themselves from, a game one observer described as nothing more than a 'street battle'.

What, you feel compelled to ask, had driven both sides to suddenly engage in the type of football that they had so long strived to avoid? Had the pressure to deliver, to win the tournament, got to them? That seems unlikely. Both teams knew how they liked to play and were confident in their system; its improbable that they would have abandoned that under any circumstances, particularly the Austrians who had tossed aside the pressure involved in playing Italy in Turin a few months earlier and played it their way, winning handsomely. They had no need to revert to the ancient footballing type; more to the point, they didn't have the players for it, either. Star man Sindelar, if you recall, was known as the 'Paperman' due to his slight build, and he was certainly rendered anonymous by the roughhouse tactics employed by the Hungarians which the Austrian's, losing some of their focus and discipline in doing so, felt compelled to replicate in response.

They had, after all, pretty much had things their own way on the football field for some considerable time, so it is hardly surprising that, when an opposing team chose to take the match to them in such a manner, they lost their heads somewhat, and the ensuing 'street battle' was the end result. Austria eventually won the game 2-1, but, despite the victory, they were clearly rattled at the nature of the game and their opponent's approach to both it and their players. This meant they were not, psychologically, in the best of moods with that semi-final against the hosts in Milan three days later. Word had, by now, got around on how to stop the Austrians, and, for the second consecutive game, Sindelar was effectively marked out of the game by Luis Monti, whose game and approach might, in some ways, have been modelled on that of Kinnaird himself.

Monti was a very effective footballer who had managed to marry both the old and the new ways of the game into his play and who, as a result, may well have been able to make as much of a success for himself in the English club game at that time as he did in both his native Argentina and with Juventus in Italy. His approach was rugged and occasionally ruthless, qualities that would have made him an easy pick to mark Sindelar out of the semi-final. He was able to combine those physical attributes with no little technical ability, essential qualities for the position he played which was what we might now call the defensive midfielder but was, at the time, seen as the role of an attacking centre half.

That position was the key one in the variation of the 2-3-5 (Pyramid) formation that had dominated the game since the late 1890s and that, for all their emphasis on short passing and free movement around the pitch, had only been tweaked at the edges by the likes of Meisl and Hogan. The Italian coach, Vittorio Pozzo, had observed that games were, more often than not, won by the side that controlled the midfield area of the pitch, and, if his teams were to do that, he would need to strengthen in that area. He did so by bringing two of his attacking five players back to a position just in front of an otherwise 'conventional' three-man midfield, and turning 2-3-5 into 2-3-2-3, a formation which not only gave a side more defensive options and strength but also set them up to effectively counterattack, with Monti being the player key here. He would have been expected to mark the opposing teams centre forward, in this case Sindelar, when his team were defending but, when they were able to switch from defence to attack, he would drive forward with the ball, acting as *his* team's playmaker. These double duties and a busy on-field persona earnt him the nickname *doble ancho,* meaning 'double wide'. It is an epithet that pays tribute to his ability to cover all areas of the pitch and, in doing so, become the first true box-to-box midfielder of the modern game, a player who well and truly mapped the pitch in all senses of the word and as much a pioneer for where the game was heading and what it would eventually become as any cited in this book so far.

Vittorio Pozzo in 1920

Pozzo's adaptation of the Pyramid formation was known as the Metodo formation, quite literally a method or procedure which allowed for all eventualities on the pitch. This was the increasing desire, to switch effectively and seamlessly from defence to attack (or vice versa), something which the traditional and positionally rigid Pyramid formation did not easily allow for.

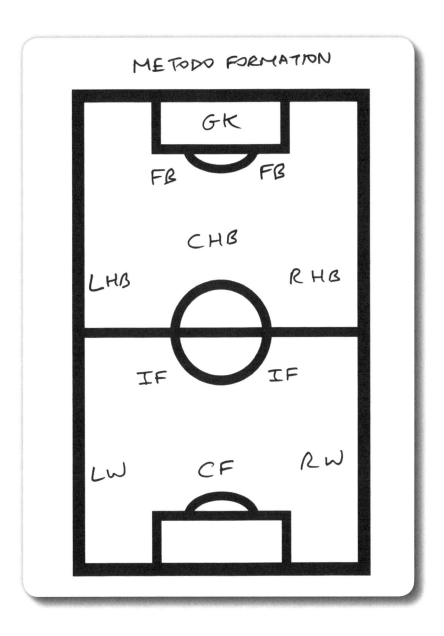

Most of all, Metodo was, like its coach, a pragmatic and sensible approach to the game but was devoted, above all, to retaining possession as much as possible with the prime intent being not to concede a goal, an approach and football philosophy that has been attributed to Italian clubs and its national team ever since. It was certainly too much for Meisl and his wonderful Austrian side in that semi-final. Yes, they were an attractive footballing side to watch; yes they played with a great deal of flair and freedom with the will-o'-the-wisp figure of Sindelar dictating the play. But pragmatic they were not; in fact, they didn't know how to be. Thus Pozzo and his new pragmatists won the day, their cause aided by a wet and very heavy pitch where Italy's numerical advantage in midfield proved to be decisive with Enrique Guaita's scoring as Italy won 1-0. It wasn't the first time *Gli Azzurri* had won a critical game by that scoreline in a World Cup (they'd previously beaten Spain 1-0 in that quarter-final replay), and it most certainly wouldn't be the last.

Metodo had more than proved its worth to Italy as Pozzo's master tactic and formation saw them win the tournament with a 2-1 win over Czechoslovakia in the final. It had been Europe's World Cup with all four semi-finalists hailing from that continent; although, in truth, with all four of the non-European nations[20] that were competing in the tournament being knocked out in the first round, the tournament was more of an unofficial contest to decide which national team was the best in Europe rather than globally. And yes, both at the tournament itself and the two years leading up to it, Austria were, on paper at least, probably the best and most in-form national side in world of football, but, on more than one occasion, the winner of a World Cup wasn't necessarily the best team at the tournament. Austria *were* good, their hybrid 2-3-1-4 formation which permitted the mercurial Matthias Sindelar to play in a more withdrawn position a sign of where the game was heading, one which now relied

---

20   *Argentina, Brazil, Egypt and the USA.*

heavily on short passing and individual skills rather than a free for all which didn't start and finish at dribbling into a wall of opposing players.

Hogan's influence on the game cannot be underemphasised at this point. He had spent time coaching in four of the eight quarter-finalists prior to the tournament (Austria, Czechoslovakia, Hungary and Switzerland) as well as being a friend and contemporary of Italy's winning coach, Vittorio Pozzo. Yet, for all that, once Hogan had left Bolton Wanderers as a player in 1913 to commence his coaching career, he neither had, nor was offered, a position coaching back in England until 1934 when he was invited to take over at London-based Fulham.

Fulham would, at least, have known what they were in for when they appointed Hogan to the accompaniment, no doubt, of severe tut-tutting and shaking of heads from those in power at other clubs as well as within the English FA. Their previous manager, James McIntyre, was very similar to Hogan in terms of both his playing experience and with his commitment to coaching He had also been somewhat of a journeyman as a player before starting his coaching career at Coventry City when he was just 26. Like Hogan, he had ideas regarding the coaching of players and tactics that went far above what was considered the norm. Again, like Hogan he was confident of his methods and not a little unspoken, regarding the equally confident if rather more well-known Herbert Chapman (see chapter 4) as both a role model and mentor. His time at Fulham certainly more than justified the methods; he won promotion with them in his first season from Division Three (his second at that level) and, in the 1932/33 season narrowly failed to get a second consecutive promotion with them. Yes, he was unorthodox, outspoken and ahead of his time, but so was Hogan, and it shouldn't be regarded as a surprise at all that they took a chance on Hogan, as his successor for they, like Hogan, and all his contemporaries, were ahead of the footballing times in England.

Herbert Chapman

McIntyre never worked in football again after he left Fulham in 1934, his character and methods still regarded as too 'off the wall' by other club owners and chairmen around the country. He could probably have, like Hogan, exported his coaching talents to a far more appreciative and understanding audience in Europe, but he chose not to take that route, preferring to return to life and work outside of the game in Southampton. As for Hogan and Fulham, it turned out to be a potential match in heaven (progressive football club meets pioneering coach) that turned out to be a mutual disappointment with Hogan's style not finding favour with some of Fulham's favoured players. Good enough, it would seem, for some of the leading international sides of the time, including World Cup semi-finalists, but not for those of an English team muddling its way along in that country's second-best division.

Not that his dismissal after just 31 games back in England phased Hogan. He promptly returned to Austrian football to a warm welcome, where he coached the Austrian international side to the 1936 Olympics football final where, just as they had two years previously, they fell to Pozzo and his Italian side. He wasn't, even then, completely finished with British football, both as coach and opponent, and his presence and influence on the game will be referred to again in a later chapter.

CHAPTER FOUR:
WM VS METODO

Both club and players lacked direction; there was no plan, no ambition and, seemingly, no hope; the type of football they played and the players who represented the club were, and remained, a throwback to the mob football of yesteryear – disorganised, unruly and with little to no finesse or thought.

Football's offside law remains one of the most controversial issues in the game as well as, to this day, its most misunderstood. Yet, as we have already realised in this book, nothing is really new in the footballing world, and the law and its various interpretations have been a cause of controversy and debate since the very earliest days of the organised game.

Rule changes often affect the way that teams play the game or set themselves out to play. As recently as 1992 when the back-pass rule was introduced to stop goalkeepers from picking the ball up after it had been passed back to them by a teammate, the ramifications of what was, after all, the introduction of a law implemented in order to make the game faster were, for some clubs, severe and not at all positive. It had been introduced to the game as an antidote to the perceived dull, stop–start football witnessed during the 1990 World Cup in Italy,[21] a tournament riddled with back passes to the goalkeeper, and not always from just inside his own penalty area. In addition to that, the flow of the game was also affected by goalkeepers frequently dropping the ball, dribbling it around and then picking it up again once an opponent had run towards them in order to put them under a bit of pressure.

Simple enough. You can still pass back to your goalkeeper. But he can no longer pick the ball up.

Some teams and players couldn't handle it at all. Leeds United, the English League Champions of the 1991/92 season, were nearly relegated the following campaign, following up their points won total of 82 that season with just 51 the following time around, losing a total of 15 games against 4 in their title winning season. It was a disastrous defence of a title, whoever you were and whatever league and country you played in.

---

21   *Was banning the passing back of the ball from a teammate for his goalkeeper to pick up a very late response and consequence of Vittorio Pozzo's introduction of the Metodo formation and type of play, that 'pragmatic and sensible approach to the game' (see previous chapter), which encouraged possession of the ball at all costs. Surely the ultimate in possession for any football team is for the ball to be safely in the hands of their goalkeeper?*

Yet the team, one that was famous throughout Europe during the 1960s and 70s, had the same manager and core group of players. So what had gone wrong?

As far as the Leeds players were concerned, it was outlawing back passes to the waiting arms of the goalkeeper. They, and their defenders in particular, had been used to playing the ball back to John Lukic, their goalkeeper, and often from distance. He would then take his time by bouncing, rolling and tapping the ball from foot to foot whilst his teammates got themselves into position, ready for Lukic to launch the ball into the air, long and high now they were in their 'starting' positions again. That Leeds United team played a very simple form of the 4-4-2 formation (more on that in a later chapter), which involved aiming the ball at the head of their tall and powerful striker, in this case, for Gilbert Smith, read Lee Chapman. In amending the back-pass law as they did, the revised laws of the game meant that Lukic no longer had time to dwell on the ball, let alone pick it up. This meant, in time, his teammates would no longer pass it back to him, seeing that as a risk rather than an opportunity. Leeds, therefore, struggled to adjust their game and the way they played and suffered an appalling follow-up season to their championship success as a consequence. That success had been almost entirely built on the concept of playing your goalkeeper as a playmaker, the player who started moves and dictated play.

The Leeds United captain and former Scotland international Gordon Strachan looked back at that time at the club and his experience of the rule change, admitting that whilst it was beneficial to players like him, it did indeed prove to be problematic for some of his teammates. Writing in his autobiography, Strachan said, '...[it] was one of the best things that have happened in the game during my career. It forced defenders into closer contact with their keepers as opposed to pushing up to squeeze the play, and gave everybody more space to settle on the ball and use their skill. But it caught Leeds out in a big way. Our central defenders, Chris Whyte and Chris Fairclough – outstanding ball winners – found it difficult to adjust suddenly to a situation where they were also called upon to involve themselves in the creative play as well. It also presented problems to Lee Chapman, in that the ball did not come through to him as early as it did before, and he had to hold it longer.'

Strachan went onto admit that whilst Leeds had struggled, their biggest rivals at the time, Manchester United, had adapted to the rule change perfectly, going on to admit that they had been able to do so as, he is honest enough to say, '...they had better footballers than we did.'[22]

What was even more of a mystery was how the Leeds United manager at the time, Howard Wilkinson, had failed to see the problems this would cause his team and plan an alternate strategy. Wilkinson was, after all, a very highly qualified coach who not only had two spells in temporary charge of the England team but was also coach of the England U-21 team (the cream of the nation's young footballers) from 1999-2001. In 1997, he was also appointed as the English FA's technical director. Thus, he had been given an esteemed and hugely visible role, one of the most influential in the English game at the time, a position of great responsibility awarded to someone who hadn't been able, a few years previously, to work out how to adjust his team's tactical approach in order to cope with a rule change that everyone had known was coming and had, presumably, taken into consideration.

But then this was an FA which had once steadfastly refused the expertise and proven CV of Jimmy Hogan. With a reputation such as that, is there any surprise the suits that succeeded those who ruled by committee appointed a man like Wilkinson as their 'chosen one'?

---

22   *Strachan, G. 2006.* My Life in Football. *Time Warner Books. 140.*

Wilkinson hadn't seen how the introduction of a new rule was going to affect the game and the way that teams played it and were coached. Which is not an accusation you could have levelled at Herbert Chapman nearly 75 years earlier.

Chapman, if you recall, was one of the names on Hugo Meisl's short but illustrious list of contacts, evidence of his networking coaches from across Europe who he admired. And with good cause. Very good cause, in fact. Because Chapman, unlike Hogan and a plethora of other names, had succeeded where so many British-born coaches had failed by making both a name and good reputation for himself *within* the English game. Anyone, Meisl would have mused, who had defied the rampant conservatism of both the English game and its FA (although, in truth, those two were as one, the English FA 'owned' its game and with an unremitting grip) in order to successfully introduce new innovations into both training and tactics had to be worth allying yourself to. Both Chapman's background and his developing career and reputation in the game had rebuffed many perceived disadvantages and setbacks which might have held a lesser man back, either in himself or as others might have regarded him. He was born in 1878, the eleventh son of a solidly working-class family near Rotherham in England's then heavily industrialised South Yorkshire where tradition didn't just expect, it demanded that lads from a coal-mining family followed in their father's footsteps as soon as they were able and the law allowed it. So Chapman might have been lost to the game even before his life really began. Fortunately, he had options as well as the strength of mind to seek them out.

His (and football's) saving grace was his aptitude for learning where he was considered bright enough to win a place at Sheffield Technical College to study mining engineering. So, whilst he may well have spent his days at the pit, it would, at least, have been in an office rather than bent double underground. He also enjoyed playing football and, like three of his brothers, one of whom had won two League Championships as well as an FA Cup winner's medal, Chapman soon realised he was a more than competent player. Thus, as a teenager he was able to play for his local pit team before moving on to play as an amateur for three non-league clubs, the last of which was Rochdale.

Like so many other football coaches, both of his generation and later ones, Chapman never reached the heights as a player. His best years were spent at Northampton Town and Sheffield United from 1901 through to 1903. Through all of this, he remained committed to his studies, playing as an amateur in Sheffield before ending his career at Tottenham at the end of the 1906/07 season. Once that was done, Chapman was intent upon moving on, fully determined to pursue a career in engineering. It's extraordinary to think that one of the great early coaches in the British game was seemingly so completely uncommitted in what are normally the formative years in any professional footballer's life: establishing themselves in the game and at the club, identifying their ambitions and working towards achieving them. Chapman was anything but this. He'd preferred to play at Sheffield United as an amateur whilst later deciding at Tottenham to retire from the game, stating that he'd had a 'good innings' when he was still only in his late twenties. One of his last active roles in the game had been to recommend a former Tottenham teammate, Walter Bull, to his former club Northampton as their new manager.

And had Bull accepted the recommendation and been appointed as manager of Northampton Town, then that may well have been the last time anyone in football had ever heard of Herbert Chapman who would, no doubt, have gone on to have a long and locally distinguished career in engineering. Who knows, he might even had ended up having an innovative new piece of engineering technology named ('keep that Chapman pivot well-greased') after him, before eventually retiring and being awarded a carriage clock for his services to the industry.

Yet Bull decided he didn't want the job and returned the favour to his friend and one-time teammate Chapman by suggesting Northampton could do little better than offer him the job instead.

It seems improbable at this stage that Chapman would have taken on the role, even allowing for Bull's recommendation. He hadn't shown any interest in it himself, neither had he shown much predilection for coaching or football administration of any kind. He had, as he'd previously declared, that good innings in the game and was set to devote himself to the technical nuances of the drawing board rather than those of the football pitch. And yet something about the possibilities that the role with Northampton conjured up must have had sudden and immense appeal to him, for he accepted the challenge and was appointed as Northampton's player-manager in time for the start of the 1907/08 season.

Maybe the appeal of football coaching was there all along? Chapman was a clever man, an intelligent one with a flair for all things technical, for making plans and designs, for working out how to make things better. Why not try to apply his analytical mind to football and see if he could get footballers to work as efficiently as one of the machines he had previously applied much rigorous thought and application to? It must have been a tantalising prospect to the young Chapman (he was still only 29), a challenge he may well have taken on for himself as much as he did for Northampton Town.

Chapman may have been a prospect, but his club were anything but. The two seasons prior to his appointment had seen Northampton finish bottom of the Southern League. Both club and players lacked direction; there was no plan, no ambition and, seemingly, no hope; the type of football they played and the players who represented the club were, and remained, a throwback to the mob football of yesteryear. They were disorganised, unruly and played with little to no finesse or thought. And perhaps it is that which attracted the club and the job to Chapman. Maybe if they had been a half decent side with some good players and signs of progress being made in the way the club was playing, he might not have been interested. But they were far from that. Northampton Town were broken and not far from being irretrievably so. The challenge of putting them back together again, of mending and making them work again, must have been an irresistible one to Chapman.

Broken they most certainly were. Chapman once remarked of his players that they never even attempted to discuss either pre-match or during a game means which they might adopt in order to best give themselves a chance of winning, adding that the best he might expect could be an 'occasional chat' between two players in close proximity to each other on the pitch. Football in England was, as we have already seen, devoid (at best) of any semblance of tactics or serious coaching and training of players. On another occasion, shortly after he had witnessed his side lose a Southern League fixture to Norwich City, Chapman summed up the reasons as to why his team had lost, saying, 'a team can attack for too long.' Northampton had indeed attacked, relentlessly, in the game, meaning that a slightly more organised Norwich City side would have been able to exploit the massive gaps on the pitch and in their defence.

Chaos and a lack of any kind of order and organisation was, and will always remain, anathema to anyone with a mind that craves discipline and technical efficiency. Chapman wanted just that – efficiency. He wanted his team to be as affective and reliable as the machines he had designed and worked with, the whole being the result of its working parts. He, therefore, modelled his Northampton side as well as the other teams he went on to coach in the same manner, ensuring that each was built within a defined framework, only in this case, a tactical one rather than a physical one. The major problem, as he saw it, was that the framework so beloved to the game, the Pyramid, was inefficient and a waste of the available space on the pitch. He thus decided to utilise this much ignored resource more.

He did this by withdrawing his teams half-backs back towards their own goal in order to give his forwards more space to work in, something he then improved upon by withdrawing two of the existing five forwards back to fill in the space vacated by the half-backs. This was an early and not yet refined version of the 3-2-2-3 formation that he would go on to master with Arsenal in the 1920s. Chapman had, by doing this, not only given his team prominence in all areas of the pitch (2-3-5 was, of course, very top heavy, the proliferation of forwards meaning some parts of the pitch would look virtually deserted during some passages of play), but also enabled them to play a short passing game, the one that had been so beloved of the Scottish players and coaches. As the players were now in close proximity to one another, his formation invited an advancement up the pitch in that manner rather than by long balls to isolated forwards whose sole objective seemed to be to attempt to dribble the ball into the net.

Whisper it quietly but, in the Southern League and with Northampton Town, a team that, even today, has a history that remains modest at best, Herbert Chapman was turning the English game on its head. There was something clinical, yet pleasing on the eye about his teams highly organised passing game, one that even encouraged his defenders to pass rather than kick their way out of trouble. It was effective enough to see Northampton, who'd finished bottom of the Southern League in each of the 1904/05, 1905/06 and 1906/07 seasons, to finish in 8th place at the end of the 1907/08 season before winning the Southern League Championship at the end of the following season, six points clear of 2nd placed Swindon Town, whose England international Harold Fleming had commented to Chapman in a mixture of both admiration and disdain that he had '...something more than a team, [he had] a machine.'

A *machine!* Chapman would have been utterly delighted at the comparison.

He had, by now, decided to see just how far he could take his interest and career in football coaching. It was giving him opportunities to question the conventional as well as plan and implement new strategies and designs, something he would have done and enjoyed as part of his work as an engineer. So why not apply the same thinking to football?

He'd certainly get the opportunity and on a bigger shop floor than he could ever have with Northampton. In the summer of 1912, he was offered the post of manager at Leeds City, the forerunners to Leeds United, and, from there moved on to Huddersfield Town in 1920. There, as he had done at Leeds City and Northampton Town, Chapman completely changed the football culture of the club, working on introducing a strong defence allied to a midfield and attack that could swiftly counterattack with the focus again on quick, short passing all across the pitch with his two wingers, the only players he truly entrusted to run with the ball. His teams were instructed to play in such a way that, at times, you could have witnessed a defensive line of four who in turn were protected by the two deep lying midfielders he had withdrawn back from that original attacking five, and on either side of that central two, two more attacking wingers whose aim was to provide the ammunition for two central strikers.

It's conventional enough now. We call that formation 4-4-2, and it's played by teams throughout the world. And, although Chapman had not introduced or championed that particular formation, there was a way about his sides, the way they played and set themselves up for a game plus the manner they spread themselves out all over the pitch that more than hinted at things to come and that familiar 4-4-2 shape of today.

He and his football were massively successful. After the First World War, he was appointed as manager of Huddersfield Town, winning the FA Cup in 1922 followed by two successive League Championships, making, in the process, Huddersfield the leading team in England football. In doing that, he had continued the domination of northern club sides in the English game in both competitions, that marker having been laid down as long ago as Jack Hunter (see chapter 1) with his Blackburn Olympic team, FA Cup winners in 1883. The subsequent 39 finals since then had seen northern-based teams lift the trophy on all but two occasions whilst in the League; the champions had come from that region on every single occasion from its inaugural season in 1889 through to the 1921/22 season which was won by Liverpool. Southern England and its London-based and -centric FA might have drawn up the games rules and regulations and been its great administrators, not just in England but throughout much of the world, and yes, they might also have been the driving force behind so many of its original clubs – Wanderers, Old Etonians, Oxford University, Royal Engineers and Old Carthusians – but they'd all been left behind. By a northerner. Who was the son of a coal miner. Pass the smelling sales, Charles.

Those once formidable and prominent southern clubs and their players had remained staid, conservative and complacent, content to play their metaphorical fiddles as their Rome burnt whilst the adventurous, progressive and imaginative clubs from the north of the country, many of them buoyed by coaches like Hunter and Chapman, as well as a fair sprinkling of gifted players from Scotland dominated the game and hogged the glory. You might have asked yourself why they let it go on for so long. Well, maybe they thought the natural order of things would return. Maybe they thought that winning wasn't what mattered (this was certainly how things were regarded at Corinthian Casuals, the team that refused to accept penalties as they were seen to be 'unsporting'), and what *did* matter was the way they did things and behaved themselves. Maybe some of them thought the northern upstarts with their proliferation of Scottish players and wiry little coaches with big mouths and even bigger ideas would, eventually, go away.

Which, of course, they most clearly were not going to do.

Which is why Chapman became such an attractive option for Arsenal when he applied for the manager role there in the summer of 1925. He'd done all he could at Huddersfield: an FA Cup win and two League Championships. How could that run of success be improved upon? Arsenal, on the other hand, had not only fought against relegation for two consecutive seasons (Chapman's Huddersfield side had seen them off 3-1, 4-0 and 6-1 in recent league games) but had also been subject to severe financial restrictions with a board and chairman particularly reluctant[23] to spend any money on new players. In other words, they, like Northampton, were broken, defective and needed fixing: a potentially mighty machine that needed an injection of imagination. They were, in short, just what Chapman, who might even have been getting slightly complacent, or, if not that, then certainly a little bored himself at Huddersfield, needed.

He also had the chance to bring some much needed footballing success to a club based in London. No doubt the normally parsimonious Arsenal boards offer of a yearly salary that doubled what he was earning at Huddersfield helped make up his mind for him.

---

23   *Modern-day Arsenal fans might say that nothing much has changed in that aspect.*

It would be easy at this point to list the successes that Chapman had with his Arsenal team – trophies won, players celebrated and plaudits earned. But he should also be remembered and praised for what he did within the game, both on and off the pitch. Amongst the developments in the coaching and tactical side of the game, he can be credited for introducing the tactics board, the promotion of floodlights at leading grounds so that matches were no longer restricted to daylight hours and even the proposal of what he called a 'West Europe Competition'. This involved matches between the leading sides from leagues all over Europe, one that was a far-reaching idea at the time and would have been better received in some countries than others. Unsurprisingly, England was indeed one of those where the concept was summarily dismissed as unworkable, impractical and, as far as the English FA was concerned, eminently undesirable.[24] Needless to say, Chapman's vision of a Europe-wide contest for club sides eventually became the competition that is now seen, throughout football, as the most desirable to compete in, let alone win, by just about every player who has ever played the game professionally, one seen by many as even more professionally prestigious to take part in than the World Cup.

Chapman could see where the game was going, both on and off the pitch. He wasn't just rebooting the shape and way that things were done on the pitch as being the master coach and strategist behind the blueprint for the modern game.

He mapped the game with one of his most long-lasting and effective tactical innovations: the development and introduction of the famous WM formation to his Arsenal side and the game in general.

---

24   *Chapman's vision for a European-wide club football tournament eventually came into being in the 1955/56 with the first-ever playing of the European Cup (Champions League since 1992/93), a competition that the existing English champions, Chelsea, were 'persuaded' not to enter by the English Football League.*

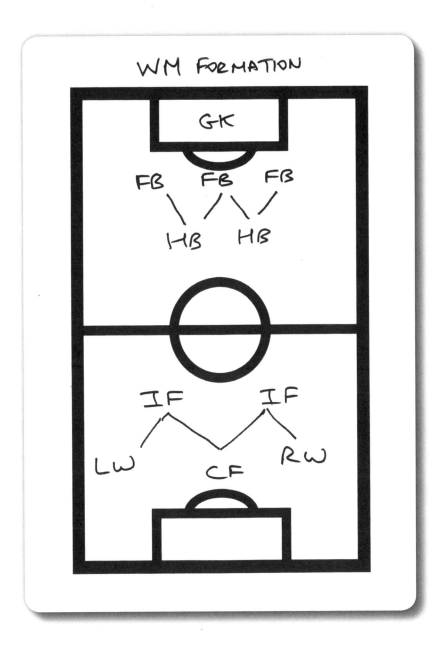

He'd certainly made an impact at the club and as a coach par excellence, repeating his achievements with Huddersfield at Highbury with consummate ease and with a further two League Championship triumphs in 1931 and 1933 as well as another FA Cup in 1930, ironically won at the expense of his former club who were beaten 2-0. This was Arsenal's first major trophy win in a run of successes that led to them becoming one of the most famous club sides in the world. But not just for the way they played the game. It was also because of what the club stood for, the very peak of professionalism and the application of high and exacting standards in whatever they did, a reputation that the club holds proudly close to its heart to this day.

This included him insisting on the club vetting any potential signings prior to them being made, a method that garnished much publicity and comment when it was revealed that former Manchester United manager Sir Alex Ferguson did exactly the same thing with regard to new signings during his time at Old Trafford from 1986 to 2013. Ferguson, like Chapman many decades earlier, was only interested in signing players of perceived 'good character' for his club, the latter's comment that it was '... not enough for a man to be a good player... I am convinced that all round intelligence is one of the highest qualifications' and one that would raise quizzical eyebrows within the game today, not to mention in the 1930s.

Character was, therefore, hugely important to Chapman as regards his players, with the emphasis very firmly on 'his'. The Arsenal players were *his* players; they were expected to be company men, to live, work and breathe the club and the culture he wished to surround it with, whether that was on the field of play, in training, or in their everyday lives. He admitted that when he was looking at making a signing for the club, one of the first things he took into consideration was the sort of day-to-day life that the player led, adding that, for him, any signs of personal weakness ('I will never tolerate slackness') would almost certainly mean a player would never play for him. His interest in the conduct and approach of his players even extended to what they did in their own time, arguing that one popular leisure pursuit was certainly forbidden as far as he was concerned, namely a night at the dogs!

'I have been told that attending dog racing is better than dancing or the cinema. I emphatically disagree. Dog racing! Gambling can have a very serious influence on footballers. A day on the golf course appeals to them. But they must not have too much golf.'[25]

A man way ahead of his time in every regard. And one who, unlike the unfortunate Howard Wilkinson at Leeds United over six decades later, was able to eventually respond favourably and with great effect to a change in the game's rules rather than continually struggle to adapt. The change in question here was a consequence of the offside law, then, as now, one of the most contentious and oft debated issues within the game.

It had certainly been debated enough in the early 1920s for the FA to make a change. Previously, an attacking player was deemed to be offside if as many as three opposing players stood between him and their goal, something which meant that teams could simply and effectively play the offside trap, which they inevitably did as all they needed to do was ensure at least three players stayed behind the ball at all times. It was hardly rocket science. Although, as a consequence of the negative games which ensued as a result of this, rocket science was probably a lot more entertaining as a spectacle. Determined to do something about this, the FA changed the law in the summer of 1925, decreeing that only *two* players were now required to play an opponent onside rather than three. The most immediate and obvious effect of this change was that the game became more stretched out over the pitch with, to their presumed delight,

---

25   Chapman, Herbert. 1934. A Life In Football. *Robert Blatchford Publishing.*

attacking players finding themselves with more room and options. One of these was the preference of teams to revert to playing the long ball out of defence for their attacking players to run onto, confident that there was less chance of them being flagged offside as they did just that.

Teams struggled to adapt to the change at first, and, just as it had done to Leeds under Wilkinson in 1992 with the change in the back-pass law, coaches and players alike found it difficult to change the way they had been used to playing. As a result of this, the beginning of the 1925/26 season saw some extraordinary games and results, those of Arsenal included. After comfortably beating Leeds United 4-1 on September 26th, they travelled to Newcastle United a week later, only to lose 7-0! Yet, two days after that game, they went to West Ham and won 4-0.

This continued into October with a 5-0 win over Cardiff immediately followed by a 4-0 reverse against Sheffield United. Huddersfield Town, Chapman's former club and the reigning champions, fared no better. One early-season game for them against Tottenham ended in a 5-5 draw, and, despite their also ending the 1925/26 season as League Champions, they suffered some heavy defeats away from home, including at Sunderland (4-1), Bolton Wanderers (6-1) and Notts County, who finished the season in bottom place and relegated (4-2).

Not what you would expect from either Chapman's former side or the one he had just joined. For Chapman, a man devoted to order and organisation, it must have been an enormously frustrating time as everything he had worked for, both at Huddersfield for the previous four years and now at Arsenal, became obsolete overnight. A game that had been evolving, thanks in no small part to people like Chapman and some of his less illustrious predecessors such as Jack Hunter, now looked as if it was set to go backwards with the 'old ways' of hitting the ball hard, long and high up the field returning at the expense of the pass-and-move game that the new breed of coaches, men like Chapman, Hogan and Meisl had been developing and introducing.

You wouldn't have been blamed for thinking the FA had changed the law in order to wrest back what they had always considered to be 'their' game away from its modernisers – the working class men of the north.

The change to the law and the resultant disorganised chaos it brought to both clubs and the game as a whole was too much for one Arsenal player to bear. Charlie Buchan, a centre forward who'd played nearly 400 games for Sunderland (and winning a League Championship medal with them in 1913), had been one of Chapman's first signings at Highbury, a star name and attraction whose acquisition was not only a statement of intent from both Chapman and the Arsenal board, but as a man whose experience and influence would play a big part in the club's growth. Chapman would certainly not have needed to vet Buchan with the zeal he usually reserved for potential new signings. Buchan had long been regarded as one of the game's more intelligent players, one who expressed himself well and who had clearly looked after himself throughout his career. He was, after all, nearly 34 when he signed for Arsenal. Clearly there had been few, if any, days at the dog track for Buchan throughout his career, and Chapman very much hoped that his presence at the club would both inspire and motivate his existing squad of players. Yet he almost lost Buchan only a few games into that 1925/26 season as a result of the way the game had changed because of that amendment to the offside law, so much so in fact that Buchan told Chapman he had every intention of retiring from the game and returning to the northeast.

Arsenal, Buchan argued, needed to adapt to the new rules and quickly. He hadn't, he added, uplifted himself from a club and area that he called home (despite being born in London) in order to play football for a club that seemed to be devoid of structure and without any sort of plan or organisation. And he certainly wasn't going to stay put if all of that meant he'd have little to no chance of winning anything with them and would merely be going through the motions every week. He was, in short, furious and felt as if he had joined the club on false pretences.

His attitude to both his club and manager at that time bordered on heretical. Professional footballers were regarded at the time as nothing more than the personal property of a club, paid to play and do as they were told. Having an opinion, especially a public one, was most definitely frowned upon. His outburst could have meant the end of both his Arsenal career and his life in the game, yet, to Chapman, his words were footballing manna from heaven of the highest order, thoroughly vindicating his decision to sign Buchan. They were the signs of a man who cared deeply about the game and how it should be played. One who had no compunction whatsoever in letting Chapman know what he thought and how it should be resolved.

Which was, of course, one of the qualities that Chapman had seen in Buchan when he signed him in the first place.

The game that Buchan cited to Chapman as evidence of where things needed to be addressed on the pitch was the 7-0 defeat to Newcastle. Buchan had noted in that game that the Newcastle centre half, Charlie Spencer, had played in a very deep role throughout the game, offering little to nothing in an attacking sense to the Newcastle side but doing a great deal to break up embryonic Arsenal attacks, allowing his midfield players to dominate both possession and, crucially, territory. He was, in effect, playing in the position of a sweeper, albeit still a little farther up the pitch than where we might expect a player in that position to be in today.

Playing a centre half in such a withdrawn position wasn't an entirely new idea as Chapman had done so himself at Huddersfield, the means then being to offer a little bit of defensive cover for his team. The difference now, argued Buchan, was that the player in that position was not just helping break up opposing sides attacking play, but he was also being used as the originator for his own sides attacking play as well. In that aspect, Spencer was unique in English football at that time, there simply wasn't a player or position like his anywhere else in the game. He was, and remains, the prototype sweeper, the player who was, and is, his team's first line of defence as well as its first line of attack.

Charlie Spencer, born in Sunderland in 1899 was, in effect, a Franz Beckenbauer-type player nearly four decades before the imperious Beckenbauer made the first of his 103 international appearances for West Germany.

Spencer's argument, one that Chapman found himself agreeing with, was that whilst withdrawing the centre half to a far deeper position was an effective one, its one flaw was that it left teams with a shortage of players in the middle of the pitch, the tried and trusted 2-3-5 formation turning into a 3-2-5 as a result. Thus, to counterbalance this, Buchan suggested that he should also drop back a little, thus making the formation of the team more of a 3-3-4, albeit a slightly unbalanced one as Buchan would be operating in a wide right position still with two central midfielders playing alongside him. Chapman's agreement with Buchan didn't, however, extend to him permitting Buchan to drop back himself as he greatly valued the player's goal-scoring prowess and felt, rightly, that it would be compromised if he played in a deeper role. Chapman, therefore, switched tactics in accord with Buchan's suggestion but chose to instruct Andy Neil to drop back instead, going on, in time, to withdraw another inside forward as well to give the side a little more balance, meaning his side were now playing a 3-4-3 formation, albeit with two of the four midfielders sitting back whilst the other two stayed slightly more forward. With two half-backs and two inside forwards (or two defensive and two attacking midfielders as it would be seen today), the resultant team shape from above looked like a W in the attacking side of the pitch and an M in the defending side, that appearance leading only too naturally to it being known as the WM formation, a 3-2-2-3 shape.

It was devastatingly effective, a formation that bought players both time and space in the game, gave them time to think and evaluate their options, the latter being possible simply because, more often than not, a teammate would be close at hand and available to take the ball. Thus the brief resurgence of the long ball game that had come about as the initial consequence of the amended offside rule sank back, once again, into history as teams chose to pass the ball amongst themselves and focus on retaining possession with a free role given to the centre half. The centre half then patrolled just ahead of his defence key, dictating play and breaking up opposition attacks before becoming the basis of his own teams reciprocal efforts. WM swiftly caught on with Chelsea and Southampton, two more English club sides to abandon the Pyramid in favour or its more flexible approach.

Chelsea found themselves adapting to WM particularly effectively with one of their players, Andy Wilson, revelling in the new role given to him by Chelsea manager David Calderhead, himself an ex-centre half. Wilson had played for most of his career as an orthodox centre forward who was able to extend his playing career up until the age of 38, so easily and successfully did he take to that physically less arduous role, his playing days coming to an end after a two-year spell with Nîmes Olympique in France. Wilson became one of the first English footballers to play on the continent in that role, which is now synonymous in French football, with such names as Marius Tresor and Laurent Blanc amongst the most well-known exponents of the position.

Chapman's Arsenal, therefore, became renowned as a fast, counterattacking side, inspired by his tactical intelligence and vision as well as the ability they now had to dictate play thanks to the introduction of a player in that anchor role. This was eventually mastered by the unheralded Herbie Roberts, a player whose expertise in that position soon saw him the subject of abuse from opposing fans who saw his deployment there as a negative tactic, one designed to limit opposing sides to as few chances as possible against the Gunners. This was true enough, but it also crucially gave his side as many opportunities as possible to score goals. It's effectiveness is perhaps best illustrated at the end of the 1930/31 season, one that not only saw Arsenal win their first League Championship, but doing so by scoring 121 goals, a very great proportion of which was scored by their famous trio of attacking talents, Alex James plus Cliff Bastin and Joe Hulme. Chapman had set up his team to combine a organised and ball-playing defence with an attack that countered with great pace and penetration with both Hulme and Bastin averaging a goal per game between them from 1929 through to 1935.

Hardly the hallmark of a negative side. Yet that is exactly what label was attached to Chapman's Arsenal at the time, one that has stayed with them ever since, notably during the years that saw George Graham's similar playing model gain a reputation for being negative with a popular terrace chant at the time being 'boring boring Arsenal'. It should be noted, though, that when 'boring' Arsenal won the League Championship under Graham in 1989, they did so with a total of 73 goals scored in their 38 league matches, easily the highest number scored in the top division that season.

Chapman had based the WM formation on the existing and traditional Pyramid formation, the 2-3-5 which is what, as we have already briefly seen, the Italian team coach Vittorio Pozzo had done with his Metodo system. Pozzo's 2-3-2-3 formation, like WM, also allowed for a stronger defence and for counterattacking football to be played with the two systems identical in both look and intent in the attacking half of the pitch with a central striker and two flanking wingers supported by two inside forwards. The essential difference between the WM and Metodo formations was in the defensive part of the pitch. Pozzo opted for two traditional centre backs positioned just in front of the goalkeeper with three central midfielders ahead of them, the central member of that trio acting as both an attacking and defensive pivot with much of the play each way going through him. Chapman, on the other hand, preferred to have three players in defence with the central man of that back three having the same responsibilities as Pozzo's more advanced man.

Chapman's main motivation had been to counter the increased pressure on defenders that the change in the offside law had brought about by putting an equal number of players on both the offensive and defensive ends of his team, the engineer technician in him wanting the sort of balance and on-field equilibrium that he would have demanded of any and all of the machines he had worked during his engineering studies. The four midfield players were crucial to Chapman's game plan as they were expected to 'double up' and be part of Arsenal's attacking *and* defensive play, achievable through the half-backs moving forward when the team attacked with the inside forwards dropping back into defence when the game demanded it.

Pozzo's Metodo was a more defensive adaptation of 2-3-5 than Chapman's WM, one that had an emphasis on man-marking with his two centre backs protecting the goalkeeper whilst the right and left halves would have been detailed to mark the opposing wingers out of the game, denying them both time and space in which to play. It was essentially a formation that had its foundations built upon a solid and organised defence, the tried and trusted concept that as long as you prevent the other team from scoring, then you only have to get one yourself. That preferred winning margin of 1-0 is one that has long been associated with the Italian national team ever since. WM was slightly more offensive, focusing on equal priorities given to both defence and attack. In other words, when Chapman's teams were attacking, they had to be set up and ready to defend the second the game demanded it just as if they were attacking. Every player on the side knew what his defensive responsibilities would be as soon as the emphasis swung back from attack to defence.

But was one system superior to the other in any way?

You would have to say that was unlikely. Both brought about unprecedented success to their architects. Playing the WM formation at Arsenal, Chapman led his team to two championship successes in 1931 and 1933 as well as success in the FA Cup in 1930. Even after Chapman's tragically early death from pneumonia in the middle of the 1933/34 season, Arsenal won a further three championships during that decade, that season as well as the following one and the 1937/38 season, five titles in eight seasons, those subsequent three being won under the management of Joe Shaw. He'd been the club's reserve team manager during Chapman's tenure at the club and was therefore as good a man as any to carry on the professional and playing legacy set in place for him by Herbert Chapman, a man who transformed the game in England as well as being the lasting inspiration, to this day, of one of the most famous and well-respected club names in world football.

Pozzo was equally successful, albeit on the international rather than national stage. His Italy side won two consecutive World Cups (1934 and 1938), an Olympic gold medal (1936) as well as two triumphs in the now long gone Central European National Cup[26] (1930 and 1935).

---

26   *This was a competition held by central European national sides that ran from 1927 to 1960. Participating nations included Austria, Czechoslovakia, Hungary, Italy, Poland, Rumania, Switzerland and Yugoslavia.*

Proof, indeed, that his methods and ideas not only worked but would, if correctly applied, bring about success. The prospect of Italy under Pozzo meeting Chapman's Arsenal when both sides and their managers were at their respective peaks is a tantalising one, a game that would have been such a close call that I am not going to even attempt a prediction at how it might have ended up. The closest it ever came to taking place was during the 1948 Olympic Tournament in London where Pozzo saw his nation's reign come to an end in a 5-3 defeat to Denmark in the competition's quarter-finals, a game that was played at, of all places, Highbury, home of Arsenal and Chapman from 1925 through to 1934. One wonders whether or not Pozzo made an effort to visit the bronze bust of Chapman which stood proudly in the famous marble hall at Highbury at some point during that day.

As footballing peers and brothers in arms, it would not be at all surprising if he had done just that.

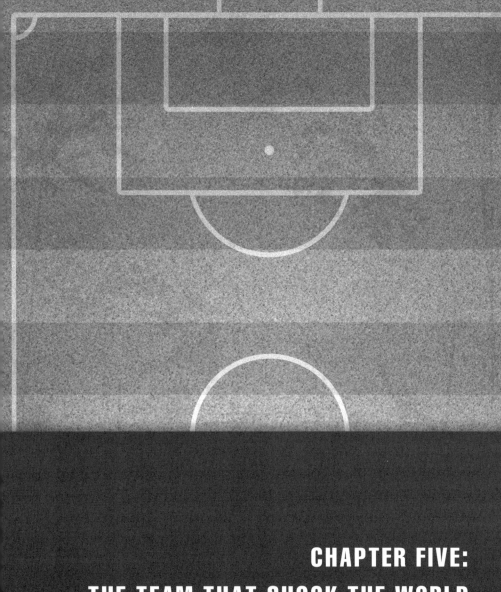

CHAPTER FIVE:
THE TEAM THAT SHOOK THE WORLD

When you fully consider the hapless manner in which the England manager and players had approached the game, it's perhaps something of a surprise that the Hungarians 'only' ended up scoring six goals.

On 25 November 1953, England met Hungary in a friendly international match at Wembley stadium in front of an expectant crowd of 105,000 spectators.

Team Hungary, 1954 World Cup

The game was billed by the English press as the 'match of the century' – a much anticipated clash between the nation that had given the game to the world against that which, at that time, was by far the finest international football team in the world. This fact no doubt was stuck in the collective craws of the FA dignitaries who attended on the day, determined to see England win and win convincingly and, in doing so, not only reminding the Hungarians but the rest of the world who the real 'top dogs' in international football were. That little bit of footballing triumph certainly made sense at the time. England was, after all, a nation on the sort of high that it has probably never come close to approaching again. A new queen had just been crowned whilst Mount Everest, previously seen as insurmountable, had been conquered, for the first time, by a British lead team. Good times indeed for a country who would, four years later, be addressed by a conservative Prime Minister Harold MacMillan who claimed in a speech that '...most of our people have never had it so good.'

Hungary were seen as lambs to the slaughter on that afternoon, players in another sign of the strength and resurgence of the English game which had shaken itself down and recovered from its disappointing World Cup campaign of a little over three years previously. That tournament in Brazil had seen England lose two of their three games, including a humiliating 1-0 defeat to part-timers USA who were coached by a Scot by the name of William Jeffrey. He, like so many of his peers, preferred the pass-and-move 'combination' football that had originated all those years ago with the Queen's Park Football Club, so, unsurprisingly, he employed that game against the English, the USA lining up in what is best described as a 2-3-4-1 formation utilising both the length and the width of the pitch, thus ensuring they could play that passing game so beloved of the Scots with the players in close proximity to one another and always offering support and another option. It was too much for the static English who ended up chasing shadows with inside left John Souza, in particular, causing them all sorts of problems. It was, and probably remains, one of the biggest shocks in World Cup history. But was the lesson learnt? Seemingly not. The period of mourning and reflection was brief and, by the time England has beaten Belgium 5-0 two years later, all was well with the newspapers of the day proclaiming that the recovery was 'complete' and that England were 'on top' again. There was even insinuations of cheating levelled at the US team with suggestions made that their team was made up of players imported to the country especially for that game. This was not the case as eight were American born with five of them all hailing from Missouri.

True or not, it eased the pain, explained the result in a satisfactory manner ('cheating foreigners' again) and all was well.

What that defeated and humiliated England side were actually 'on top' of what is unclear, but one thing that they were most certainly not on top of was the world of international football as the game against Hungary would, finally and irrevocably, illustrate.

Hungary's 6-3 win has long gone into both English and Hungarian sporting folklore. That they won at all should not, maybe, have been a surprise, even if it was the home nation's first-ever defeat at their famous Wembley home. Hungary were, after all, the world's number-one ranking team and reigning Olympic champions, a team that would almost certainly at least have got to the final of the 1950 World Cup had they (and the Soviet Union) not withdrawn on the pretext they would not play international sides based in Western Europe. As it was, Hungary were still on a 24-game unbeaten run and would be going to the following year's World Cup as favourites. So they were a good side, a very good side, one that could at least give England a game, maybe even beat them. But by as convincing a margin as they did? It would have been thought impossible.

England went into the game playing the WM formation made popular by former Arsenal manager Herbert Chapman when he took over at Highbury in 1925. Formation-wise, WM was now becoming as old and dated as the Pyramid formation it had superceded. The game had moved on, but England had not, their belief in the old system, again, an unshakable one. Hungary, in contrast, elected to play in their conventional 2-3-3-2 formation, one that was a reboot of the Metodo system developed and practiced by Vittorio Pozzo with the Italian national side in the 1930s. That had been a 2-3-2-3 formation which Hungary's coach, Gusztáv Sebes, had tweaked to allow for an extra man in midfield at the expense of a conventional attacker. He did this by turning 2-3-2-3 into 2-3-3-2 using József Bozsik as a deep-lying playmaker, allowing Nándor Hidegkuti to play as an attacking midfielder with Ferenc Puskás and Sándor Kocsis playing as strikers. The team's width and pace was provided by Zoltán Czibor and László Budai who played on either side of Hidegkuti in that forward three.

1954 quarter-final, Hungary vs Brazil, 4:2

'Deep-lying playmaker' and 'attacking midfielder'. These could be modern-day buzzwords within the game used to describe any contemporary team, their players and tactics. Yet this is a team, a formation and a method of play that relates to a game that was played over 60 years ago, a tribute and testimony to how advanced and farsighted the game was in Hungary at that time, a game that was lightyears ahead of the one that was still being practiced and preached in England.

The Hungarians weren't just mapping the pitch. They were tearing up all of the old maps and introducing some new ones, maps and plans that covered every single aspect of the game with Sebes at the forefront, the Budapest-born coach developing what he called 'socialist football'. He defined this by expecting every player to have equal responsibility on the pitch, both to themselves and their teammates, able to carry out a teammate's role in the side as capably as they could their own. This form of footballing ideology is more well known today as Total Football, that much vaunted and praised method used by the Netherlands in the 1970s which we will look at in a later chapter. Its earliest origins were first practiced by the Hungarians with Sebes' predecessor from the late 1920s, Márton Bukovi. He was credited with turning Herbert Chapman's WM formation into a WW-shaped 2–3–2–3 by turning the M 'upside down'. Sebes was the coach who was able to fine tune that formation through a combination of having some truly world-class players available to him as well as the most famous stage in world football to demonstrate how effective it could be – as England were about to find out.

A famous photograph taken on the day of the game in question shows the two teams walking onto the pitch prior to kick-off. England's Billy Wright affords a wide smile for the waiting camera; immaculate and confident looking, he manages to look as if he is wandering down a country lane rather than out to play in front of an audience of 105,000. For Hungary's leading two players, Ferenc Puskás and Gyula Grosics, the look is different. Grosics is deep in thought and has his head down, almost as if he is trying to block out the occasion from his mind and is preferring, instead, to focus on the game ahead. Puskás, on the contrary, looks as if he is calmly taking in the scene around him, but calmly and objectively and with no show of nerves or anticipation of the game that awaits him and his teammates. It's a look and attitude that maybe, just maybe, England would have matched had Herbert Chapman, the purveyor of the professional approach to everything you did as a footballer, had been the England coach. Calm, detached, focused and in control. An efficiently running machine. England's coach, however, was Walter Winterbottom, a man with no prior managerial experience in professional football up to his taking the position with England, one now given the onerous role of developing and improving the standard of football coaching throughout England. These were two massive roles and responsibilities that would surely have been better given to two men, and, ideally men with far more experience of both playing and coaching the game than Winterbottom whose sole experience as a player was just 26 appearances for Manchester United from 1936 to 1938. He then gave up the game altogether in order to study physical education in Leeds, eventually becoming a lecturer before serving as an officer in the Royal Air Force, reaching the rank of wing commander during World War II.

Fernec Puskás

Little wonder that, in 1946, Winterbottom was FA secretary Stanley Rous' first and only choice to be appointed as the FA's first director of coaching with the added 'extra' responsibility of looking after the England team. He not only knew a lot about physical education (so there'd be none of that new-fangled coaching and tactics nonsense) but was also, like Rous, an ex-British Armed Forces Officer.

He ticked all the boxes. It was just a shame that none of them applied to football. As an added insult, he was also not permitted to pick the England team himself. That responsibility was entrusted to a motley collection of blazers and old school ties who sat on an FA selection committee.

That state of affairs is, quite rightly, laughable now, even embarrassing, given the massive strides forward the Hungarians were making in their national game with the very great irony that the best man for the job as both the FA's director of coaching and England manager was a certain Jimmy Hogan. He remained, as far as the English FA were concerned, the very last man they would have appointed to either post, having previously regarded the work he did with the MTK club in Hungary as that of a 'traitor'. Thus Hogan, perhaps secretly supporting the Hungary team, sat and watched at Wembley, accompanied as he did so by the youth team players of Aston Villa where, at 71, he was still coaching, such was his love for the game. Hogan was finally and belatedly put forward for a coaching role with England following the defeat against Hungary only for the FA, no doubt with some relief, to say it wasn't a practical situation as he was now 'too old' for such a role.

Stanley Rous, it should be noted, a longtime critic of Hogan, held his senior post with the FA until he was 67 as well as holding the post as president of FIFA until he was 79, making a mockery of the FA's claim that Hogan was 'too old' to hold a coaching position within their organisation when he was nearly 10 years younger than Rous. The simple truth of the matter is that the FA wanted nothing to do with Hogan and had steadfastly and openly ignored his outstanding candidature throughout his coaching career, just as they did that of another English coaching maverick, Brian Clough, during the 1970s and 80s. Hungary's emphatic win at Wembley would certainly have come as no surprise whatsoever to Hogan. He knew the Hungarian system, the clubs, the players, administrators and coaches. He would certainly have known, and worked alongside, Sándor Barcs, president of the Hungarian Football Federation who, in the aftermath of Hungary's victory, dedicated the win and performance to Hogan, adding that 'Jimmy Hogan taught us everything we know about football.'

Hungary's emphatic win and display was partially down to some woeful tactical naivety displayed by both Winterbottom and some of his players. Man-marking is an example. Teams that played the WM formation would always brief their centre half to mark the opposing team's centre forward. In other words, number 5 marked number 9; in this case, Harry Johnston of Blackpool and England sticking close to Nador Hidegkuti. Standard procedure. Hidegkuti wore the number 9 shirt, so he would have played up the middle, a traditional targetman of the type that Johnson played against and, more often than not, dealt with on a weekly basis. Except, of course, Hidegkuti was not a traditional centre forward. In fact, he was anything but, operating instead as an attacking midfielder, in effect, an early version of the false number 9, that position that we see players like Lionel Messi carry out for Barcelona and, previously, Francesco Totti for Roma. The result of this saw Hidegkuti roam the pitch in his nominal position of an attacking midfielder, meaning that Johnson, conditioned to carry out his individual instructions without fail, chased him everywhere he went, inevitably finding himself drawn out of his normal defensive position as he did so. This gave Hungary's other attacking players more than enough time and space to exploit the England defence, which they did to great effect with Hidegkuti himself opening the scoring for Hungary after barely a minute had elapsed, running onto the ball from a deep position and scoring from outside of the penalty area. Johnson was nowhere to be seen.

But England's confusion didn't end there. Kocsis and Puskás were playing as Hungary's two strikers but, as they were wearing the short numbers 8 and 10, respectively, the England players regarded them as inside forwards, which is exactly what they would have been had Hungary been playing the conventional WM formation. As a result of this, no one really knew who was meant to be marking them, leading to more uncertainty and conceded space and possession. Indeed, when you fully consider the hapless manner in which the England manager and players had approached the game, it's perhaps something of a surprise that the Hungarians only ended up scoring six goals.

Another significant advantage that the Hungarians had over England was their approach towards international games and their national setup as a whole. For England, international matches had always been arranged and played in a bit of a haphazard way. Indeed, for many on the FA board, away trips were regarded as something of a 'jolly' with the suits travelling and staying in first-class accommodation overseas whilst the players had to make do with second class. England had even shown considerable disdain towards the World Cup, choosing not to enter at all in the first three tournaments, instead choosing, if you recall, to give preference to the British Championship, a yearly league contest between England, Scotland, Wales and Northern Ireland. International matches were, therefore, not a priority, and, as was the case with this particular fixture, if one did happen to take on a greater than usual significance then it was usually accepted that England would only have to turn up to win, such was their natural superiority to any other team.

The skilful and organised Hungarians were now blowing that long-held self-belief out of the water. Future England manager Bobby Robson, then an established player at Fulham and a man who would go on to make 20 appearances for England, later admitted that both he and England had seen '...a style of play, a system of play that we had never seen before. None of these players meant anything to us. We didn't know about Puskás. All these fantastic players, they were men from Mars as far as we were concerned. They were coming to England, England had never been beaten at Wembley—this would be a 3-0, 4-0 maybe even 5-0 demolition of a small country who were just coming into European football. They called Puskás the "Galloping Major" because he was in the army—how could this guy serving for the Hungarian army come to Wembley and rifle us to defeat? But the way they played, their technical brilliance and expertise—our WM formation was kyboshed in ninety minutes of football. The game had a profound effect, not just on myself but on all of us. That one game alone changed our thinking. We thought we would demolish this team—England at Wembley, we are the masters, they are the pupils. It was absolutely the other way.'

England captain Billy Wright, whose confident smile and manner was so obvious on that pre-match photo, partially admitted to a feeling of complacency before the game when he had noted the type of boots that the Hungarian players were wearing, saying, 'We completely underestimated the advances that Hungary had made, and not only tactically. When we walked out at Wembley that afternoon, side by side with the visiting team, I looked down and noticed that the Hungarians had on these strange, lightweight boots, cut away like slippers under the ankle bone. I turned to big Stan Mortensen and said, "We should be alright here, Stan, they haven't got the proper kit."'[27]

As it turned out, it was England who hadn't got the right kit – playing or otherwise. Their boots were heavy and cumbersome, hardly contusive to the sort of fast, athletic passing game practiced by the Hungarians who were, in every detail, so far ahead of their English counterparts it was embarrassing. Yet the immediate aftermath of that heavy defeat saw blame placed, unfairly but very squarely, on the shoulders of six members of the England team, none of whom would ever play for the national side again.

---

27 Puskás, Ferenc. 1998. Puskás on Puskás: The Life and Times of a Footballing Legend. Robson Books.

The unfortunate six were Bill Eckersley, Alf Ramsey (who, as England manager guided them to World Cup success in 1966, more on that and how he transformed the national side in a later chapter), George Robb, Stan Mortensen, Ernie Taylor and, last of all, the unfortunate Harry Johnson. He'd been run ragged throughout by Hidegkuti, one man of six blamed for failings that had nothing to do with them as men or footballers but everything to do with a national Football Association which, time and time and time again had stuck its head in the sand as regards the progress that the rest of the world was making in football. England had paid a humbling price for their easy complacency and insular attitude with a humiliating defeat at what they liked to call, then and now, the 'home' of football. England would now spend the following 60 years or so trying to catch up with the rest of the world, both at club and international level.

You could argue that, even now, they have yet to do so.

Willy Meisl, watching the game and, no doubt, catching up with Hogan at the same time, was moved to comment after that, 'To the British fan, Hungary's game must have looked like soccer telepathy. If one player had the ball, all his colleagues moved as if they saw a kind of "astral" ball which at any moment might materialise into the real leather globe at their feet.'

Hungary's win was as much for the game of football as it was for themselves. They had proven, beyond all doubt, that the way ahead for the game involved the sort of tactical innovations and specialised coaching and preparation that had become more and more a part of the game. And not just in Hungary and Europe as a whole, but in South America where the beginnings of a great Brazilian side was already taking shape, one that would captivate the world by the end of the decade.

One consequence of Hungary's famous win at Wembley was the realisation amongst English coaches and managers that they would have to accept looking to Europe and farther afield for both the latest advances and developments in training and tactics. The nation that had exported the game to the world now looked to that same world to remind it how to play the game in the first place. One of the first to do so was Matt Busby at Manchester United who did not want to see his side go backwards in the same way the England side clearly had through a reluctance to play in regular competitive games against continental opposition. Busby did this by ensuring that his team entered the European Cup, which they did in time for the 1956/57 tournament, barely a year since the FA had grandly announced that it would not be entering a team for the inaugural competition the previous year, despite Chelsea, the reigning English Champions wanting to take part. The FA refused to allow them to do so. Manchester United thus became the first English side to take part in the tournament, acquitting themselves well in the process by knocking out Belgian champions Anderlecht (12-0 on aggregate), Borussia Dortmund and Athletic Bilbao before falling to Real Madrid in the semi-finals. It was the start of a passionate love affair between the club and Europe's premier football competition that lasts to this day.

One English admirer of the Hungary team was Don Revie, another man who would go on to briefly be in charge of the national side. Revie had noted the effectiveness of the Hungarian line-up and, in particular, the role and performance of Nador Hidegkuti, the false number 9 who had led England and, in particular, Harry Johnson such a merry dance at Wembley. Revie was a player at Manchester City at the time and felt that his club would be able to play a similar system with him assuming the role filled by Hidegkuti for Hungary. Manchester City duly based their game on Revie playing as a deep-lying centre forward, drawing opposing players out of position in much the same way as Hidegkuti had.

Perhaps, unsurprisingly, the tactic and method took a little time for the Manchester City to get used to. They lost their first game playing it 5-0, but, as the players got more and more used to it, they started to excel, and the system worked. Manchester City went on to reach two consecutive FA Cup Finals playing to the Revie plan. They lost to Newcastle in 1955 but won against Birmingham City the following year.

Revie went on to have a great deal of success at Leeds United where, perhaps surprisingly, he chose to play a far more conventional (as it was becoming) 4-4-2 formation. He had not, however, totally forgotten his admiration for continental football, adopting some of the professionalism that had seeped into the game in Spain and Italy and introducing it to the English game with Leeds. These were, however, some of the more unsavoury elements of 'professionalism' that included time-wasting, surrounding the referee in order to try to get him to change his mind with regard to a decision or simply play-acting in an attempt to unfairly win free kicks and penalties. One particular image that will forever remain iconic as far as that Leeds side is concerned is the sign that was placed in a prominent position in the home dressing room, one that would forever be visible to the players within. It read 'Keep Fighting'. Managers and players of other clubs knew exactly what it meant as did their support with the 'fighting' being all too often literal.

That was a pity as Revie's Leeds side when they were at their peak were one of the most exciting to watch in English, maybe even European, footballing history. Their reputation went before them and even let them down as it most certainly did in 1975 when, with Revie, now the England manager watching his old team from a TV studio, they lost the European Cup Final to Bayern Munich 2-0, outwitted and outplayed by a team wary of their reputation for gamesmanship and a referee who was even more so. His team played 4-4-2 and was one of the finest exponents of that formation in contemporary footballing history, each player given the fixed role and responsibility as well as position on the pitch it involved. Rigid, yes. But played with exceptional players, as Leeds all too briefly illustrated, extremely effective.

Then there was Bill Nicholson and Tottenham Hotspur. Nicholson, like Don Revie, had been a long-time admirer of the game played on the continent and how much more effective and attractive that type of game was in both club and international sides. Hungary was the epitome of this in 1953. Nicholson vowed to bring the same kind of attacking flair and excitement to Tottenham when he was appointed as the club's manager in 1958, five years after Hungary's demolition of England just down the road at Wembley. The formation that Nicholson chose to introduce, and not just to Tottenham but the English game as a whole, was based on Hungary's successful 2-3-3-2 formation with the exception that it had an inside forward (as opposed to a centre forward) deployed as a midfield creator, meaning Nicholson was going to go with the attacking midfielder of which Hidegkuti had been the shining example and a traditional centre forward in what was a very attack-minded line-up, one that was, if anything, more inclined to that type of game than the Hungary one was.

It was risky. Yet Nicholson felt he had the players to make his version, a 3-3-4 formation, work. His first choice midfield trio was very strong indeed, featuring, as it did, the physical presence of Dave Mackay, the guile and artistry of Danny Blanchflower and the speed and directness of John White. In front of those three was an attacking quartet that featured two wingers in Cliff Jones and Terry Dyson, that 'traditional' centre forward in Bobby Smith plus an inside forward in Les Allen. Attack-minded? Just a bit. But it was also an extremely flexible line-up with, if necessary, Jones and Dyson able to slot back into the midfield, giving Tottenham a more solid-looking 3-5-2 formation, or, if necessary, Allen slotting in just behind Smith as a false number 9, giving the formation more of a look of 3-4-1-3 or even 3-5-1-2. It was hugely adaptable and, in time, one that opposing teams found hard to play against. And it was even harder to defend against, such was the way the Tottenham players would constantly push into space, interchanging with one another and, in doing so, dragging staid and unprepared markers all over the place.

Bill Nicholson, Tottenham Hotspur Manager in 1969

It could, of course, have been a spectacular failure, just as Argentinean World Cup winner Osvaldo Ardiles attempted to partially recreate it at the beginning of the 1994/95 season was when he opted to field a team with five attacking players in it, his contemporary take on the Pyramid formation of old featuring a front quintet of Darren Anderton, Nick Barmby, Teddy Sheringham, Jurgen Klinsmann and Iliie Dumitrescu. It was a formation that promised goals and got them; a 4-3 win over Sheffield Wednesday in their opening fixture of the season was a sign of things to come, the problem being that having such a formation means that whilst you are capable of scoring a lot of goals yourself, you are equally prone to conceding as many at the other end.

This inherent weakness in such a vulnerable formation was that it was great for attacking but comparatively useless when defending due to the fact that so many forward players means there is a lot of space behind them for opposing teams to exploit. Thus, Tottenham suffered some humbling defeats, and Ardiles lost his dream job at the club he had graced for so long as a player. Bill Nicholson had realised that whilst a formation with clear attacking intent was one thing, it also needed to be able to switch from attack to defence in an instant with even the most attack-minded of his players clear on their responsibilities, something which his side had in abundance unlike that of Ardiles whose side switched from attack to rushing back en masse in a panic.

One thing Nicholson did have in common with Ardiles was a high-scoring debut game as manager: seven in the Argentinean's opening game but double that in Nicholson's as Tottenham beat Everton 10-4 at their White Hart Lane ground with rumours abounding after the game that the new man in charge was furious at the way his new charges had conceded four goals. But was that and Nicholson's own contribution to mapping the pitch a one-off? No. Less than two years after his appointment, Tottenham won English football's League Championship and FA Cup double, winning their first 11 league games and, by the end of the season, scoring a total of 115 goals. The following season, they won the FA Cup again as well as reaching the semi-finals of the European Cup (beating Gornik Zabrze, Feyenoord and Dukla Prague on the way). In 1963, they broke totally new ground by becoming the first English club side to win a major European trophy when they beat favourites Atletico Madrid 5-1 in the European Cup Winner's Cup Final.[28] That game, the result and the manner of Tottenham's triumph is perhaps the biggest tribute that can

---

28   *Atletico Madrid played a 4-2-4 formation in the game, therefore matching Tottenham's compliment of four attacking players. This left them a man short in midfield which is where Nicholson's side took control and won the game, Danny Blanchflower and John White dominating in both terms of possession and physical presence.*

be paid to Bill Nicholson; the fact that he wasn't afraid to look beyond his homeland to find the best way of playing the game and, when his methods proved to be both highly effective and successful he had done so by taking on, and beating, the best in both England and on the continent by playing that continent's top sides at their own game and beating them. Nicholson's success. But made in Hungary with just a little bit of Jimmy Hogan thrown into the mix, as close, maybe, as Hogan ever would come to having any kind of influence, however indirectly, on the way an English team played and the success it duly brought them.

The 3-3-4 formation created by Nicholson had been lauded as a one-off, a unique formation that belonged to one man and his special team at that time. In truth it was a formation that came right at the end of a footballing trend that was, by the beginning of the 1960s, set to change with coaches preferring to play four rather than three defenders at the back with the 4-2-4 formation favoured by the great Brazilian side of the 1950s considered the first to focus on having four defenders at the base of their team (see chapter 6). The 3-3-4 formation did, however, enjoy something of a renaissance under Dutch coach Co Adriaanse who used it at Portuguese side FC Porto during the 2005/06 league season during which they won a domestic League and Cup double. Its effectiveness there is evident in the fact that, at the end of that season, FC Porto had scored 54 goals whilst conceding only 16 in their 34 league games, a tribute to the effectiveness of a system that, with little defensive width, demands a very high level of tactical discipline throughout the side. This would not have been a problem for Adriaanse who has a reputation for not only for being a strict disciplinarian but for championing training methods that could be, at best, described as unorthodox, such as the time when, as a youth team coach at Ajax, he instructed his players to lie on the ground whilst a teammate, wearing football boots, would be told to run over their bodies, an approach which, as his career progressed with the unorthodoxy accompanying it, he was given the nickname 'Psycho Co'.

Nicholson had a similar reputation as a strict disciplinarian at Tottenham with an approach to both the game and his players to match. Writing in British newspaper *The Guardian* soon after Nicholson's death in 2004, David Miller recalls a man and coach who '...chastisingly entrenched the fundamentals of the game: simplicity, to eliminate error; repetition of moves, to breed familiarity; honest sweat, so as to leave the field wholly spent.' Nicholson was, he added, 'First to arrive each day, last to leave, without his nod no stone turned at White Hart Lane. Even training balls were inspected before being replaced for wear and tear. No player was fined, because players conformed out of respect. Anyone spitting at an opponent was straight out of the door. No parent was paid as inducement for the signature of a promising boy.'

No one would have dreamt of calling Nicholson a 'psycho' in the way they had coined the phrase for Adriaanse. Yet the similarities between both coaches, in terms of their disciplinarian approach and their strict attention to detail in every aspect of the day-to-day running of their respective clubs and their players' lives is what made their adoption of the 3-3-4 formation so successful. It demands discipline; it demands that every player in the team knows exactly what his role is, but, not only that, what the role of each and every one of his teammates is, so much so that, if any one player has to slot into a position normally held by another, he isn't a square peg in a round hole but one that fits into it perfectly. Take Tottenham's convincing win in the 1963 European Cup Winner's Cup Final, for example, one they achieved without Dave Mackay, one of their most influential players, a leader on and off the pitch and someone whose rich mix of determination and skill would have made him a key man in the final and one that Atletico would, for certain, have feared. Mackay missed that match because of injury, but did Tottenham miss him? Clearly not as the margin of their victory shows, one of the reasons for this being how effectively Tony Marchi stood in for Mackay in the final, understanding the responsibilities of the role and the way Mackay was expected to play perfectly.

Therein lies the secret to making 3-3-4 work as a football formation.

It's a formation that needs discipline, clear thinking, intelligence and a certain amount of self-sacrifice on the part of a player. Your role is defined; you stick with it. To the letter. To roam, to wander needlessly, to depart from that role in any way can, and probably will, affect the team in a negative manner. It is, in effect, a formation that can only be played by teams that have a fair share of clever players, players who are amongst the very best at what they do, the best available in their on-field position.As Miller goes on to say in his wonderful tribute to Nicholson in the afore mentioned *Daily Telegraph*[29] article, he once spent time with Nicholson at Cambridge University '...where, besides working us to the point of physical sickness, he chastisingly entrenched the fundamentals of the game: simplicity, to eliminate error; repetition of moves, to breed familiarity; honest sweat, so as to leave the field wholly spent.' A formation that offers alternatives whilst a team is attacking but which requires near perfection to succeed. The four attackers must consistently apply pressure, play with pace and with an understanding of what their teammates are doing as space can be limited for them and running into one another's would be counterproductive. At the other end of the pitch, the defence must constantly be alert, particularly to the possibility of having to deal with the long, high balls that the opposition, under constant pressure from that ever present, pushing and pacy front four, will tend to send their way.

Strenuous responsibilities for both offence and defence. Yet the part of the pitch where the game is won or lost for a team playing the 3-3-4 formation is the midfield where exceptional players are needed, exceptional players being exactly what Nicholson had at his disposal with Blanchflower, White and Mackay, all of whom were capable of playing in all three areas of the pitch, if necessary. Mackay was

---

29   Miller, David, The Daily Telegraph *(Nicholson spent a lifetime putting his heart into White Hart Lane, October 25th 2004.)*

particularly strong as an additional defender with White equally as capable in the front line. They must, therefore, have infinite energy levels and be able to track up and down the pitch without a break for the entire 90 minutes either to support the attack or to provide defensive cover (and remember, at the time Tottenham were playing this formation, in-play substitutions were not yet part of the game).

Got all that? It's complicated. And that's the whole point. It was a very different, very difficult, formation to play. Yes, it was an innovative one to create in the first place but was, and remains, one which, in practice, is even more difficult to play well and effectively as it makes so many demands of both the team as a whole as well as the players in question. It's a tactical one-off. No wonder, in Miller's words, Nicholson espoused the qualities of simplicity, of eliminating error, of repetition, breeding familiarity and, with this particularly relevant to his midfield which must have, by the very nature of the way 3-3-4 was played, been one of the hardest working and running in Europe, to ensure that 'honest sweat so as to leave the field wholly spent'.

But what of that Hungarian team which had been an inspiration to these and so many others in the game at the beginning of that decade?

Six months later, England's swift acceptance of the invitation to play a return match in Budapest saw them take on the side that had the previous November given them the shock of their footballing lives and had, in doing so, shaken the foundations of English football and the nation that had, as it keeps telling everyone, given the game to the world, to its very core.

As you might expect, the reaction to that 6-3 defeat had been swift and decisive. Walter Winterbottom had been replaced as England manager whilst the old practice of selecting the team by committee had been abandoned with the role and overall responsibility for coaching the team as well as its selection had been given to an eminently qualified and experienced replacement manager, one who also headed up a nationwide group of coaches charged with modernising the game in England from top to bottom. This would start with school teams and work its way all the way to up the national side, including an ambitious seven-year plan to learn from and adopt techniques and procedures learnt from specially invited coaches and representatives from overseas nations, including some from South America, with representatives from the Brazilian, Uruguayan and Argentinean associations already invited to visit FA headquarters with reciprocal visits in the process of being arranged.

Except, of course, none of that happened at all.

There was, admittedly, a sudden and rather desperate initiative turned obsession to make the players fitter, the belief at the time being that continental players 'lasted longer' than English players and that the defeat had been nothing to do with football at all. It was more to do with the pesky Communists ensuring their men were so much stronger and fitter than anyone else, so the honest artisans from England never stood a chance. The obsession for strength and physical fitness being the optimum requirement for any footballer had, of course, started to go out of fashion back in the late 19th century when Scotland's smaller, quicker players had first shown that guile could always outwit strength. It was now widely believed that England had been beaten at their own game, at least, their own, *old* game, and the traditionalists leapt upon the chance to re-inflict it on the England players with one unnamed player known to protest during one particularly exhausting session by asking the trainer, Charlie Cole, 'What are we training for, Charlie? The ruddy Grand National?'

No one would have been surprised, you suspect, if England had gone into the match by reverting to the 1-1-8 formation of old and taking a bemused Hungarian side on at mob football.

England made eight changes to their starting line-up from the previous game, one of which saw the return on the left wing of the incomparable Tom Finney who had missed the first match and, as a consequence, was free of the tarnished reputation that it had given those eight who hadn't made it for the second, of which, six would never play for their country again. Decisive? Yes. Papering over the cracks? Not really. The time for English football to attempt to do that had been at least 20 years previously.

The English game had already fallen into the chasm and was at rock bottom, way behind both their European and South American peers in terms of technique, coaching, fitness and their approach to players' health and diet. Hungary's 6-3 win at Wembley had shown all that up for what is now, without any doubt whatsoever, a failed and backwards system. However, rather than attempt to address the real issues, the FA committee decided to pin the blame on the players, pick almost an entirely different team and, in doing so, with the help of Finney, look to show that all was well at the home of football and that the home defeat to Hungary a few months earlier had been an aberration. Here they were in Budapest, Finney included, to prove just that. This included, of course, the retention of the tried, tested, out-of-date and very much wanting WM formation which the Hungarians had so systematically and gleefully pulled apart in that corresponding fixture with Hidegkuti the star of the show. He must have been delighted to realise that he was going to have the opportunity to do it all again, albeit, this time at the expense of Luton Town defender Syd Owen who would have the onerous task of marking him, or, to be more accurate, of trying to work out where he was at any one time during the match.

Owen had made his England debut in their previous fixture, a disappointing 1-0 reverse against Yugoslavia where, once again, he and the other England defenders were constantly pulled out of position by the Yugoslavs' use of a false number 9 as well as midfielders given a free role to roam at will anywhere on the pitch. Yugoslavia's tactical superiority in the game ended up being rather more emphatic than the result suggested.

England and WM had been found out. No question. Yet, doggedly they stuck to it, buoyed, no doubt, by a 4-2 win over Scotland in the first game they'd played after that first defeat to Hungary at Wembley. Maybe the win against the Scots made some feel England were vindicated in continuing to play the way they did, who can tell? It made no difference to the end result in the Hungary rematch. England lost 7-1 in Budapest, and, if Syd Owen had done fairly well in keeping Hidegkuti fairly quiet on this occasion, it was only because Hidegkuti had pulled Owen out of position a sufficient number of times to let his teammates, led by Puskás, sweep at will through the gaping hole that was left as a consequence. As Puskás himself said of the Hungarian approach, one that led to an aggregate victory of 13-4 over England in the two games (a result which more closely resembles a rugby match), 'When we attacked, everyone attacked, and in defence it was the same. We were the prototype for Total Football.'

Which was no exaggeration, at least, not in the way in which Puskás had described the Hungarians way of playing as 'Total Football'. The phrase has been widely attributed to the Dutch side of the 1974 and 1978 World Cups with its origins in the Amsterdam-based club side Ajax and their progressive coach Rinus Michels who had two spells at the club (1965-71 and 1975-76) as well as one in charge of the Dutch national team at the 1974 World Cup Final held in the then West Germany. Both Ajax and the Dutch team that took part in those two consecutive World Cup Finals (and reaching the final on both occasions) were widely praised for the type of football they played, one that saw any of the outfield players being able to take over the role of any other player in the team.

Yet this was not done in a haphazard manner; indeed, and paradoxically, the fluidity and freedom of movement that this football allows is the very reason that it is so strong from an organisational and formation point of view. Players are able to switch positions and responsibilities so effectively that the shape of the team is never lost. It means that no outfield player is fixed in a nominal role and that anyone can play as an attacker, midfielder or defender, with the only fixed position in the team being the goalkeeper.

Naturally enough, this places enormous physical and technical demands on all of the players in the team. Players had always been thought to have either one or the other of those qualities in their favour. For example, Paul Scholes was always considered one of the most technically gifted players to play for England, but, as far as his tackling ability and ability to last 90 minutes in a full-blooded match, both were questioned, with former England manager Sven Goran Eriksson saying of Scholes, '... [he] was England's best football player. He had everything except the ability to tackle without earning a yellow card.'[30] To add to this, Scholes suffered from asthma, meaning he was rarely, if ever, able to play a whole match, especially in warm and dry conditions, admitting to Eriksson that, 'If I last an hour, that's good.' Contrast that to the player with the greatest technical ability in both the Ajax and Netherlands teams of the time, Johan Cruyff, who was, for all his astonishing technical qualities as a player and all-round skill and vision, someone who could look after himself on the pitch, who wasn't, it appeared, particularly interested in looking after himself off it with his one-time habit of smoking 20 cigarettes a day. Michels had taken a team of 10 very good footballers plus, in Cruyff, one immortal and successfully married their excellent technical qualities with physical strength and the type of stamina required to run for 90 minutes without a break. He was, as Bill

---

30   *Eriksson, Sven-Göran. 2013.* My Story. Headline.

Nicholson had once demanded, ensuring his players always left the field 'wholly spent'. Anyone who has seen post-match images of Cruyff, his shirt soaked in sweat and his face pale with exertion, will know he had done just that and, for all his otherworldly skills, was a player neither unable, or too proud, to put a shift in. Yet hadn't Hungary an equivalent to Cruyff in their team? And weren't they, as Puskás claims, playing 'Total Football' long before the world awarded the phrase to Michel's, Ajax and the Netherlands?

One thing that the Hungarians did have, in abundance and over England, the Netherlands and just about any other team you can care to name throughout football history was total control of how they played and the players that performed their respective roles. This privilege and insistence fell onto the shoulders of their coach, Gusztáv Sebes, the Michels of his day and another footballing visionary who, like all of the names already mentioned in this book was a man who could see the bigger picture. Not only where the game was going and how big it might be on the world stage, but, significantly for Hungary, how much international and political kudos, not to mention strong affirmation for the nation's politics, an all-conquering football team might bring both him and the nation. Hadn't, after all, Sebes described 'Total Football' as, first and foremost, 'socialist' football? Sport didn't mix with politics on this occasion. Sport was politics and politics was sport, the vindication of a political system demonstrated by a football team.

It wasn't an unreasonable claim to make. Socialism is traditionally seen as, well, social, that is, collective ownership of a product as well as the collective responsibility for it. Its links with football have been made before. One example was that of former Liverpool manager Bill Shankly, who said, 'The socialism I believe in is everybody working for the same goal and everybody having a share in the rewards. That's how I see football, that's how I see life.' Everyone working together, everyone working for the same reward, collective responsibility and ownership? Wouldn't that be characterised by a football team where all the players also have a personal responsibility, not only for themselves but for their teammates, with each one of them being able to step in and take on another role or responsibility? Wasn't that exactly the way Hungary played the game at the time, the ethos behind their game and their ultimate strength? The fortunes of the national team were certainly seen to come above everything else, players included. Military conscription, compulsory in Hungary at the time Sebes was putting his great side together, meant that all of the country's most promising young footballers found themselves, after Sebes had a word in the ear of the military official who mattered, stationed together in the village of Kispest, the home of the great club side Honvéd. Sebes would then watch them playing for Honvéd with the very best singled out to do their spell of military conscription as a sinecure. In other words, they had little to no exposure to military life at all, but rather spent all of their time playing football.

This is how Ferenc Puskás – overweight, out of condition and about as far removed from being a soldier as it was possible to be but who was, for all of that, one of the finest footballers Sebes (or anyone) would ever have the privilege of seeing – ended up having a very successful 'military life', one that eventually earnt him the ironic nickname 'The Galloping Major".

In the game's modern era, national team managers often lament the fact that the nature of their jobs means that they do not have any day-to-day contact with players, that their contact with them, when they do have it is minimal at best – around 3-4 days, including match day. Even then, they don't always have access to the players they want in the squad, such are the pressures and expectations that come from their parent clubs who are often reluctant to even release their players to join a squad, much less play in a game, especially if it is only a friendly. What Sebes managed to do back in the 1950s, albeit more out of the political circumstances of the country of the time than through design, was to successfully create the togetherness that you might normally expect from at a club side at an international level. The players spent time together, learnt each other's respective strengths and weaknesses and the way the coach wanted them to play, day after day, week after week. It was relentless with the national side; by the time they played England in those two matches, they had been together for years, assembling every week for three days to practice and be coached as an international team, playing all the top club sides in the country and going on tours together. In that way, the Hungary players were not only learning from and about each other but they were also, through repetition that eventually became instinct, picking up the way Sebes wanted them to play, and he had all the time in the world to implement and introduce as many new ways of thinking and playing as he wanted.

One of the tours the Hungary players took was to England in the guise of club side Honvéd a little over a year after their win at Wembley when they accepted an invitation to play English club side Wolverhampton Wanderers (Wolves) as part of that club's celebrations in having had floodlighting introduced at their stadium. That match, although it was a friendly, broke all sorts of new ground as far as the game was concerned, not only raising more interest and excitement at the prospect of having a European-wide club knockout competition but also, as it did, tempting the BBC to televise the second half of the match live, such was the interest. Two signs of things to come then. A midweek game between two of Europe's foremost club sides but also one that was to be televised live, and, bear in mind that, even today, midweek friendlies are unlikely to be shown by any of Europe's major broadcasters as a live attraction. It did, however, show there was curiousity, an appetite for fixtures between Europe's elite club sides, something which came to fruition in 1955 with the first-ever European Cup competition.

Chelsea, as we have already seen, were prevented from entering (imagine the English or any other national FA preventing one of their leading sides entering the Champions League) that season, but there was an entry from Hungary,[31] together with clubs from 15 other European nations.

Hungary's representatives in that first-ever European Cup were Budapest FC (MTK), the club that Jimmy Hogan had done so much of his early pioneering work with in coaching from 1914 to 1921. His time spent in Hungary then led to claims from the FA that he was a 'traitor', given the then kingdom of Hungary's allegiance to the Central Powers during World War I. Paranoid gibberish, of course, yet, more than reflect Hogan as someone who had let both King and Country down by refusing to come home and sign up (he wasn't wanted in England for his prowess as a football coach but was more than welcome to represent his country in a war) it showed, again, what an enormous impact his vision and approach had made on both the game and his club, both then and into the 1950s and MTK's entry into the European Cup.

MTK had, when Hungary became a Communist state in 1949, been taken over by the country's secret police, the AVH, in the process going through a procession of name changes, including Vörös Lobogó SE which was the name they were playing under when they entered the European Cup. One of MTK's, or Vörös Lobogó SE's, leading players was our old friend Nándor Hidegkuti whose role as a false number 9 had tormented the England defence, in particular the unfortunate Harry Johnston in Hungary's 6-3 win at Wembley two years earlier. He played a similar

---

31   Along with Hungary, club sides were entered by the FAs of Austria, Belgium, Denmark, France, Italy, Netherlands, Poland, Portugal, Saar, Scotland, Spain, Sweden, Switzerland, West Germany and Yugoslavia. No surprises in seeing that the Scottish FA was as progressive and willing to break new ground as it had always been with regard to playing the game, one that continued to put their insular and pompous neighbours from England to shame. Scotland's entrants, Hibernian, went as far as the semi-finals, losing that tie to French side Stade Reims 3-0 on aggregate.

role for his club side, and, in this instance, it was enough to do the same to Belgian champions Anderlecht who were convincingly beaten 10-4 on aggregate in their first-round game with Péter Palotás' hat trick in the first leg, the first ever to be scored in a European Cup/Champions League game.

A dominant and irresistible national team plus, in Honvéd and MTK (and all their other guises, how apt a team owned by the Hungarian secret police had a propensity for repeatedly changing their identities, one of which was the innocent and rather harmless sounding Textiles SE), two potentially great sides, ones that could, and should, surely have gone on to dominate both club and international football for years to come? Yet that turned out not to be the case, for, despite the great players that the Hungarian game produced; the great coaches (including Hogan); the emphasis on technique and skill placed in coaching in favour of strength and stamina, their 'socialist' footballing revolution that, all too briefly, not only deservedly blew away the conservative old guard but made the rest of the world sit up and take notice, ultimately, faded away to nothing with no reward, no longterm glory, just memories and a dark case of just what might have been.

Hungary should have won the 1954 World Cup. They reached the final through an intoxicating run of wins. South Korea were beaten 9-0, West Germany 8-3, Brazil 4-2 and Uruguay, two-time winners and the holders, again, by four goals to two. A total of 25 goals scored in just four games prior to the final where they were due to meet West Germany again, the side they had already beaten 8-3 in their group stage. There was no reason for anyone to think they couldn't repeat that achievement in the final, even less doubt when, after just eight minutes of the game had elapsed the Hungarians were 2-0 up, courtesy of goals from 'Galloping Major' Puskás and Zoltán Czibor. Victory and, with it, the reward and ultimate justification of their great football experiment, one that Jimmy Hogan had done so much to help initiate over three decades earlier. Yet West Germany still went on to win in what turned out to be one of the biggest shocks to date in the history of football, a match that, to this day, is referred to as the 'miracle of Berne'. It was also one of the last times Germany would go into any international match as the underdogs as they went on to defy footballing logic and expectation by winning the game 3-2.

Many reasons have been given for Hungary's defeat. Some claim that the weather on the day, cold and very wet, prevented the Hungarians from easily playing their fast-moving, quick-passing game on what was a very heavy pitch. Others look to the technical advances made by Adidas, the German footwear company whose boot the German players were wearing was as far in advance to the 'slippers' (as quoted by England's Billy Wright in 1953) worn by the Hungarians as the latter had been to the English boots from that game. These technologically superior boots had screw in studs, meaning the German players could wear the ones they were comfortable with by just changing the studs to reflect the weather and the state of the pitch. Then there was Puskás. Clearly unfit (he'd missed the previous two games due to injury), he'd been rushed back into the side and seemed to justify his selection with the first goal, but he struggled in the inclement conditions, his selection a rare sign of favouring an individual at the expense of the team, one thing you might have expected the Hungarian philosophy to expressly forbid. Perhaps then, Puskás, of all people, was the weak link? Perhaps it was the weather, perhaps it was the difference between the boots the sides were wearing, perhaps it was the 3-2-2-3 formation that the Germans played on the day, one that gave the Hungarians little room to open up and make the most of the space in midfield that their expansive game demanded. This lack of space crucially denied Nándor Hidegkuti the room he needed to make his decoy runs. And maybe, just maybe, having already played them once, the West Germans had worked out how Hungary had played and sent out a team and formation aimed at stopping them doing just that which they were eventually successful in doing.

Which is precisely what Wolves did to combat Honvéd in that prestigious friendly that had been arranged between the two sides in December of that year, having unquestionably noticed, it should be added, of what means and advantages the West Germans had utilised to secure their own win. It was now up to Honvéd to restore a little pride to a nation whose footballing pride had, briefly, suffered a blow to its confidence, something which they could most effectively do by dismantling one of England's leading club sides as easily as the national team had done to the esteemed three lions.

Honvéd took their overseas tours very seriously. There was no question of resting their star players or leaving them at home in order to play a shadow side or give some of their promising younger players a run out. The squad that travelled was strong, and their team that started at Wolves featured six of the players that had beaten England at Wembley. Honvéd didn't take long to get into their expansive stride either, taking a 2-0 lead into the break with Wolves, just like England, struggling to cope with Honvéd's wide variety of tactical plays which ranged from lightning raids down each wing to, horror of horrors, aping the English game by hitting the ball long out of defence. It's little wonder Wolves struggled initially. English football had been stuck in the WM mire for a long time; it consisted of one way and one way only of playing. But it wasn't just that. English club sides were still used to their opponents playing in pretty much the same manner. For an opposing team to actually play with two, three, four, maybe even more players interchanging positions and roles at will, the Wolves players were run off their feet in much the same way England had been, and there must have been some sympathy for Wolves captain Billy Wright who had gone through it all twice before and was now looking at suffering a third consecutive heavy defeat at the hands of the Hungarians.

It was clear that Wolves would not be able to play Honvéd at either their own game or by relying on the tried, trusted but now doubted tactics of WM. So, mindful of what had happened at the World Cup Final some six months earlier, Stan Cullis, the Wolves manager ordered the pitch to be heavily watered in an attempt to make the pitch as muddy and near to unplayable as possible in order to prevent Honvéd from playing what one observer had called their 'delightful' football (this was not needed, of course; remember, the game was played in December when the pitch would have been wet and heavy anyway). Delightful it may have been, but the Wolves boss was in no mood for his side to suffer a heavy defeat on his own ground, and to a continental team at that. So the pitch was watered until it began to resemble something more akin to a bog than a field of sporting conflict, one that, according to the *Daily Mail*, looked like '...a cattle ground at the end of a four-day show in the rain.'

You'd be excused for thinking the Wolves manager was engaging in a bit of gamesmanship here. You'd be right to think that way. Was soaking the pitch in that manner unsporting? Yes. But was it against the rules of the game? Absolutely not. Did it work? Yes. Honvéd, clad in a lightweight strip and a version of the football boots turned slippers on their feet, the same boots that had amused Wright so much at Wembley, began to get bogged down in the thick mud, completely unable to play their fast, passing game and, as a result, attempted, manfully but with little effect to match Wolves at their own game. With the Wolves players bigger, stronger, heavier and used to a far more physical type of game, Wolves long-ball game and constant pressure began to have an effect as the home side scored three goals in the now atrocious conditions to seal a victory which *The Guardian's* Nick Miller later admitted was a '...triumph of grit over skill' in a game where Puskás was, surprisingly, largely ineffective, mainly due to the solid man-marking job that was done on him by Wright, able, at last, to get some sort of payback for the two heavy defeats he had previously experienced as England captain.

The secret of beating sides like Hungary was now out. This game and that earlier World Cup Final had shown that, however tactically superior and skilful one team might be, the nature of football means that they will always be vulnerable to sides that take the game to its physical limits, employing tactics that, as much as possible, win games through a method that focuses on stopping your opponents from playing rather than looking to outplay them yourself. It's one that countless teams have since adopted in an attempt to defeat both the odds and more illustrious opponents, something which was famously achieved by the national team of Greece in order to win the 2004 European Championships in what was described by the BBC as '...a triumph of negative football over the beautiful game.'

Which was no more and no less than what Wolves had done in order to beat Honvéd on that wet and chilly December evening in 1954 in a display that the *Daily Express* claimed was proof positive that '...English football was still the genuine, original, unbeatable article... still the best of its kind in the world.' When you consider the lengths that Cullis had gone to win the game, including soaking the pitch at half-time, it is rather sad and something you would think they'd be rather more inclined to condemn rather than use as a reason for posturing and preening. The *Daily Mail* went as far as claiming that Wolves were now the 'World Champions', nationalistic posturing that was ridiculed by Gabriel Hanot, a former French international who was editor of *L'Equipe*, the French sports daily. Hanot, clearly annoyed, responded by writing, '...before we declare that Wolverhampton are invincible, let them go to Moscow and Budapest. And there are other internationally renowned clubs: Milan and Real Madrid to name but two. A club world championship, or at least a European one – larger, more meaningful and more prestigious than the Mitropa Cup[32] and more original than a competition for national teams – should be launched.'

---

32   *The Mitropa Cup was one of the first international major European football cups for club sides and was competed for by clubs from Austria, Czechoslovakia, Hungary and Italy from 1927. The winners in 1954 were the previously mentioned MTK Budapest FC, or Vörös Lobogó SE, Hungary's side made up of the state secret police.*

Defeat in the 1954 World Cup Final for Hungary followed by Honvéd's high-profile capitulation to 'Champions of the world', Wolverhampton Wanderers weren't the prime reasons for Hungary's consequent fall from the summit of world football. Vörös Lobogó SE went on to make the semi-finals of the following seasons (1955/56) European Cup competition with Honvéd taking up the mantle the following campaign (1956/57) only to make a surprising first-round exit at the hands of Spain's Athletic Bilbao. Honvéd had narrowly lost the first leg of that game in Bilbao by the odd goal in five, but, before they could get the chance of revenge and what was expected to be a convincing victory in the return leg that October, revolution that was anything but related to football broke out in the country and, stranded and very much in limbo whilst violence raged in their homeland, the Honvéd players decided to not even attempt to return home, arranging for the return leg of the game to be played in the Heysel Stadium in Brussels. This was a last and rather magnificent gesture of sporting solidarity and an ethos of 'the show must go on' despite the bloodshed and turmoil at home. Undoubtedly distracted and ill at ease, Honvéd had lost that game as well, and, once it was over, the players summoned their families from Budapest. Despite opposition from FIFA and the Hungarian football authorities, they organised a fundraising tour of Italy, Portugal, Spain and Brazil. After returning to Europe, the players parted ways, and the nucleus of both a great club and international team was lost, their promise, potential and beauty gone forever.

Sándor Kocsis played in Switzerland for a short period before spending seven years with Barcelona whilst Zoltan Czibor had a brief spell with Roma before joining Kocsis at Barcelona. The most high-profile Hungarian player of them all, Ferenc Puskás played in Spain as well, joining Real Madrid before eventually assuming Spanish nationality and making four appearances for the Spanish national team. He did, at least, get the European Cup winner's medal he and his football deserved as part of the Real Madrid side that beat Eintracht Frankfurt 7-3 in the 1960 final, contributing four of the goals himself.

What of Nándor Hidegkuti, the man who, playing in that false number 9 position more than anyone else personified that great Hungary side and the vision of Sebes? He returned home to Hungary later on in the 1956/57 season, post-revolution, to play for MTK, also having two spells as a coach with the side. He eventually ended up coaching in Egypt with the Al Ahly club, successfully introducing the 5-3-2 formation there. Post-revolution Hungary, a people's spirits crushed and their footballers scattered all over Europe, saw both clubs and country struggle. It wasn't enough to have innovative coaches or to devise new ways of playing; you had to have intelligent players to carry out the master plan, and the standard of players was clearly not quite as good as it had been.

Vasas, the 'club of the iron workers' reached the semi-finals of the 1957/58 European Cup before going out to Real Madrid (their quarter-final win over Ajax of the Netherlands would have been a fascinating clash of two sides who played a form of 'total football'), whilst a post-Hidegkuti MTK, competing in the 1958/59 season also went out at the first-round stage, their exit to the Swiss side Young Boys symptomatic of the fall the Hungarian club football had been experiencing in the post-revolution years.

The national side didn't have much luck in the 1958 World Cup either, struggling in their group and eventually going out after a sudden death place-off match against Wales who defeated the previous near unbeatable Magyars 2-1. That defeat came less than five years after their two crushing wins over England and long unbeaten run. From that and being overwhelming favourites to win the World Cup to going out of the next World Cup to Wales whilst, in the same year, your leading club side is bundled out of the European Cup, a trophy made for those great club sides from Hungary to win by a team from Switzerland. It had been a hard, painful and spectacular fall from grace for a side that looked, for a while, if it could be Europe's version of Brazil and one to match them at every World Cup that was ever played. Sebes had, by now, been sacked. Yet his influence and presence remained in the Hungarian game with his taking on the position of president of the Hungarian Olympic Committee from 1948 to 1960 whilst, from 1954 to 1960, he held a senior post with UEFA.

There is little doubt that Hungarian football could, and should, have been magnificent and dominant for several decades. The infrastructure was in place as was the philosophy, that of identifying and acquiring all of the best young players, keeping them together and, through that continuity, creating something special, that communal, socialist sporting ideal of 'all for one and one for all'. Perhaps one of the reasons that the English took their two heavy defeats at the hands of the Hungarian national side so badly was not so much that they lost but the fact that they had lost to an ideology that they very clearly opposed and disagreed with, one that they would have happily gone to war for in order to prevent its doctrine being repeated in that country. It was as if it wasn't just their football that had been proved inferior by the Hungarian side, but the way they lived their day-to-day lives as well. No wonder the English media had trumpeted Wolves victory over Honvéd so loudly and proudly. The Empire had, finally, struck back.

Hungarian football had, whether you happened to agree with the politics that shaped it or not, made three huge and very significant changes to the game on a worldwide basis, practices that are still preached today as being an inherently positive aspect of the game, something to copy and aspire to.

Firstly there is the development and introduction of new formations and tactics. Sebes introduced a starting formation so fluid and adaptable in terms of where his players were on the pitch that, even today, contemporary accounts about his team and their line-up vary about exactly how they played. Some argue it was a 3-2-3-2 formation, others that it was 3-5-2 or 3-2-1-4. In truth it was perhaps all of them plus some more, and then none of them at all. Because the second significant change that the Hungarians made to the game was the idea, that dream of 'socialist' total football that saw every player in the team able to play in any other position or role in any game seamlessly and without the need for transmission – a gift and ability that, surely, throws the rigidity of a strictly pre-planned starting formation out of the window.

Finally there was the idea that a team could only benefit if they gathered together a core of exceptionally talented and well-coached players and kept them together, for weeks at a time if necessary, in order that they might get used to playing as a team and to fully understand not only their roles, but that of their teammates. That time together was crucial if they were to perfect the 'socialist' football that they preached, practiced and played.

In the midst of all this, of course, stood Gusztav Sebes, that master coach who bridged the gap between ancient and modern football like no one else has. His place in footballing history is assured, yet his name was little known outside his homeland. The unique match tactics he devised and introduced revolutionised the game to such an extent that other international teams and coaches could only hold up their arms in a weak gesture of submission and look to copy rather than beat them, acknowledgement, if ever there was one, that the old ways of the game were no more. Amongst his most revolutionary ideas was to popularise the role of the false number 9,[33] the freedom given to Nándor Hidegkuti

---

33   *Popularise rather than introduce – the first player to make a name for himself in and of that position was probably Matthias Sindelar, the captain of Hugo Meisl's Austrian team in the 1934 World Cup. Sindelar was a virtual 'one-off' of the time, a footballing oddity, albeit a very effective one who scored 27 goals in 43 appearances for Austria, but, despite that, it was only after Hidegkuti had, amongst other teams and equally bewildered players, so mesmerised England that the concept really took off and teams started to play it themselves.*

to roam, at will, all over the pitch, the number 9 on the back of his shirt no more identifying him as a (then) traditional centre forward than it did a right back or centre half. That position, the role and responsibility of the false number 9 as well as his effectiveness has been one adopted by teams all over the world ever since with famous names like Francesco Totti, Ezequiel Lavezzi and Carlos Tevez being amongst the more contemporary masters of the role with, further back, Johan Cruyff, fittingly, playing a similar role to that of Hidegkuti in the second great team to play 'Total Football', the wonderful Netherlands side of the 1970s.

Sebes insistence on continuity in his national team selections was also one that other teams began to follow. All too often, football teams had been selected by picking the best 11 players available before hoping they'd somehow be able to play together as a team, a practice that was patently not always working for England who famously had a selection committee charged with picking the players that the coach was expected to turn into a team. Sebes used a core of players who were used to playing alongside each other at club level, players who already had an understanding of how each other played, an understanding that could only have been enhanced whilst they were away with the national team by virtue of the fact that they spent so much time together anyway. Indeed, had the Hungary coach not had the opportunities he had been given by the state in order to get the best players in one place as much as possible, it is extremely unlikely that they would ever have had the impact on the world game that they did. It was certainly one that was eventually copied by coaches of other nations. England were a prime example in 1966 when their World Cup winning side, one that was certainly missing one, if not two of the best players in the country in Brian Labone (the classy Everton centre half electing to withdraw from the World Cup squad as he was getting married!) and Jimmy Greaves, injured early one but available for the final, won it with a core of

West Ham players; Bobby Moore, Martin Peters and Geoff Hurst, the perceived all-round qualities of the hard-working, hard-running Hurst being preferred to world-class goalscorer and widely perceived better player Greaves in that game.

Geoff Hurst comes too late against Sepp Meier during the World Cup 1970.

Therefore, much of what we now take for granted as being part of the modern game can be traced back to the Hungarian footballing revolution of the 1950s, one that marks a midway point in the game. At the time the Hungarian national team was at its peak, arguably in 1954 after their 7-1 win over England, 82 years had lapsed since the very first official international football match had been played, the 0-0 draw between Scotland and England in 1872.

Football was no longer the 'new kid in the block'. Most European nations had organised domestic leagues by now whilst a fourth World Cup was about to be played. The European Cup, now the Champions League, was also just a year away from being held for the first time, it's first winners, Real Madrid, as familiar and dominant name in the sport then as they are today. Hungary had made the rest of the footballing world wake up to the possibilities that the game held. National team managers wanted to rise to the challenge of beating Sebes 'Magnificent Magyars'[34] whilst those at club level wanted to pit their wits against their club sides with Honvéd, as we have already seen, only too happy to give them an opportunity.

Football had finally arrived. It was now the dominant sport throughout Europe and South America and would, in time, make its presence felt in both North America and Asia. In those two traditional powerhouses, however, the dominant nations and clubs were pretty much the same as the ones we watch and admire today. Take the 1958 World Cup for example and its last four of Brazil, West Germany, France and Sweden, three of whom would go on to win the tournament in future years whilst Sweden would reach the semi-finals stage again in 1994. In contrast, two of the early international heavyweights, Austria and Hungary, have never again reached the heights that they either threatened to do

---

34 *Something which Josef Herberger had done as coach of the West Germany side that had defeated Hungary in the 1954 World Cup Final.*

with Austria, or did so as far as the Hungary team was concerned. The Magyars early run of international eminence saw them reach the World Cup quarter-finals in 1934 before finishing as runners up in both 1938 and 1954. They then, and this was probably as good an achievement as any given the ever harsher political control the Soviet Union had over the nation following their crush of the Hungarian revolution in 1956, made the quarter-finals of the tournament again in 1962 and 1966, beating England in 1962 en route. In addition to this and, remarkably, in what was their last-ever demonstration of what a footballing powerhouse they were, or rather could have been, they also defeated holders Brazil 3-1 in a group game during the 1966 tournament, one they could, feasibly, even have gone all to the final in had they not been unfortunate enough to have to play their political masters the Soviet Union in the semi-finals.

That win against Brazil, however, turned out to be Hungary's last hurrah at international level. They failed to qualify for the next two World Cups, and, although they were back in the 1978, 1982[35] and 1986 tournaments, they went out in the first group stage of each of those finals whilst, from 1990 through to the 2014 finals in Brazil they have not qualified. For a game that still dotes upon tradition and history despite its drive towards the corporate riches and all the commercial opportunities that come with it, a World Cup without Hungary will always feel incomplete. A reappearance at the finals by the once mighty Magyars in 2018 or 2022 will, therefore, be both welcome and somewhat overdue because, for a nation that gave so much that was new, exciting and wonderfully controversial to the game of football, it is a sporting tragedy that the country's contribution to a game that they once dominated, ideas that have been, as we have seen, since copied (with some nations getting all

---

35   On 15 June 1982, Hungary briefly stole the world footballing headlines again, albeit briefly, when they defeated El Salvador 10-1 in their Group 3 World Cup match in Elche, Spain. It was, and remains, the biggest scoreline in World Cup finals history. Substitute Laszlo Kiss scored a hat-trick in the game, the only one to be ever scored in a World Cup by a substitute and, with the three goals scored in the space of seven minutes, it is the fastest in tournament history.

the credit[36] for implementing what the Hungarians had done first) with relish by coaches and teams across the world is now largely forgotten or else reduced to nostalgic references to a game thought to belong to another era.

Which is wrong. Hungary were, and are, of the current footballing era. They were its progenitors, a coach and team that mapped the football pitch in the same manner that Mercator mapped the world.

---

36   *Don't let anyone tell you that the Netherlands were, in 1974, the 'inventors' of Total Football. Imitated it they might have done, brought the concept to near perfection even. But invent it they did not, that honour goes to the Hungarians and Gusztáv Sebes.*

CHAPTER SIX:
THE BOYS FROM BRAZIL

...there was something different, something pleasing about the way the team played, the way the midfield two would alternate between defence and attack and back again in the blink of an eye; the manner in which the players would always be in close proximity to each other and ready for a pass yet, at the same time, always seeming to have the space required to receive the ball, control it, move it on. They were a team that loved to have the ball, and, when they did, they treated it as if it was something precious that had to be handled with care, short passes, gentle touches, clips, chips and caresses.

Brazil's national team in 1958

Brazil had cut a swathe through football in two successive World Cups, and, in doing so, had got the world talking. Most of it was about Pelé, yet, in truth, just about any one of them could have been held up at the time as one of the finest footballers in the world. Recent years have seen Lionel Messi and Cristiano Ronaldo jostle for position as the world's best player with few, if any, rivals for the accolade. From 2008 to 2014, they were the only winners of the FIFA World Player of the Year award, or, as it has been known since 2010, the Ballon d'Or with, in six of those seven years, whichever one of the duo didn't win, finishing as runner-up.

Is this lack of genuine world-class players a result of the dearth of attacking football within the modern game; the fact that there are so few players out there who guarantee excitement whenever they get on the ball, are known for their unique and explosive talent, standout artists in a game that has forsaken the attacking possibilities of 4-2-4 in favour of the conservative 4-4-2 (see next chapter) and deviations of same?

Consider again the Brazil sides that won those two World Cups in 1958 and 1962; any one of several could have laid claim to be the best player in the world at that time. Didi? Most definitely. Or also Garrincha. Mario Zagallo. Nilton Santos. Four of the very best. As in ever. And I haven't even mentioned Pelé yet!

Attacking formations, positive and expansive football. Breeding grounds for the great. Think of any list claiming to be of the 10 greatest footballers of all time. It's a fairly safe bet that those names will include Meazza, Puskás, Di Stéfano, Eusebio, Best, Beckenbauer, Platini, Maradona and Zidane. Add Ronaldo and Messi to the mix plus those five Brazilians. Sixteen stellar names, the very best of the best.

How many of them were defenders? One.

Many of the greatest names in the game's history came from an era when the game was, unashamedly, focused on attacking play and scoring goals; a time when, perhaps, the game was a little more naive than it is now. Naive? By that I mean that the stakes weren't so high, the pressure so immense and the expectation to deliver, week in, week out at club level, wasn't as relentless as it has become in the last couple of decades or so. Take another look at the 16 names listed and compare the decades when each of those players was, arguably, at his professional peak. The decades that dominate the list are the 1950s and 1960s with the 1970s tucked in, rather like an attacking midfielder, just behind those two front runners.

Coaches who encouraged attacking football with formations that set out their intentions from the outset were, by default, indulging players with those same tendencies in their game, giving them a mandate to express themselves the only way they could, by going forward, looking to beat opponents and creating or scoring goals. And in abundance. Players like that never had that ability coached out of them; they were never expected to take on any defensive responsibilities or bring some discipline into their otherwise free-form game. Some weren't encouraged to toe the expected line at all. Take Ferenc Puskás of that great Hungary team from the 1950s, a man whom some of the England players referred to, pre-match, as '...that little fat chap', adding, 'we'll murder this lot.' Famous last words. Puskás was, admittedly, anything but an athlete, at least in appearance, with a figure that would never be tolerated. Indeed, it would be ridiculed in the modern game, the preserve of a Sunday league player representing his local pub. But Puskás was a genius footballer. And that, then, was all that mattered. Neither he nor his many equally famous and skilled contemporaries were shackled by the need to cover their man, to track back, to man mark, work hard and run all day. His remit was to entertain, score goals and win games.

The modern game is different. Players are athletes as well as footballers, and tactics and formations reflect a team's desire to not lose rather than to win. Flair players, players who excite fans (and, no doubt, infuriate their own coaches), are seen as a luxury, and all too often an unwanted one.

When Spanish midfielder Juan Mata joined Manchester United from Chelsea for £37 Million in 2014, some of his critics immediately labelled him just that, a 'luxury player', arguing that role as a playmaker, someone who was allowed the freedom to roam around the final third of the pitch without the need to track back or press opposition players, meant he struggled to track the runs of opposition players and was, as a result, not a tactically aware defensive player.

Why would you pick a player like Juan Mata in your team and then expect him to contribute defensively? It is an obsession which blights the modern game, this expectancy for all the players in a team to 'do their bit' and defend from the front backwards rather than attack from the back forwards.

No wonder the modern game only has two real superstars in Ronaldo and Messi. The creative life is being squeezed out of them and their contemporaries. Who knows, they could even be amongst the last of their type, players with a remit to roam, to excite, to get people off their seats.

To entertain. And where, after all, is the entertainment in a rigid defensive display that kept a clean sheet?

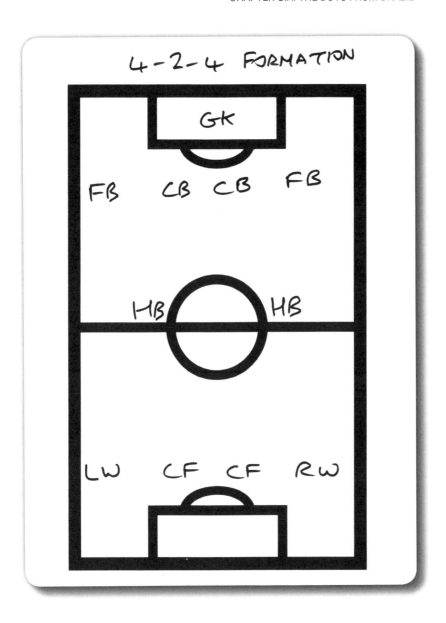

The greatest entertainers of all, Brazil, certainly 'found' a football formation that suited their team of entertainers with their bold 4-2-4 line-up. As well as being one of their first formations to play the now conventional four players right across the defence, it's front four included two players who played as out-and-out attacking wide men, or left- and right-sided wingers. Fleet of foot and often small of frame, their task was to get the ball and run it to the opposing by-line before swinging in a cross for the two strikers to feed off. If anything, 4-2-4 was developed as an antidote to the perceived rigidity of WM, a formation that made the very best use of professional footballers' increased fitness as well as their tactical awareness and skill. Long, long gone by now (for the most part) were players, teams and formations that relied upon the old 'kick and rush' tactics, of kicking the ball long and high out of defence before chasing after it en masse. England had originally one of the most formidable international sides in the world because of the manner in which the game had been practiced for so long, one that focused on players who could run all day and had a great physical presence and venomous shot, players like Steve Bloomer (refer to chapter 2). Bloomer was made for the old-fashioned Pyramid formation that focused on getting the ball to the main attacker as quickly and in as uncomplicated a manner as possible. He excelled at the time *because* of the Pyramid formation that he played at the peak of – he was quick of thought and speed of movement as well as being exceptionally strong. Yet he, and players like him (and this implies no disrespect to Bloomer whatsoever), were limited in that they had one way of playing and one way alone. The modern game expected more of its forward players; think of Nándor Hidegkuti, who, like Bloomer, wore the number 9 shirt. Bloomer played in attack, and that's primarily the part of the pitch he could be seen in and found around, in other words, the opposing team's penalty area. His teammates would have been given instructions to give Bloomer the ball. Bloomer's would have been to put the ball into the opposing team's net. Simple, the role and responsibility of the classic number 9, the archetypal centre forward.

Hidegkuti was similar to Bloomer in one way and one way only: the number on the back of his shirt. His brief was to roam the attacking third of the pitch, whether that saw him playing wide and near the touchline, in the penalty area or pushed out a little deeper into the area immediately short of that penalty area. He could never have played the sort of role and game that Bloomer played; neither could Bloomer have played his. The game was getting smarter as were the coaches and players. The emergence of 4-2-4, a formation and philosophy that has been attributed to both Hungary and Brazil, was how the game responded to this fact that its coaches and players were now becoming as greedy for knowledge and both personal and team development and tactics as they had previously been for 'mere' possession of the ball alone.

The credit for developing and playing 4-2-4 is shared by two men, Flavio Costa who was Brazil's national team coach in the 1950s, and, no surprises here, another enterprising and farsighted Hungarian, a man by the name of Bela Guttman. Budapest-born Guttman played as a competent, if not outstanding, midfielder for MTK in his homeland as well as Hakoah Vienna in Austria before spending some time playing in the US.

He is better remembered, however, as another of the fine Hungarian coaches who came to the fore in the game from the 1930s onwards, a long and hugely distinguished career that began with Hakoah Vienna in 1933 and ended with a short spell at Porto in Portugal in 1973. His was a life in football coaching that encompassed four decades, 19 different club sides and, in 1964, a short period as coach of Austria.

He was everything that many coaches weren't, especially those in England: adaptable and ready to travel and take on any job that took his fancy as well as confident, if not somewhat verbose and radical about his abilities – an earlier version of Jose Mourinho according to some

contemporary sages in Portuguese football. This comparison comes as
no surprise. Both had spells at Porto; both felt that a coach could stay
with one club for too long (Guttman was once quoted as saying, in terms
of coaching longevity, 'The third season is fatal.') Amongst the clubs he
spent time at as a coach are AC Milan, Benfica, Penarol, Sao Paulo, and
of course, Porto. Guttman became, in the process, one of the first men to
successfully coach in both Europe and South America. Along with Sebes
and Marton Bukovi, who won three Hungarian Championships with
MTK in the 1950s, he justified the introduction of the 4-2-4 formation
by championing its combination of a strong attack with an equally strong
defence, thus bringing a sense of balance to teams that had often, in
the past, been anything but balanced; England's early use of the 1-1-8
formation was proof positive of that.

A balanced formation indeed. Four in defence, four in attack and two in
the middle. It could almost be seen as a pair of counterbalanced scales
with the midfield duo given the responsibility of being spare men that
could help out as and when they were needed. They'd either be tracking
back to bolster up the defence if their team were under pressure or else
pushing forward to join the attack if the team were going forward,
meaning that the original concept of 4-2-4 was only that in terms of how
teams started matches for, as soon as the game started, its natural ebb
and flow meant that it was either 6-0-4 (defending) or 4-0-6 (attacking).
That's not to say that the midfield unit didn't exist. It did, in the fact that
they were either playing as a defensive midfielder or an attacking one.
Versatile and adaptable, they were perhaps the forerunner of what we
now call the 'utility' player, the one who is a jack of all positions but
master of none. It's a phrase that has, at least in the modern game, come
to be seen as almost derogatory in fashion, referring to a player who is
able to slot in anywhere and, for that reason, is seen as a good squad man
and someone who, because of his versatility, is best used as a substitute
as he can then cover a number of options. Yet there have been some great

footballers who excelled at more than one role, one of them being John Charles who was able to play with ease as either a centre half or centre forward. Charles was just the type of player who Guttman would have loved to been able to call upon and just the sort of player that tactically aware European coaches wanted in their team. He spent his peak years playing for Juventus in Italy where his skills in both defence and attack were widely respected and valued. He was also one of the very first British professional footballers to sign for and represent a successful continental European side.

Charles would almost certainly have been good enough to play in such a role for Brazil had he been born in Sao Paolo rather than Swansea. Brazilian coach Costa would have revelled in seeing Charles leading the line in one of his teams at one moment before defending his own in the next; his versatility in each role echoed the belief of Sebes that every player in his team should be able to play in and understand all of his teammates' positions and responsibilities as well as he did his own.

Costa was, if not an intellectual, a very intelligent man, one who cared for and studied the game, so much so that he felt bound to first publish his ideas on how the game should be played in the Brazilian newspaper *O Cruzeiro*. He illustrated his formation of play and tactical beliefs with the sort of simple overhead graphic representations of those that are so familiar in the game today and which, as a matter of course, are used in this book to illustrate them. He was also the first to refer to his formation by numbers. They had previously been described in words or letters – for example, the Pyramid, the Danubian School, Metodo, WM and WW formations and schools of thought.

Costa cut through the terminology and made things clear and easy to understand. In doing so, he made that part of the game more understandable to the fans. His formation was comprised of four defenders, two runners or utility players and four attackers – four then two then four. 4-2-4. It was so easy it beggared belief that no one had thought to do it that way before, but then Costa was exemplifying the Brazilian way of doing things on the pitch with his description of how his team would line up on it. Simple but effective. And how.

Thus, in 1958, Brazil, coached by Vicente Feola, won their first World Cup in Sweden by employing the 4-2-4 method developed and introduced by Costa. Their team beat hosts Sweden 5-2 in the final, lined up with Gilmar in goal, a back four of Djalma Santos at right back, Bellini and Orlando in central defence with Nilton Santos playing as left back. The two midfield runners were Didi and Dino Sani with a front four of Garrincha, Vava, Pelé and Mario Zagallo, with Bellini and Zagallo under instruction to push forward and track back as and when required, giving the team a more balanced appearance of 3-4-3.

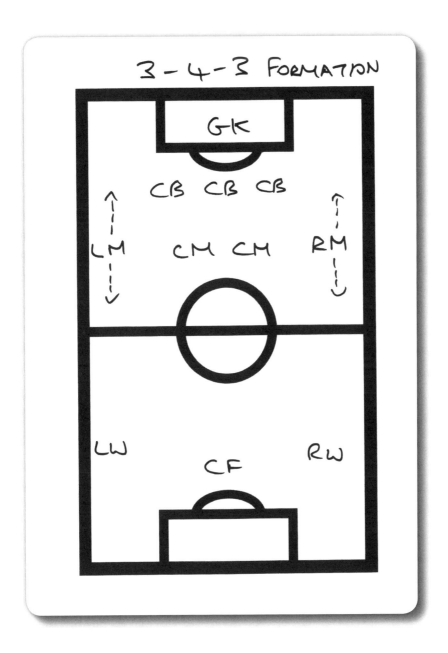

In truth, 4-2-4 was a formation made for Brazil and their surfeit of outrageously talented and very attack-minded players. You only had to watch their games at the 2014 World Cup to see Brazil players urged on by their fans to push forward at all costs; their players, compelling urge to attack best represented by centre half David Luiz who all too often abandoned his defensive role completely to join in with the attack. But you cannot attack in a gung ho fashion without having some sort of defensive plan and responsibility. Brazil and, in particular, Luiz's anarchic obsession of going forward with scant regard for his defensive duties ultimately, as it turned out, cost them dearly, as they departed the tournament in spectacular and painful, even embarrassing, style. That was not the case in 1958. That Brazilian side was not only better organised, but it also had, particularly in their defence, better players, defenders who, unlike Luiz, were tactically aware, disciplined and conditioned to play and perform for the good of the team rather than their own personal glory. As a formation, 4-2-4 looks unbalanced with its lack of midfielders. The joy of that team was that it was flexible enough to switch as and when the occasion demanded, but, whatever form it took, there was always a player near the one in possession ready to take a pass and offer support. Brazil were, therefore, able to practice and perfect a game based on quick, short passes and one-touch football, that pleasing on the eye game that was made possible for them by the sheer versatility offered by the formation, one that allowed teams to be either expansive, making full use of the width of the pitch and playing an attacking game that threatened to overwhelm an opposition defence, or, paradoxically, allowed them to be compact and tight with an organised defence that gave that opposition no time and space in which to create chances and attack.

It certainly worked for Brazil at the 1958 World Cup where they were drawn in what was, perhaps, the first ever 'group of death'. In addition to Brazil, it also featured reigning Olympic champions the Soviet Union; Austria, who had finished third at the previous World Cup; and, just to make matters really interesting, the 'old guard' themselves in England. They were the pre-tournament favourites, at least in their own minds, especially as they had been given some support pre-tournament by Sepp Herberger, the coach of the much-fancied West Germany side who had said England were '...a team of hard fighters, and pure football teams do not win the World Cup.'

Sepp Herberger, Team Germany's long-time national coach

To be fair to both Herberger and England, still labelled as 'fighters' at a time when teams like Brazil and Hungary had been redefining the sport with football that was based on flair, skill and technique, he might have been correct and England may well have won the tournament had it not been for the Munich air disaster in February 1958. This tragedy robbed Manchester United and the world of some of its best young sporting talent, including the peerless Duncan Edwards who was just 21 when he died as a result of injuries sustained in that crash. People talk now of the Diego Maradona-inspired Argentina that won the World Cup in 1986 even if they had not been necessarily the best team at the tournament. The same might have been said about Edwards and England after the 1958 World Cup.

Edwards was primarily a defensive midfielder but such was his level of skill and technical ability that he could, and often did, play in any role required of him on the pitch. In one game, for example, he started it as an emergency striker in place of an injured player before, in that same game, switching to centre half in order to replace another who had been injured. And seamlessly. In addition to that, Edward's game seemed to possess absolutely no weaknesses – much like Maradona's. He was strong in the tackle but was hardly someone who just 'stopped' other players. He could start, continue and finish moves as well as, if not better than any player in the game at the time he was playing, able to pass and shoot with great precision and power and equally well with both feet.

After England had beaten Herberger's West Germany 3-1 in a friendly match two years before the finals (when Edwards was only 19), the local press gave him the nickname 'Boom Boom' due to the power and accuracy of his shooting. He was, without doubt, England's best player and one who they, along with his Manchester United teammates Roger Byrne and Tommy Taylor, would have built their World Cup campaign around, just as Argentina had successfully done with Maradona nearly two decades later. Would they have had a chance of winning the tournament with the three of them making up the midfield in England's otherwise tired 2-3-5 formation? You have to concede and admit that, as limited as English football was tactically at that time, the addition of those three players to the side would have given them a very good chance of success. Sadly, all three players perished in Munich, leaving England to travel to Sweden with a side that was both under strength and, not surprisingly, low on morale, one that Simon Briggs observed was 'a mish-mash, a side that was neither fish nor fowl.'[37] England did indeed struggle, but there was no disgrace in that or their performances in the four games they played which ended in three draws and a defeat in a group playoff match to the Soviet Union. One of the draws was significant, however, in that it had seen England grind out what could perhaps best be called a 'gritty' 0-0 draw against Brazil, the only game of the six that the eventual champions played in the tournament that they failed to win or even score in. It was also the first game in World Cup history that had ended goalless.

The significance of that result can be attributed to the fact that, in an previously unprecedented move, England had not only scouted the opposition in their previous match (a 3-0 win over Austria) but had then, as a result of that, devised a bespoke tactical approach for that one game.

Hell duly froze over.

The tactic England chose to deploy was devised by the real footballing brain of the their coaching setup, Winterbottom's assistant, Bill Nicholson (later, if you recall, he devised a 3-3-4 formation for Tottenham Hotspur, one still based upon a strong midfield spine but in a much more balanced side). He suggested a man-for-man marking system that included sitting one player, the versatile Bill Slater, on Didi, Brazil's most influential player. With the creative Didi now shackled, the vital connection in Brazil's 4-2-4 line-up, the pivotal midfielder who sat between defence and attack dictating the pace and pattern of the play as

---

37   *Briggs, Simon. 2007. Don't Mention the Score. Quercus. 167.*

he did so, was rendered tactically impotent. Impotence then for Brazil but a triumph of sorts for England, the end result being that they only had to keep their own shape and discipline in order to get the draw. It was an excellent result given the circumstances and a sign, at least for them and the FA, that the 'modern approach' to football could, if applied correctly, yield a dividend or two. They had suffered the ignominy of a 1-0 defeat to the USA eight years previously, both the result and the dire performance that went with it down to a woeful lack of planning as well as serial complacency. They had now redeemed themselves and could, providing the shift in attitude and approach that had been shown prior to the Brazil game, look forward to future World Cups with perhaps a degree of optimism.

This World Cup, however, was all about Brazil and their 4-2-4 formation which they were showcasing to the world. They weren't exactly setting the footballing world on fire with free-scoring, fast-flowing attacking football (the game against England illustrated that), but there was something different, something pleasing about the way the team played, the way the midfield two would alternate between defence and attack and back again in the blink of an eye.

There was also the manner in which the players would always be in close proximity to each other and ready for a pass yet, at the same time, always seeming to have the space required to receive the ball, control it and move it on.

It was like watching Hungary.

This wasn't Hungary, though. This was Brazil, Hungary upgraded and improved, Hungary with added *joie de vivre,* a team free of the political and ideological shackles that had bound them together. They played because they loved the game rather than because it was what they did.

They were a team that loved to have the ball, and, when they did, they treated it as if it was something precious that had to be handled with care: short passes, gentle touches, clips, chips and caresses. They didn't even introduce Pelé to the tournament until their last group game which was against the Soviet Union, a 2-0 win that saw Vava, a striker in the mould of later Brazilian (but inadequate in comparison) centre forwards like Serginho, Gil, Casagrande, Robinho, Jo and Fred, score both the goals. That win ensured Brazil qualified for the quarter-finals from where they advanced to the final, winning all three games, scoring 11 goals in the process.

It is worth referring to that short list of Brazilian strikers at this point. Vava excepted, none of those named have gone down in footballing history, even in Brazil, as great and revered players. Brazilian football fans regard both the position of centre forward and the identity of the man in possession of the shirt with mild disinterest, accepting, perhaps, that he is an important member of the side but only in a functional manner. He is seen as someone there to do a job, to carry out team orders. The real crowd favourites, the artisans and idols, are the midfielders. These are the free spirits and creative geniuses who control the rhythm of the game, dictate play and have a far wider and more responsible role than those who provide the simple denouement to a quick passing move that probably thrilled those fans as much, if not more, than the actual act of scoring the goal.

Fred's performances in the centre forward role for Brazil at the 2014 World Cup were so disappointing that he drew widespread criticism for his efforts, with one former player and centre forward, England's Alan Shearer observing at the time that, 'I just don't understand why Brazil are still picking him [Fred] – he doesn't move, he doesn't shoot and he's dragging the team down. I don't know if Brazil should change the system or play Neymar as a false nine, but the fact is that Fred is not the answer for what they are doing now.' Clearly Fred felt the same way about things as he quit international football immediately after the World Cup. Yet he is not the first, nor will he be the last, Brazilian centre forward to suffer the collective ire of his fans with Serginho (1982) and Jo (also in 2014) being the subject of a lot of criticism. Serginho had the misfortune of being part of a squad and side that included the stellar talents of players like Junior, Socrates, Zico, Eder and Falcao who, to this day, are revered in Brazil.

Following a dour 1-0 win against Wales[38] in the quarter-finals, Brazil opened up in spectacular style, winning the semi-final against France and final against hosts Sweden 5-2. Pelé scored five of their goals with Vava adding another two. The majestic Pelé had everything, a player who, in a decade where the possibilities of Total Football were first witnessed was the total player himself, one without a fault or weakness in his game. He was a natural athlete who moved with easy grace, a player celebrated for his pace, dribbling skills and ability to pick the most precise of passes.

More often than not he would see and casually execute a pass that no other player would have seen, let alone attempted. He also possessed a venomous shot and exceptional heading ability, allied to being a prolific goalscorer – 77 in 92 games for Brazil. But, on top of all of that, he was a player with a sharp mind and clarity of vision that sometimes defied logic. There had not been a player like him in the game until then, someone who thought the game as well as he played it. Maybe, just maybe, the Hungarian Hidegkuti might have ended up being mentioned in the same breath as Pelé. Politics denied the world that opportunity whilst tragedy denied it the chance to see if Edwards could have been

---

38   *Encouraged by England's perceived success in man-marking the Brazilians in their group game, James Murphy, the Welsh coach, whose players all represented club sides in England sent out his side with a similar approach, one that so nearly had the desired effect in stifling Brazil's attacking talents but at the expense of Wales creating very little for themselves in terms of chances.*

the same for England. Positionally, Pelé was, just as Hidegkuti had been, a false number 9; a player given license to roam the area between the midfield and attack. Opponents could no more work him out than spectators and critics could identify his place in the 4-2-4 formation Brazil played. Pelé was everywhere, always ready to receive the ball and to do something with it, something positive, something that, invariably would result in either a goal or, at the very least, a chance, for either himself or one of his teammates. He also had a touch of audacity about the way he played the game, a sense of its theatre and how people were there to be entertained. As evidence of this, look at two examples of both his and Brazil's play. Firstly there is Pelé's shot from the halfway line in that tournament against Czechoslovakia, one that just missed. Since then the feat has been achieved, most notably perhaps by David Beckham, yet, for all that, Pelé's near miss is still treated with more reverence than Beckham's goal. Then there was Brazil's final goal in that year's final and their 4-1 rout of Italy. The start of the move that led to the goal is highlighted by a jinking run from Clodoaldo, the Brazilian number 5, a now largely overlooked member of that fabulous team who took the ball past four Italian players with consummate ease, as if he were Fred Astaire on ice. The assist for the goal is Pelé's; lurking just outside and to the left of the Italian penalty area, he receives the ball, looks up and waits unchallenged for the advancing Carlos Alberto before knocking the perfect pass into his feet with all the nonchalance of a man kicking a ball back to a group of schoolchildren playing in a park. It is simple, unrushed, casual and made to look breathtakingly easy. It is pure Pelé and the very purest of Brazil.

Brazil's success at the 1958 tournament caught the public imagination – not least because of the emergence of Pelé but also because of the sheer scope of the football they played. Costa had outlined this in his articles for *O Cruzeiro*, arguing that 4-2-4 allowed for improvisation and allowed a team to defend well in order that they might be able to attack even more effectively. In other words, this was a formation for a team that attacked from the back. And that suited Brazil more than it would any other team in the world. It was a formation that suited their collective abilities, their wish to entertain and their propensity for flair and artistry above hard work and organisation. It also allowed for the fact that just about every footballer ever born in Brazil wants to do one thing and one thing only: to attack (remember David Luiz) despite any and all responsibilities they might have in defence. Even defenders like Junior (1979-1992) and Roberto Carlos (1992-2006) were more renowned for the qualities they brought to the side in an attacking sense and at set pieces than they ever were for their defensive qualities. The simple truth of it was, were they able to (and they might just have pulled it off), Brazil would have played a 0-0-10 formation. The 4-2-4 formation had been visualised by Costa as the best way of playing a vaguely sensible attacking formation and utilising the talents of so many fabulous players.

As far as footballing formations and on-field tactics are concerned, 4-2-4 was the most important change in playing systems that the game had seen for several decades. Much of this has been because of how the game had changed. Players were fitter and faster; kit and playing equipment was becoming lighter; and coaches, many of them ex-players, were having more and more of an impact on the game tactically, rather than just being employed to make players run around a bit and throw medicine balls at one another. Football, once hallmarked by the conservatism of the English approach, was becoming progressive. The game as a whole was also changing. Those faster, fitter players meant that the pace of the game increased and with it came the need for players to have much more technical ability. This meant that, whilst the old-fashioned 'battering ram' number 9, the warrior centre forward of old with mud on his boots and blood on his face, would never totally go out of fashion; he was rapidly being seen as an option to a team's armoury rather than an obligation.

Thus skill and technique were winning the day over strength and power. Or, rather the 'old-fashioned' virtues of strength and power were being successfully married to the brave new football world of skill and technique, as exemplified first by Hungary and now by Brazil. Hungary's failure to win the World Cup that everyone had thought was theirs (no one seriously expected them *not* to walk away with the Jules Rimet trophy after the 1954 World Cup in Switzerland) four years prior to Brazil's exciting triumph might have led to some sceptics to the 'new ways' to declare that whilst football's brave new world was exciting, it was never going to be practical nor beneficial to club or country in the long term.

After all, West Germany, crushed so very emphatically to the tune of 8-3 in their group match by the Hungarians, had rallied enough to be able to use the time between that game and the final to work out how the Hungarians could be beaten, put it into practice and, against all the odds, won the match and the trophy. Similarly, Wolves in England had, using similar tactics and techniques – not forgetting that watered pitch – sent Honvéd packing. Socialist football was a dream, a very nice one admittedly, but not a game plan that was going to last. West Germany had proven that. The old ways were, after all, the best. Sighs of contented relief abounded amongst the leather armchairs and cigar smoke of the London clubs.

Brazil had now shown, four years later, by playing a type of football that wasn't so very far removed from how Hungary had been playing four years previously that expansive football like the type which 4-4-2 encouraged could be effective. Yes it *did* demand very high levels of skill, intelligence and appreciation of what you were, as a team, looking to achieve (Jack Hunter's pioneering work with Blackburn Olympic in the 1880s can now be truly appreciated for what it was[39]), but, in

---

39   *See chapter 1.*

balancing those demands, the new system also brought a wonderful simplicity to the way a team could approach a game. It was a subtle difference which saw modern coaches aiming to score one goal more than the opposition to win rather than conceding one less. A subtle difference (football had never previously been known for being 'subtle'), but a telling one. It was about going into a game with the objective to win rather than to not lose, as had been the case for so long

Brazil's win and eventual dominance of the international game from that decade onwards overshadowed the achievements of Sebes' great Hungarian side with one great team just starting to fade as another began its rise to prominence. Yet much of the credit for Brazil's success must go to the Hungarians, even to the extent that you could argue that the great tradition of Brazilian football owes much to its earlier origins in Eastern Europe. Then, of course, there was the influence of Bela Guttman. He first travelled to South America with the Hakoah All Stars[40] in 1930, returning in 1957 when he was coach of the legendary Honvéd Club side. A tour of Brazil included games against leading club sides CR Flamengo and Botofogo as well as a combined 11 drawn from the players of both those Brazilian club sides. Once the tour was complete, Guttman elected to remain in Brazil after being invited to become the coach of Sao Paulo FC. His impact was immediate as he led Sao Paulo FC to their first championship success in the Campeonato Paulista, their first win in the state league since 1953. Both his presence, character and eventual success with his new club drew the attention of the wider Brazilian footballing community, and it was during his time here that he helped develop Costa's original ideas, those that he had originally shared with *O Cruzeiro* into what eventually became the classic 4-2-4 formation that was employed by Brazil during their successful 1958 World Cup campaign.

---

40   *A New York-based team formed by the merger of Brooklyn Hakoah of the American Soccer League and New York Hakoah from the Eastern Soccer League. Both clubs had been initially formed by players from the Austrian club SC Hakoah Wien who Guttman had played for from 1922-1926.*

Conceived in Hungary and fine-tuned in Brazil. 4-2-4 had made its mark thanks to the work of those two remarkable men, Flavio Costa and Bella Guttman. Most Brazilian football fans will never realise it, but they owe more to their success to a Jewish Hungarian footballer than they will ever know.

The strength of 4-2-4, apart from its great emphasis on attacking and philosophy of 'however many you score, we'll score more', was its sheer flexibility. The fact that it was came down to the two central midfielders, defenders turned attackers or attackers turned defenders, depending on your outlook. They were the team's strategists, the football equivalent of military generals safely watching the battle from afar, directing operations and troops from behind a pair of binoculars. They were expected to not only be part of their own team moving forward, to precipitate and be part of attacking intentions but also to help out in defence. They were the first line of both defence and attack, something which not only demanded extraordinary levels of fitness but also a thorough understanding and appreciation of the game and how it ebbed and flowed. They had to be, in short, extraordinary footballers – something which the Brazil side of 2014, with one exception, was not.

One of the hallowed pair of Brazilians from 1958, Waldyr Pereira, better known as Didi, most certainly was extraordinary. Bill Nicholson, working alongside Walter Winterbottom at that tournament, had watched the Brazilians play, concluding that if you want to stop Brazil, then you stop Didi. Man-marking a team's most influential player may seem common sense now, but it was a new strategy then, or, at least, a brand new and vaguely heretical one as far as England were concerned. They had, after all, tried the experiment before, only to see Harry Johnson's international career finished by Hidegkuti. But mark Didi they did, and, as we have seen, it so very nearly worked. Such a tactic doesn't stop other players from benefitting from all the attention given to another. Vava, for example, hit the bar during that 0-0 draw whilst a goal-bound shot had been cleared off the line by one of the England defenders. Had either, or both, gone in and England had suffered a 2-0 defeat as a result, then the experiment of man-marking and closing down might have been abandoned there and then, but it hadn't. That result was treated as a major triumph in England with one newspaper, the *Daily Herald*, announcing it in a headline that read 'It's A Golden Draw: Those Super Senors Held By England.'[41]

Despite the presence of Pelé, Didi, midfield strategist and on-field general, was the pivot around which Brazil's challenge and the 4-2-4 system depended. Had those two places been filled by mediocre players, then Brazil would have struggled for all the quality they had elsewhere in the side, including Pelé. He ended up being named the player of the tournament in Sweden, going on to make 68 appearances for the Brazilians, winning another World Cup with them four years later. He was, arguably, football's first great playmaker, a man worthy of any team's number 10 shirt (Pelé wore number 10 of course; Didi's shirt number in 1958 was 6) and the harbinger of a whole heavenly host of equally skilled exponents of the art. Start the line at Didi, and the succession of great playmakers that followed were: Coluna, Baxter, Gerson, Netzer, Falcao, Scholes, Pirlo and Alonso.

Dream makers, all.

Yet the game demanded more of the playmaker than just an eye for strategy and ability to hit a 40-yard pass to feet. These players had to be fit, had to be athletes in their own right, and ready, as they had to be by virtue of the formation employed, not only press the opposing defence when they were attacking but to be the first back to assist their own defence when the play switched. Prominent within the game at all times, and, in many cases, prominent in life as well, for many of them were big personalities

---

41   *Not that it bothered Brazil. They still went on to win the tournament and, in their next eight fixtures against England, won seven of them, including a 5-1 victory in 1964.*

with a happy knack for creating headlines off the pitch as well as one it. With great responsibility and artistry comes, more often than not, a larger-than-life personality as Günter Netzer, the maestro at the heart of the West Germany side for a decade as well as a club player who, having impressed at hometown club Borussia Mönchengladbach, enough to win two Bundesliga titles with them, their first ever, in 1970 and 1971, shows.

Such was Netzer's growing reputation and unquestionable skill that, when he signed for Real Madrid in 1973, he had done so, as far as Real were concerned, in response to Barcelona's earlier signing of Johan Cruyff from Ajax. Real Madrid president Santiago Bernabéu was adamant that, of the two players he had got, in Netzer, he had the better of the two. Like the formation that spawned the need for players like him, Netzer was a one-off, the David Beckham of his day, a man who cultivated his looks and media personality with the same craft and precision as Beckham, and as he caressed a football. As well as opening and frequently being in attendance at his own nightclub Lovers' Lane, he expanded into the media, establishing Borussia Mönchengladbach's in-house magazine *Fohlenecho* at the same time as he developed his nightclub. One visitor to the club was Sepp Herberger, the coach of West Germany's 1954 World Cup winning side, the man who had found a way to silence Hidegkuti. One wonders if he would have played Netzer had he been available at the time?

West Germany were again victorious in international competition with Netzer in their side, the conductor of the orchestra, winning the 1972 European Championship title. West Germany had en route to that success absolutely destroyed England at Wembley, winning 3-1 with Netzer beyond imperious as the lynchpin of Helmet Schön's adventurous 4-2-4, dictating play and running at the England defence, causing pandemonium amongst the massed ranks of white shirts every time he did. That particular West Germany side had been an extraordinarily positive selection from coach Schön playing the equally adventurous Uli Hoeness alongside

Netzer in the midfield; although Schön had previously admitted that, given the choice between Netzer, whose performance was a talking point throughout England over the subsequent few days, and Wolfgang Overath, he would always select the latter, intimating that Overath was more reliable as a player. He was also, suffice to say, less of a playboy, something which might just have helped sway Schön's judgement.

Günter Netzer playing for Germany during the 1974 World Cup.

Netzer was, as can be the case for players of his outrageous talent, a little distrusted by the West Germany management. He did indeed have a career with the national side that lasted a decade, but, in that time, he only made 37 appearances for his country. In a playing career with West Germany that lasted just two years longer, Franz Beckenbauer made 103 appearances, so it seems reasonable to think that Netzer, had he been a valued member of the team and the 'must pick', his performance against England as well as those for both Borussia Mönchengladbach and Real Madrid should perhaps have ended his career with at least 80 appearances for West Germany to his name. Sadly for him, his reputation went against him and was all too often considered first rather than his prodigious talent as a professional footballer. Not that West Germany were in particular need of him as they went on to win the 1974 World Cup with Overath and Hoeness preferred as the central midfield pairing.

England's short but passionate love affair with all things Netzer following his dismantling of an English defence which included the equally peerless Bobby Moore was hardly that of a nation deprived of similar players, however. Throughout its history and certainly since the playmaker role became an essential part of not just the 4-2-4 but also the 4-4-2 and 4-3-3 formations, English club football had been blessed with individuals whose talent was comparable to Netzer's, players who could, had they been trusted and given license to do internationally with England what they all too often did with the club sides, make a difference. The list of shame (the shame being the FA's and those England managers who didn't pick them, including Don Revie, a man who indulged a team of mavericks at Leeds United but who didn't let one near his England side for the long term) includes Stan Bowles (5 appearances), Tony Currie (17), Matt Le Tissier (8), Alan Hudson[42] (2), Frank Worthington (8) and Ian Crook (0). Six gifted players who, with one moment of genius could change, could win a game, 40 caps between them. Criminal. Compare that to the case of one Gareth Barry, a

---

42   *Hudson drew plaudits from the great and the good in football regularly. Bill Shankly, the legendary manager of Liverpool once entered the Stoke City dressing room after a game against Liverpool to tell Hudson that the performance he had just seen from him was one of the best he had ever witnessed.*

proverbial 'tireless midfield battler' who made 53 appearances, preferred and favoured by no less than eight different England managers for, well, being a 'tireless midfield battler'.

Then there was Glenn Hoddle, one of the most gifted English number 10s ever who made 53 appearances for England himself, albeit over an 11-year period. Clearly, like Netzer for West Germany, he was a player who just could not be trusted by the management even though, as both Brazil and Hungary illustrated, if you pick the right formation for players of this ilk then they will excel. And Hoddle would have been picked, and regularly, by both Hungary and Brazil.

To this day, the formation of legend, 4-2-4 remains, despite Brazil's success with it, a formation that is tried only by the very brave or those teams with exceptional players, not least the central two. When a player like Didi is the 'default' for the type needed in order to make the system work, you can understand the reasons why. But, unsurprisingly, it has had its detractors. Many coaches were, and are, unwilling or unable to play the system, or, more likely, extremely reticent to authorise a formation that was defensively risky and went the other way, advocating formations that focused on a strong and well-organised defence rather than a gung ho attack. One coach who very much opposed this type of play was Argentinean Helenio Herrera, winner of two European Cups as coach of Inter Milan in 1964 and 1965.

Herrera advocated the *Catenaccio* system of play, a tactical system with a strong emphasis on defence, something which was the polar opposite of 4-2-4 and a reaction to it. This was not surprising. Teams that could not, or would not, play a 4-2-4 formation would be very wary of playing those that did; the only solution they had was to stop them playing and to match their front four, or even six, with a solid bank of up to six defenders. It is a highly organised and effective system which focuses primarily on reducing your opponent's chances of scoring whilst, at the same time, hoping to catch them on the counterattack and get one yourself. They try to score more goals than you, you try to concede less than them. Attack versus defence. It is football's equivalent of Cape Horn, the place where the Atlantic and Pacific Oceans meet, two irresistible forces clashing and forever cancelling each other out in the process.

Helenio Herrera (left) with the Italian national team in 1967

Any team playing one of Herrera's outfits knew what to expect, but that didn't matter. Keeping 10 men behind the ball might be an open secret, but it is very hard to break down. To watch a game which saw a Herrera side go 1-0 up in the first few minutes would be to watch a game that ended with the same scoreline as it would be considered 'job done', all 10 players would then drop back in defence and spend the rest of the match devoted to preventing the other team from scoring, rarely even venturing into the opposition's half, let alone their penalty area. For spectators, watching a game in which one of the teams has this formation (which could be as negative as 1-4-4-1) can be rather unforgiving in terms of entertainment value. Not that this ever bothered Herrera who commented, 'I get paid to produce a winning team; I don't get any extra if they play attractive football.' He was correct, of course. And his methods were successful. Aside from those two European Cup triumphs with Inter Milan (in winning the tournament in 1964, his side scored just 16 goals in their nine games, an average of 1.77 a game whilst their opponents in the final, Real Madrid, scored 28 goals in their nine games at 3.11 a game), he also won four La Liga titles (two each with Atletico Madrid and Barcelona) and three Serie As, all with Inter. As he racked up the trophies and accolades, he became one of the most feted and in demand football coaches in the world in the 1950s and 1960s. And that reputation never left him, so much so that, when he accepted the invitation to have a second spell with Barcelona in 1979, he had already been involved in top-class football for nearly half a century and was 71 when he left the role two years later.

The moral of this tale of packed defences and caution? Playing attractive football is one thing. But playing, coaching or owning a side that plays winning football is something else, something far more important. Herrera's way of playing didn't particularly entertain anyone who watched them – playowners, players, fans, you name it. But did they care? Hell no. Because they were winning things, and that was all that mattered. Brazil had discovered football's mother lode in Sweden – gloriously entertaining attacking football and winner's medals. They were an exception. Even Sebes' fabled Hungary side had been unable to combine that with success, just as Hungary's club teams hadn't, for all the advantages they were given. Football teams and coaches, therefore, had a choice: entertain or win.

It was a no brainer. Brazil in 1958, 1962 and 1970 were one-offs, at least in as far as they were a team that played glorious football and won trophies. And, with clubs and coaches now as aware of how to play against Brazil as they were aware of how not to play against them, allowances began to be made, allowances which meant for the 1962 finals, which were held in Chile and for which Brazil were overwhelming favourites, they were also now seen as targets. Opposing teams would look to nullify their overwhelming attacking prowess with solid defence and by counterattacking, as Herrera had done with Spain. So Brazil had to retaliate; the result of this was the end of their pure 4-2-4 game as they introduced a slightly, for them, more cautious approach. The back four remained as it was with both the full-backs, Djalma and Nilton Santos as well as goalkeeper Gilmar, all travelling and featuring. The difference was in the attacking quartet which was reduced to three with Mario Zagallo brought back to patrol the left side of the pitch alongside Didi and Zito in a vague midfield three with Amarido ahead and to his right and Garrincha and Vava forming an attacking spearhead. It was a modified 4-3-3 or even a 4-3-1-2 with Amarido, in for the injured Pelé, charged with occupying the role of false number 9.

One reason for Brazil approaching these finals in a less gung ho fashion was, according to their coach Aimore Moreira, 'The age factor...one we had to always take into consideration. That was responsible for our tactics being less flexible...remembering the teams sparkle in Sweden.'[43] Brazil were still an entertaining side to watch despite the caution that the new coach had introduced to their play and the absence of Pelé, injured in the first game against Czechoslovakia and subsequently out of the tournament. Fortunately for Brazil and for FIFA, they still had a star name and attraction to boast; this was right winger Garrincha who ended the tournament as its leading scorer. This was a fitting testament to his explosive pace, trickery and overall mastery of the wing position – a role that, at the same time he was excelling at, was, nevertheless, one which, as *Catenaccio* took a further hold, was to all but disappear from the game within a decade.

---

43   Wilson, Jonathan. 2013. Inverting the Pyramid. Orion. 151.

A particularly damning indictment of the route that football was taking in the weeks and months after Brazil's second successive World Cup triumph in 1962 came from Gustav Sebes. He, remember, was the man whose footballing revolution in Hungary had, briefly but gloriously, seen their national side become the world's best only to be supplanted in that position by the Brazilian vintage of 1958 and 1962. He'd watched both the tournaments as a spectator, admitting, post-Chile that 'The future will belong to teams that have a well-organised defence who can effectively into attack.' In other words, he saw teams that could counterattack, swiftly and with great pace as being those that would have the most success in future years rather than those who, like his sides, had not always seen a strong defence as a priority, such was their dependence on their attacking players. This was backed up by Rudolf Vytlačil, the coach of the Czechoslovakian team that Brazil had beaten in the final, who announced that, in his opinion, this World Cup had seen a sea change in priorities and tactical approaches and that '...the WM system is dead. All players now have to be able to defend and attack. The forwards are the first line in a team's defence.'

It hadn't been that long ago that a team's defenders were the first line of its attack!

Herrera went one step further with regard to his dedication in building sides with exceptionally strong and well-organised defences by expecting his players to be as strong and well organised as the game they played. He was one of the great pioneers of psychological motivating skills; he was a man who wanted to get into the minds of his players as much as he wanted to get them on the training pitch. He regularly littered his team talks with the sort of positive quotes and phrases that are now common to sportsmen and women throughout the world today, a typical Herrera quote being, 'He who doesn't give it all, gives nothing.' He also arranged for a multitude of billboards to be pinned up in strategic positions around the grounds of the clubs he managed that stated, 'Class+Preparation+Intelligence+Athleticism=Championships.' He even got his players to chant it as they trained, quite an achievement given that he worked with some of the world's greatest clubs and individual players.

It's highly unlikely now that the stars of Barcelona, Real Madrid or Bayern Munich would entertain such a suggestion whilst they trained. Can you see Lionel Messi chanting a slogan all over again in the manner of a US Marine as he jogs around the Camp Nou? Me neither. He'd probably ask Herrera to get one of 'his people' to do it for him.

Herrera's tactics were based on discipline and so was his attitude towards the everyday lives of his players. They were forbidden to smoke or drink, and in addition to that, he outlined to them what they could and couldn't eat as part of their daily diet. All of this is part of the game today, but during Herrera's time it was hugely controversial with many in the game expressing disapproval at what lengths he would go to in order to win. This also included taking his players away to a hotel in the days leading up to a game; that very same tactic that Jack Hunter had done with Blackburn Olympic back in the 1880s, when he took his players to Blackpool pre-match and had them running up and down the famous sands there as part of their training.

Although a disciplinarian, he did, at least, recognise that teams did need to have some attacking intent during a game, broadly agreeing with Sebes' notion that teams would need to defend well first and foremost but then be able to hit opposing teams on the counterattack. Herrera pioneered the modern concept of wingbacks – that is, full-backs who are pushed slightly ahead of their normal defensive positions. They were still expected to defend, though, despite their advanced positioning, and woe betide the Herrera defender whose ill discipline led to an opposing goal or scoring opportunity. That came as standard. But they were also expected to get forward and provide crosses. So, whilst wingers weren't quite a dying breed in the game, not, at least, for as long as a wingback might be seen replicating the role, they were set to become an endangered species (and have been ever since) as that sense of defensive pragmatism settled over the game. Most teams and coaches realised that, whilst it would be nice to play like Brazil, the reality of it was that they were indeed a one-off. So, too, was 4-2-4 whose bright light would eventually fade, if not totally disappear, from the scene by the beginning of the next decade.

One man who had already decided that he could do without wingers was Alf Ramsey, who'd been appointed as manager of the modest English club side Ipswich Town in 1955. He was, like Herrera, very much a disciplinarian type of manager who set very high standards of behaviour and overall conduct for his players to follow and who didn't, by any means, appreciate or indulge in prima donnas or that sort of behaviour. For him, and there are similarities approach-wise to Sebes and the ideal of 'socialist' football here, no player enjoyed special status or treatment and that they were all, himself included, merely parts of a greater good. In other words, they were a team and responsible for both themselves and one another.

He liked his teams to be efficient, to operate effectively and for each player to know exactly what his role was and how to perform it. If you, as a player, exceeded the parameters that Ramsey set in place, professionally or personally, then you were likely to be cast aside and never used again. He made no exceptions to this rule. You could be the greatest player on the planet, it wouldn't matter. Had, for example, Pelé been English and had been late for a team meeting that he had previously arranged with the players, there is every chance that Ramsey would have sent him home and refused to pick him again. Leading players Jimmy Greaves, Bobby Moore and Bobby Charlton discovered this for themselves in May 1964 when they failed to turn up for a meeting prior to England undertaking a pre-season tour. They'd all returned to their hotel rooms later that night only to find their passports waiting for them on their beds, the inference being that, as they hadn't turned up for the meeting, they could take themselves home. They were treated rather like naughty schoolchildren on a field trip. It mattered not that they were three of the leading players in England, and, indeed, in Europe. The fact that they had failed to show the sort of respect Ramsey expected meant he, briefly, considered them surplus to requirements. He didn't only expect complete control over his players, however, but he also demanded it of the role prior to his appointment. There was to be no interference, as there had been in the past by an FA board and no trying to influence him in any way what players he should or should not pick. He demanded total control, almost on a dictatorial level.

Much to his probable surprise, he got it. Giddy with (controlled) delight at how the FA had acquiesced to his demands, he promptly caused a bit of a stir by confidently predicting, four years in advance of the actual event, that England would win the next World Cup. This was heady stuff. It's worth bearing in mind that prior to any major tournament that England have been playing in over the last couple of decades or so, the side has flown off to a media generated groundswell of optimism about their chances with many predicting that the side have a 'genuine chance' of winning the tournament. Illogical, maybe, given the team's level of performance during that time. But it sells newspapers and heightens interest in the tournament, the players and even their wives and girlfriends. Yet no one quite goes as far as to say that the team *will* win the tournament in question. But nearly 50 years ago, Ramsey had said just that, clearly, succinctly and with utter conviction. It was either a touch of genius or a sign, perhaps, that he had already lost touch with the responsibilities of his role and the huge expectations he had now placed upon his and the team's shoulders.

Ramsey was not a stranger to unexpected success, however. He'd spent eight years as manager of Ipswich Town prior to his appointment to the 'top job', quietly building a team that eventually, and against all the odds, won the First Division title in 1962. He'd done this without traditional wingers in his side simply because he didn't trust them and their often all too obvious lack of defensive qualities. Like Herrera, Ramsey believed in teams that were built to defend from the front backwards; traditional wingers were, therefore, an indulgence, players who would gently amble back to the halfway line to wait to be given the ball again rather than chase back and defend when his team lost position. That wasn't good enough for Ramsey, and he wasn't prepared to indulge wingers in his teams. This was despite the fact that during his time as a player with England, he'd been in the same squad and teams as two of the all-time great wingers in English football history, namely Tom Finney and Stanley Matthews.

Ramsey, however, was a right back by trade, and it could well have been that he had, playing in that position, endured a torrid time, defensively, on more than one occasion due to the absence of any defensive cover or support ahead of him. This was something which he avowed would not be the fate of the full-backs in his teams. Ramsey had, for example, played for England in their 3-6 defeat to Hungary in 1953 where his 'partner' on the right-hand side would have been Matthews – someone who would not, you can be assured, have made it a priority to chase back and offer cover and protection to Ramsey during that, or any other game, leaving him hopelessly exposed and vulnerable. It's easy to picture Ramsey, arms on hips shaking his head, quietly admonishing the distant Matthews as he does so: '...not good enough Stanley, really not good enough, nor acceptable at all.'

Ramsey's response to that was for his two wide players to be withdrawn into a deeper position on the pitch and to have a broad remit of supporting the team's defensive and attacking play rather than just the latter.

Simplistically, he had culled the old-fashioned attacking four from the 4-2-4 formation by bringing the two wide men into a more central role, thus 4-2-4 became 4-4-2 with the two players added to the midfield from the attack. Making the midfield stronger and looking to dominate that area of the pitch naturally made a team's defence stronger as well, with, if necessary, seven or eight players looking to get behind the ball and defend. This was something which, as West Germany's Franz Beckenbauer later admitted, opposing teams, including his own, found difficult to play against as no one had really set up their team in this way before, saying, 'Almost everyone played with wingers, so our team and others found it hard to do anything against this, because the system was strange for them.' A revelation then. Staid, conservative, predictable England who had persisted with the WM formation long after every other footballing nation had tossed it aside or even never bothered with it in the first place, had a manager and a way of playing that, to quote one of the world's leading players, other teams '...found it hard to do anything against.' Hungary had started the footballing revolution in the 1950s; Brazil had succeeded them. Were England about to take the game to the next stage? If they won the 1966 World Cup, it would be very hard to argue that they hadn't.

The team that Ramsey finally settled upon once England had gone through the formalities of qualifying for that tournament's knock-out stages wasn't, however, set out to play in a 4-4-2 formation. He had settled on Alan Ball and Martin Peters as being his wide midfielders, primarily because both players were not only good on the ball with an eye for both a telling pass or a goal, but they were also both very hardworking, willing and more than able to run all day. They'd happily track back to help out the defence or push forward to support England's two strikers, fulfilling both roles perfectly. But Ramsey did not see them as players who would either be comfortable or best utlised in a wide position, so he brought both of them slightly infield, flanking England's much feared and respected attacking midfielder, Bobby Charlton. This enabled Ramsey's other first choice midfielder Nobby Stiles to sit back farther behind that trio rather than alongside them in a conventional midfield four, meaning that Ramsey's formation, commonly seen as a 4-3-3 (the formation he actually started the tournament with) was more of a 4-1-3-2 with Geoff Hurst and Roger Hunt operating as the two strikers with Bobby Charlton, like Stiles, playing in a slightly deeper, withdrawn role than he might have been used to at Manchester United.

Putting Stiles just ahead of England's back four was a masterstroke of Ramsey's and one which may, more than anything else, have led to England winning the tournament. It made their defence, which hadn't always been the most reliable, impervious to the attacking talents of some of the world's leading sides and players as England went through their three group matches as well as the quarter-final win over Argentina without conceding a goal. It was effective, if not altogether popular. Take, for example, Ramsey's cautious style early on which, in the wake of their opening game, a 0-0 draw against Uruguay which heard a mass outbreak of indignant boos around the Wembley terraces after the final whistle. England had been cautious, yet Uruguay had been even more reticent to commit, sitting back from the start with every player behind the ball. Ramsey, however, was delighted with both the result and performance, warmly greeting his players afterwards, telling them, '... you may not have won, but you didn't lose and you didn't give a goal away either...you can still qualify, provided you keep a clean sheet and don't lose a game.'

Don't give a goal away. Keep a clean sheet. Don't lose a game. It isn't Brazil, is it?

Exciting it wasn't. What on earth had happened to that joyful, free-scoring football championed by Brazil over the last decade? Surely national teams and their coaches would be desperate to follow their lead and build a team in their image? Obviously not. It wasn't as if Brazil, winners of the last two tournaments, were cutting a familiar attacking swathe through their games either. They'd won their opening match against Bulgaria but found themselves fully sussed out by their next two opponents, Hungary and Portugal, who both beat the holders 3-1 with games based on physical power and pace, not to mention a little intimidation as the tackles flew in, not least on Pelé who ended up being hacked, kicked and bullied out of the tournament. The 'stop Pelé and you stop Brazil' approach commenced immediately in that first game, the Bulgarians tactics on him (which often consisted of two, even three players surrounding him whenever he was in possession) meaning he missed the next game, the defeat against a briefly rejuvenated Hungary. By the time Pelé returned for their last group game, one they had to win, the Portuguese merely took over from where the Bulgarians had left off, leaving Pelé so bitter that he exited the competition, along with his side, vowing never to play in a World Cup again. Football's new professionalism had claimed both its biggest superstar as well as the world's best team. It might also be fair to say that, with their last two games both refereed by Englishmen at a tournament held in England with FIFA led by, yes, an Englishman at the time in Stanley Rous (yes, that very same Stanley Rous who went from being an Armed Forces PT instructor to, unfeasibly, the head of football's world governing body, the Stanley Rous who advocated a game based on physical strength, fitness and the ability to run faster and longer than anyone else) that there might, perhaps, have been an inclination to ensure that England did not have to meet Brazil in the semi-finals.[44]

England did, of course, succeed Brazil as world champions, beating West Germany 4-2 in a final that was not short of controversy. For

---

44   *Not that I am advocating a conspiracy theory in any way, but it is also interesting to bear in mind that, out of all the 20 World Cup Finals held from 1930 to 2014, the winning team has, just once, played all of their games at the same stadium and their home stadium: England, in 1966.*

the final, West Germany had lined up in the familiar 4-2-4 formation with those two critical central midfield places taken by Beckenbauer and Overath. Crucially, neither were able to exert much influence on the game with Stiles an ever-present figure ahead of them, looking to break down and interrupt the flow of West Germany's play as much as he could. It was a game where Geoff Hurst, scorer of the first, and, to date, only hat trick in a World Cup Final has got all the plaudits but one which, in fairness, either Stiles or Alan Ball could rightfully claim to have been named Man of the Match, such was the way they dominated the play and stopped the West Germans from playing. It was just as well that the two of them were capable of playing in such a way, winning tackles and retaining the ball. Alan Ball, speaking about his midfield partner Bobby Charlton, admitted that Charlton thought that a '...tackle was what you go fishing with.'

But then it didn't matter. Ramsey had won a World Cup for England with a team that was, in essence, hard working, energetic and able to run all day – all of the qualities that the self-proclaimed home of football had always championed. Was there a Pelé, a Didi or a Hidegkuti in the England site, a maverick, a player able to change a game with a touch of genius? No. Were there any world-class players at all in the England line-up? Perhaps two, Moore and Charlton at best, although Banks would, by the time the next World Cup came around, be recognised as the greatest goalkeeper in the world. Some of the England players who'd played in that final were probably not even the best in England in their position. Was, for example, Jack Charlton a better centre half than Brian Labone or Roger Hunt a better bet in attack than Joe Baker who had scored a phenomenal 93 goals in 144 appearances for Arsenal? Then there was the question of Jimmy Greaves, the subject of Ramsey's biggest gamble and, along with Moore and Charlton, the only real contender in the squad fit to command the epithet 'world class'.

As goalscorers go, Greaves was in a league of his own. He'd become one of the first English players to join a top continental team in 1961 when he'd joined AC Milan in Italy, promptly hating every minute of life in Italy and desperate to come home almost as soon as he got out there. But, despite that, he still managed to score 9 goals in 12 appearances for Milan against some of the most uncompromising defences in world football. Yet, after his injury in England's final group game against Mexico, he was replaced by the rather less-prolific but far more hard-working Geoff Hurst. Most people assumed that as soon as Greaves was fit again he'd regain his place in the England team, but Ramsey chose to stick with Hurst all the way through to the final, despite Greaves being fit and available. Had England lost that game or the semi-final, Ramsey would, no doubt, have been pilloried by both the England fans and the media (as well as Greaves) for not selecting him, yet he stuck to his beliefs and kept his faith in Hurst, a much more, in his view, hard-working player who contributed more to the team in terms of support play and work rate than Greaves ever would.

The payback, when it came, was spectacular. But what if Hurst had flopped? The risk the England manager had taken in deciding not to restore him to the team was an enormous one. Greaves was a world star and an influential voice in the dressing room where he was also immensely popular. He was also one of a handful of England players who might reasonably have been in with a chance of being considered good enough to play for Brazil, West Germany or Portugal, three of the leading international sides in the world at that time. He was, in short, a player who you couldn't afford to leave out of your starting 11 if he was available. Yet Ramsey did.

But that was typical of the man. His England, his players, were hard working, efficient and organised. They were nowhere near as pleasing on the eye as Brazil. Had they tried to play like Brazil, their deficiencies would swiftly have been found out. It was a case of 'horses for courses' as far as England and Ramsey were concerned, and selecting the players and the formation he played was done with but one thing in mind: to win football matches. Greaves was a great player; Ramsey knew that. But was he a team player; was he as valuable a part of the collective as the hard-working, hard-running Hurst was? Had England lost the semi-final or final, the recriminations might have been long and very critical of Ramsey for leaving Greaves out. Yet he did and England prevailed.

Their success indicated another shift in how football was being played. Brazil had won the last two tournaments with an attacking side built around wingers and a creative midfielder, someone who made the team 'tick' and who linked defence with attack. England had done so without wingers and with a hard-working rather than creative midfield. They'd also done so by stopping other teams from playing rather than imposing themselves upon the opposition, concentrating, as Ramsey had reminded them after the dour 0-0 draw against Uruguay, on 'not losing'. And there, there was the big difference between the England of 1966 and the Brazil of 1958 and 1962. Brazil took to the field looking to win games; England did so looking not to lose them.

Thus a cautious 4-1-3-2 won the World Cup, if not worldwide praise for England. It brought to mind the words of Malcolm Allison, a successful if controversial coach with Manchester City who, when asked for his thoughts on Ramsey, said, '...to Alf's way of thinking, creative means lazy.' And England were not lazy. During the match, BBC TV commentator Kenneth Wolstenholme remarked that Alan Ball was, '... running himself into the ground as usual.' Yet Ball was simply playing the game as Ramsey preached it. Always be involved, always be committed, always look to have possession. Ball would never have got a game for Brazil but then again, it is likely that Ramsey would not have picked Didi for England had he been available for the same reason Ball wouldn't have played for Brazil. Neither would have fitted in with the footballing philosophy of the other nation, a statement which is a lot more damning of England than it is Brazil.

Ramsey's 4-1-3-2 was a vaguely cautious derivative of the 4-3-3 formation which was becoming a more and more popular option for football teams throughout the 1960s and 70s. It was one that, like the already disappearing 4-2-4, he had experimented with; its failings there being his latent distrust of traditional wingers. Indeed, he'd gone into England's group games with a 4-3-3 formation, choosing to utilise one rather than two wingers in those three games on the basis that he thought their pace and presence might unsettle the (widely thought to be) shaky defences of Uruguay, Mexico and France. Three games, three different wingers in John Connelly, Terry Paine and Ian Callaghan, all on the right-hand side of an attacking trio that included one of the aforementioned players alongside Roger Hunt and Jimmy Greaves. The fact that none of the three had much of an impact in either of those three games was what led Ramsey to revert to the 4-1-3-2 formation for the knock-out stages, any fading hope he had in wingers now completely at an end. Now the England careers of the three players were in question; Connolly and Paine never played for England again whilst Callaghan made just one more appearance for England, against Switzerland, 11 years later.

4-3-3 is very much, like 4-2-4, an offensive formation tailor made for sides that base their game on fast-moving, attacking football, teams that look to win a game rather than to not lose it. It relies upon an out-and-out striker to spearhead the attacking trio, someone who is able to control the ball, retain possession and, through holding the ball up, bring the two players on either side of him into play. Much like, for example, Arsène Wenger's Arsenal side that won the FA Cup in 2005 and which, for much of that season as well as the final, relied upon an attacking trio with Nicholas Anelka flanked on his left by Jose Antonio Reyes and on his right by Marc Overmars. The latter pair were traditional wingers with the ability to outpace or outfox opponents before either passing to the centre forward or by feeding off the chances he inevitably gave them with the type of little lay-offs or knock-downs that you'd expect from a central striker. Yet Anelka was never the 'traditional' number 9. Yes, at 6'1", Anelka was not short on physical presence and strength but was still far more than a target man, the much beloved big and strong number 9 of yore like Steve Bloomer and all his contemporaries. Anelka had much more about his game, enough to prosper in that role but also as a maker, as well as a taker of chances. In short, a centre forward with the complete game, a precious commodity that was clearly recognised and valued by some of the world's leading club sides, such as Paris Saint-Germain, Real Madrid, Fenerbache and Juventus, all of whom have had the Frenchman on their books, plus six clubs in England including elite sides Arsenal, Liverpool, Manchester City and Chelsea. Anelka is possibly the only footballer who has ever played for all of those clubs, quite an accolade and a tribute to his ability at playing in the middle of a front three.

Imagine, for a moment, you are one of the full-backs of a team set to play Arsenal. They are playing their usual 4-3-3 formation with Anelka leading the line, flanked by Reyes and Overmars. All three players have pace, that is no secret, no great team talk revelation. But all three of them are more than that, much more. Their positional awareness is acute; each always seems to know where one or the other is; there is no need to look up, because the pass is played automatically. Reyes knows if he is in one part of the attacking third, Anelka will be in another and vice versa. Sometimes Reyes will move into a central position and Anelka will drift out wide, and both will drag their markers with them in the process.

Overmars, meanwhile, was the perfect player for a 4-3-3, learning the system under Louis Van Gaal at Ajax who described him as a 'multi-functional player' – an apt description for someone who was made to play in a multi-functional system. These qualities were recognised, in time, by Arsène Wenger who felt at the time of signing Overmars that he would provide Arsenal with what they had been missing and that, with him in the side, they could now look to play the sort of 'expansive' 4-3-3 football that Wenger wanted to play.

No surprises then really, when Overmars eventually joined Barcelona. Having won three consecutive Premier League titles with Arsenal, he formed part of another attacking trio at the Nou Camp, initially playing on the left alongside Rivaldo in the middle and Luis Enrique on the right, the three of them providing support for striker Patrick Kluivert. With Rivaldo often leading the line alongside Kluivert, however (and ending that first season with Overmars as Barca's leading scorer), this formation, ostensibly 4-2-3-1 was nearer to 4-2-4, a real throwback to the glory days of that Brazilian team from 1958 with, fittingly, Rivaldo, another in that infinite line of attacking midfielders from Brazil leading the line as well as happily taking most of the plaudits.

Where there is light there must also be shadow, and, in the case of 4-3-3, wherever there is attacking intent and carefree offensive devilry of the type you are always likely to get from the aforementioned, then there must always also be defensive backing and support provided by the trio of players immediately behind the attacking spearhead. And, such is the onerous responsibility of the three more conventional midfielders, there to cover, supply and, no doubt, admire said offensive spearhead. The responsibilities of these three vary, but it is likely one will be there solely to break up opponent's attacks, to win the ball, and then, as quickly and cleanly as he has done that, to move the ball onto a teammate. Think again of the Barcelona team of the last few years for they are as good an example as any of a team that plays a 4-3-3 formation. The hard-working and competitive member of that team will be a player like Sergio Busquets, the pivot of both the Barcelona and Spanish national teams when he plays, for much of what they do both in defence and attack revolves around him. Crucially he reads a game well and knows where the ball or an opponent is likely to be, playing a role similar to that taken on by Alan Ball, who played in the England side that won the 1966 World Cup. Alf Ramsey had famously told Ball that his role in that team was to be their dog; whenever he got the ball he was to chase after it, get it and bring it back to a player who was able to do something with it, in this case, Bobby Charlton. Busquets'[45] role (though he would rightfully protest at being known as the team dog) is similar. Get the ball and move it into someone who can do some damage. Similar roles but different players; Busquets is totally at ease in possession and is more than capable of retaining it until such times he can see the pass that will make a difference. Look at the options he has had in his Barcelona side and who plays alongside him. He is able to do just that. Iniesta, Xavi, Messi. Ball, in comparison would be expected to off-load the ball as soon as possible.

Another example of the type of player who excelled in this type of role, playing it in a similar fashion to Ball, was Jeremy Goss, the former Norwich City and Wales midfielder who shot to prominence during his club side's run in the UEFA Cup during the 1993/94 season. Goss was, like Ball, responsible for winning possession before laying the ball off to, again, players who were expected to be able to create or take a goal-scoring opportunity. In Goss's case, he had an extremely technically adept player alongside him in the Norwich midfield by the name of Ian Crook, or, in Ruel Fox, a winger with genuine pace and skill. All three players were, admittedly, lesser-known names playing for a modest English team, but such was their skill at performing those roles. Goss was a full international and someone who played in the same Wales

---

45   *Busquets' technical knowledge and ability to read the game will almost certainly make him a leading club coach and continuing prominent figure in the European game from around the mid-2020s onwards.*

side as the likes of world stars Ryan Giggs, Mark Hughes and Neville Southall whilst Crook was constantly touted for a place in the full England side. Fox, meanwhile, went on to play for leading club sides Newcastle United and Tottenham Hotspur, costing the latter nearly £5 million when they signed him in 1995.

If you have the players, success in any given formation will come, whether you be Brazil, Barcelona or even little Rochdale from England's League One, a team who have, in their 108 year-long history never even made it to that countries second league tier, never mind the top one. Yet, in their FA Cup match against Stoke City in 2015, playing a team in the Premier League managed by Mark Hughes, a man who has played for Manchester United, Barcelona and Bayern Munich. Stoke even included in their team Bojan Krkić, a player who'd also been at Inter Milan and Barcelona, another used to being part of an expansive system rather than finding himself lining up against one. Formidable odds and an invitation, you would think, for any perceived minor team to 'park the bus' and look to fight and kick their way to an unlikely victory. Yet Rochdale approached the match with no fear and, in the face of what you might call a hopeless task, started it playing a 4-3-3 formation, a tribute to the attacking philosophy of their manager, Keith Hill. But not only that. It was also a tribute to Hill's players, none of them household names, yet all familiar with and comfortable playing in such an expansive, ambitious formation. 4-3-3, the neglected yet much admired spin-off of 4-2-4 is still out there. You just need to know where to look for it. Sometimes in the most unlikely of places.

Thus we have an attacking trio with a ball winner and ball player in the midst of the three that sit behind them. But what of the other two midfielders in that group? Their role in the team is equally important, and, as far as that and the rich legacy they are following, think back (again) to that Brazil side of 1958 and that great side that mastered

4-2-4 with the majesty of Didi orchestrating both defence and attack from his place in that slender but effective midfield pairing. Only now the responsibility of both defending and attacking goes with the wider players in that second line of three across the pitch. They do this from those wide positions, effectively playing as wingbacks. Two lines of three, therefore, and, of that six, five players with a licence to attack. If anything, 4-3-3 is as adventurous offensively, if not more so, as 4-2-4. Where it ultimately finds favour with modern coaches, however, is in its potential to go from an attacking formation to a defensive one, and more or less instantaneously. No team, no matter how good its attacking players are or how offensive their formation is or who the opposition is, can attack continuously. Therefore, whenever a team playing 4-3-3 does find itself on the back foot, you will often find the formation revert to 4-1-4-1 as the one central midfielder drops back along with two of the attacking three; Wenger's Arsenal is a good example.

Wenger emphasised expansive football played by talented and expressive players, football that initially yielded a great deal of success for him and his team. This included three Premier League titles, including, in the 2003/04 season, going through the whole Premier League campaign unbeaten; four FA Cups and a Champions League final from 1996 to 2005. Success in the way of trophies has been slender for Arsenal ever since with just a sole FA Cup win in 2014 to show for their efforts. Exciting football? Yes. Exciting players?[46] Yes. Entertaining football?

Yes. But, to both the fans of the club and the media, it mattered not one jot. What did matter was winning trophies. And if that meant a more staid approach, then so be it. Such an approach was, and remains,

---

46   *To name but a few: Thierry Henry, Denis Bergkamp, Marc Overmars, Cesc Fàbregas, Robin van Persie, Mesut Özil and Alexis Sanchez – you'd be excused for wondering why Arsenal haven't won everything going with such a galaxy of talent to call upon.*

anathema to Wenger who, when asked by the *Daily Telegraph* if he had ever considered blunting both his and his team's attacking instincts and adopting a more cautious approach in the quest to win trophies, replied, 'Not really, we have always tried to attack because we have a team that has that ability.'

Wenger is a leopard who won't change his spots for anyone.

Brazil's triumphs in 1958 and 1962 had been glorious. Yet, in 1966, the manner of their play and their leading player was brutalised, contained and made virtually impotent by teams who had learnt how to play against them. And, ultimately, it stopped them playing in the process. It was very much a repeat of what had happened to Sebes' Hungary side of the 1950s with teams eventually realising that if you couldn't play like them or even play them at their own game, you simply stopped them doing what they did best by any and all possible means. As Pelé found out to his and his teams cost in England, this could well mean by kicking them if necessary. It was almost as if, in the self-styled home of football, the culture of mob football had, briefly, made a comeback. It also saw the dawn of the age of footballing caution, one best demonstrated by the strict and tactically rigid formation which, from the 1970s onwards, slowly began to dominate the game all over the world.

And it worked.

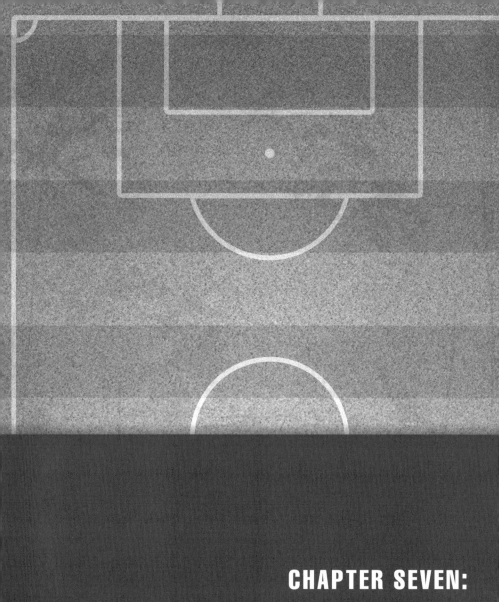

CHAPTER SEVEN:
THE CASE FOR 4-4-2

Because whilst it isn't the most attractive or fluid of formations, it is one of the strongest, one that, when the balance is right, can be devastatingly effective – as Real Madrid would testify.

Let's talk about 4-4-2.

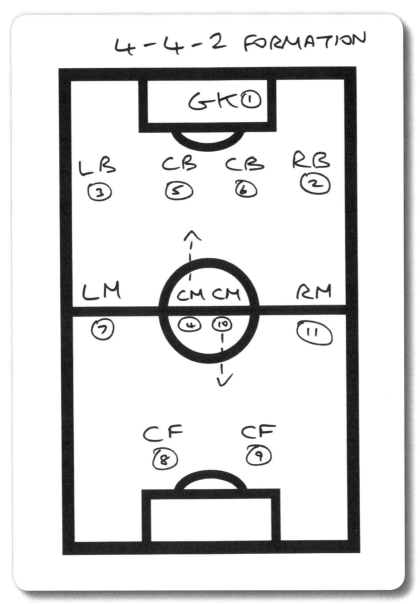

The 4-4-2 formation with classic shirt numbers.

Or 4-4-bloody-2 as it has become referred to in England in recent years.

It is, perhaps, the most well known and understood of all football formations. Tried, trusted, appreciated. One that is not all that difficult to get your head around tactically or technically – even if you aren't exactly the fastest thinker on the pitch.

The beauty of 4-4-2 is, like the game of football itself, its simplicity. The numbers 1 to 11 on the players' backs all mean something in a 4-4-2 formation, more than any other in the game's history – until, that is, the likelihood of your team starting a match with the squad numbers 1 to 11 on the starting 11 was rendered virtually impossible by the introduction of season-long squad numbers into the game. For that reason, 4-4-2 is the formation of choice for those amongst us who while away the time picking our respective 'Best Ever XIs' from the wide choice of players available to us from the history of our favourite club side or international team of choice. Every number makes a statement about the player who wears the shirt, his strengths and qualities and what he will bring to the side. Thus we have a side made up of the following:

- Goalkeeper[47]

- Right back

- Left back

---

[47] *Nothing much has changed there, fortunately, although, having said that, prior to the 1958 World Cup, the Brazilian Football Federation forgot to send the player number lists to FIFA prior to the tournament, meaning they had to allocate them in a hurry and without much apparent thought at the last minute. This resulted in first-choice Brazilian goalkeeper Gilmar ending up with the number 3 shirt, this haphazard method of allocation running right through the squad. Thus, for their opening game of the tournament, Austria, Brazil's opponents, lined up in a respectable and almost straightforward sequence of 1-2-3-4-5-6-7-9-10-11-13, the Brazilian starting 11 was numbered 3-2-5-6-7-12-14-15-17-18-21!*

- Defensive midfielder

- Centre half

- Centre half

- Right midfield

- Striker

- Striker

- Attacking midfielder[48]

- Left midfield

Simple and effective, yes, but one that crucially made full use of the pitch, including giving teams both attacking width and defensive cover for that width. Thus numbers 2 and 3 were the two wide defenders with 5 and 6 placed in between them. Next up was another line of four, the midfielders with numbers 7 and 11 situated in front of numbers 2 and 3, respectively, with 4 and 10 playing in the middle of that four. This left the two strikers, often one tall and physically strong player who is good in the air and at winning the ball playing alongside a smaller, faster partner, the classical goal poacher of the Jimmy Greaves and Gerd Muller mould.

A formation that is now perhaps rather unfairly vilified as being old fashioned, predictable and tactically unimaginative. Yet one which was, for the main part, developed and played by teams with exactly that in mind. The fact that it could be predictable and tactically unimaginative was

---

48   *The above method also contributed, quite by chance, to randomly allocating the number 10 to Pelé for the tournament, the shirt number he eventually became synonymous with.*

what made it so appealing, but not only that. It was also considered easy to coach and easy to understand with even the most technically inadequate players able to understand and excel at the roles they were given.

If 4-2-4 was the formation of the footballing elite, then 4-4-2 was the formation of the people and the people's game. A formation for everyone and anyone. If just one word could be used to describe 4-4-2 as a formation, that word would almost certainly be 'balance' and throughout the side with no great emphasis on attack (2-3-5) or defence (5-4-1). Rather than that, 4-4-2 offers balance throughout the middle of a team with what the purists in football like to call a 'good spine', that is, strong and commanding players in each of the following positions: goalkeeper, central defence, central midfield and centre forward. But it then goes deeper than that. The two central defenders are usually comprised of a big, strong and physically imposing player who is good in the air as well as dominant in the tackle who plays alongside a slightly smaller yet fast and capable ball playing defender who is as able to stride out of the defence with the ball at his feet as the other is to make a long and high kicked clearance – the further away, the better. A good example of this sort of defensive pairing would be Jack Charlton and Bobby Moore, the tried and very tested central defensive partnership of Alf Ramsey's England.

Likewise there should be balance in the central midfield pairing. Again, one of the players will be tenacious and aggressive, a ball winner, a player who likes to tackle, to break down opponents' attacking moves and generally disrupt the pattern of their play. He will play alongside a more technically gifted player, someone who is able to play a 30-yard pass to feet as effectively as his midfield partner is a 3-yard one; someone who relies on his vision and ability to read a game.

Examples? The Italy team that won the 1982 World Cup, beating West Germany in the final. At the heart of their midfield lurked Gabriele

Oriali, a player who, it would be fair to say, didn't have the best technical ability. Yet, as someone who could stop opposing players and moves, man-mark a danger man out of the game and, to an exceptionally high level, play the role of *incontrista,* he had few equals. Alongside him played the much more well-known and renowned Marco Tardelli, rated then, and now, as one of the best central midfielders to ever play the game. Tardelli was also defensively minded but combined that with exceptional technical skills as well as an ability to get forward to support the attack, even scoring the occasional goal himself. Indeed, one of the most famous goals in World Cup history was scored by Tardelli, their second in the 3-1 win over West Germany in the 1982 World Cup Final. It is a characteristic Italian goal, one made on the break: fast and deadly, with the final pass of the move made to Tardellii, unmarked and waiting, expectantly, on the edge of the D of the penalty area. That goal and his iconic celebration that followed remains one of the most memorable in World Cup history.

Finally, you have the attacking tip of the 4-4-2 formation, the two forwards. Again, these are usually two players with contrasting styles playing together with one the traditional target man, an 'old-fashioned' centre forward – good in the air, good at holding up the ball, laying it off and unsettling opposing defences with his sheer physical presence with great strength rather than height. His partner will invariably be a smaller, more mobile, faster striker able to convert half chances and to run, at pace, at opposing defences. Two completely different players but two styles that complement each other well, the classic 'big strong one and fast little one' pairing. One classic example in recent international football is that of Emile Heskey and Michael Owen for England. Heskey was unpopular with England fans for not scoring as many goals as the centre forward position might warrant (just 7 goals in 62 games), but his value to the England team overall made him a must pick for six different England managers.

Emile Heskey

Heskey is, in many ways, the typical centre forward for a typical 4-4-2 line-up, one whose qualities and strengths fit it perfectly. He has pace and physical strength in abundance and is a very hard-working player, one who will, as coaches love to see, 'run all day'. He was a player mindful of his defensive responsibilities as well as his attacking ones and who is, in the words of Paul Wilson from *The Guardian*, 'a blunt instrument with which to bludgeon defences.' Above all, and, unusually, perhaps, for a striker, he is unselfish and looks to hold the ball up in order to draw opposing defenders in, leaving space in their wake for other players to take advantage of and score. Few benefitted more than his long-time England teammate Michael Owen, a player who was everything Heskey was not. What Heskey most definitely was, apart from all the other qualities already listed (now you begin to understand why so many of the game's most renowned coaches liked him as a player) was honest, busy and reliable, someone who understood his role in the team and was able to perform it to the very best of his abilities.

Honest, busy and reliable. Ideal qualities for any player within a 4-4-2 system.

One of the England managers who put his faith in Heskey was Fabio Capello, a coach who espoused the 4-4-2 formation during his time in Italy. Capello enjoyed a lot of success at AC Milan where he succeeded another devotee of that system, Arrigo Sacchi.

Arrigo Sacchi

He'd built one of the great Milan sides, one based around what may well be the finest back four ever to have graced world club football: Franco Baresi, Alessandro Costacurta, Mauro Tassotti and Paolo Maldini. They were the mainstay of his European Cup winning Milan side in 1989, one that carved itself a place in footballing immortality by beating Real Madrid 5-0 in the second leg of their semi-final that April; the 4-4-2 formation he selected helped his side to simply overwhelm their opponents and included the considerable talents of players like Bernd Schuster, Emilio Butragueño and Hugo Sanchez. Real Madrid were neither players nor a side that ever expected to lose a match, least of all an European Cup semi-final. This was, after all, a competition which, up to then, Real Madrid had won six times, and they were beyond desperate to win again, having not lifted the trophy since 1966. To be so comprehensively beaten would have been a humiliating experience for them. And so close to the final, where their opponents would likely be Romanian side FC Steaua Bucureşti, a team they would have been confident of defeating. You might, therefore, be assuming that Milan's performance in that second-leg game was as near to perfect in terms of the football played as it is possible to get.

It was. And this, remember, was 4-4-2. The formation for the cautious, the methodical, the organised. The opposite to socialist or Total Football. This is football where every player knew his place and stuck to it rather than assuming the role and position of someone else. Sacchi himself said when describing both his coaching ethos and that of 4-4-2, 'Many believe that football is about the players expressing themselves. But that's not the case...the player needs to express himself within the parameters laid out by the manager.' It doesn't mean the football can't be enjoyable to watch. It was. But comparing the Brazil side of 1958 and 1962 (and, ultimately, 1970) to Sacchi's at Milan from 1987 to 1991 was like comparing Michelangelo's David to something by contemporary sculptor Henry Moore. Both will be regarded, undoubtedly, as great works of art. Yet one piece will always get more admirers than the other, simply because it will be regarded as more pleasing to the eye, more beautiful (like 4-2-4), whereas the other will be seen as of its time, contemporary and relevant but not always as a thing of beauty (4-4-2).

Players have to work hard to make the 4-4-2 formation effective. There are no hiding places, no room for indulgences. All four midfielders are expected to support both the defence and attack, their athletic prowess and stamina as valuable an asset to the team as their overall technique. Midfield players are now judged on how far they run during a game. One sign of just how much the physical abilities and stamina of the modern-day player are now valued is the immediate availability of in-game statistics which readily show just how far a player has actually run during a match, with one survey showing that the average distance run in any one game by a professional footballer was 13 kilometres (around 8 miles).

Unsurprisingly, this is the average distance that was covered by a midfielder with strikers and defenders averaging around 'only' 9 to 10 kilometres per match. As someone in the game once confided in me, '... they used to take athletes and turn them into footballers. Now they take footballers and turn them into athletes.'

Sacchi's legacy at Milan was eight titles in all, including one Serie A and two European Cups. Little wonder that, when he took over at the helm in 1991, Capello did little to change the way the team had played, sticking to the 4-4-2 system and making minimal changes to the team. One concession he did make was to replace the ageing Carlo Ancelotti with 20-year-old Demetrio Albertini. This was a tactical masterstroke on Capello's part, with Albertini swiftly developing into the complete midfielder, one full of stamina, power and pace (all of which was beginning to disappear from Ancelotti's game); these were essential qualities for any player playing one of the roles of central midfield in a 4-4-2. He was also, and here is another key quality for those players, extremely versatile, able to play in several midfield positions, which he did, successfully, for both Milan and the Italian national team. Again, strong, all-round physical *and* technical qualities in a player, a combination which has made that phrase 'the complete footballer' a more and more commonly heard one in the game. But does this, or rather, the fact he might be able to run for farther, and for longer, make the modern-day midfielder a better player than, say, a contemporary of 50 or so years ago?

Didi vs Albertini? Who would you rather have in your team?

Capello, therefore, continued the legacy of trophy-laden success that Sacchi had carefully and systematically laid down for him. A player in there, a tweak there. But 4-4-2, always 4-4-2. During his first full season with Milan, 1991/92, he managed something that had never been done before in Serie A, nor since. AC Milan went through an entire league season without defeat. Why? Because his midfield excelled. A total of 74 goals was scored in 34 games whilst they conceded only 21. The uber-critical Italian football media, ready to find a cloud in every silver lining, christened his side as 'The Invincibles', just as their English counterparts would do for Arsenal a decade later when Wenger's side went through the 2003/04 season doing exactly the same thing. Invincibles. It is worth bearing in mind at this point that the plaudits here are for teams that didn't win every game or even set out to win every game. But they sought out not to lose one – and succeeded. That all too subtle difference, again, between wanting to win and wanting to not lose.

Wenger's preferred Arsenal formation for their record-breaking season was also 4-4-2, and, like Sacchi and Capello's Milan sides, built around a solid defence and hard-working midfield combination. The latter central duo, which usually consisted of Patrick Viera and Gilberto Silva, was an outstanding combination of talents: the defensive talents of Silva with Viera's love of joining and supporting the attack, juxtaposing duties and strengths which, when they were brought together, created a fearsome barrier. It was one that would have been, without question, a major topic of discussion for any opposing team in the days leading up to a clash against the London side. How do you stop Viera? How do you get past Silva? Formidable talents, indeed.

Prior to joining Arsenal, Brazilian Silva had been known as 'the invisible wall' in his homeland. This was given to him because his play and presence in a game often went unnoticed as he used his exceptional skills at reading the game to position himself between his two centre backs and the rest of the midfield. As a consequence of his 'invisibility', he was able to anticipate and break up the opposition's attacking moves before they had really gained any momentum or made any forward progress. He was also a player who preferred to use those skills to nullify an opponent's influence by closely shadowing rather than tackling them, preferring to either force them onto their weaker foot, or else to put or run the ball out of play or be hurried into a quick pass, one that might be intercepted by his midfield partner and used as the basis of another attacking move. This meant, unusually, that he had an exceptionally clean disciplinary record for a player in his position. He is expected to physically impose himself both on the game and his opposite number. Silva twice managed to play over 40 games for Arsenal without receiving a single booking. This is a remarkable feat for any player, let alone one whose in-game territory is at the centre of just about everything that happens in a match.

Viera, on the other hand, was a physically competitive player, a reputation that he liked to live up to. This was something which his equally fiery Manchester United counterpart Roy Keane could testify to as Viera once made his presence known pre-match by standing toe to toe with Keane and eye balling him, letting him know, in absolutely no uncertain terms whatsoever, who was 'the boss' on that day. A tactic which, of course, is all part of the role that 'professionalism' plays in the game today, the mind games and on-field sledging included. Yet, to be fair to Viera, he knew and appreciated what his duties as a player were and followed those instructions to the letter. He would have been, no doubt, the perfect signing for a manager such as Lippi with his '... the player needs to express himself within the parameters laid out by the manager' quote. Viera was the complete midfielder. Aggressive, tenacious and incredibly powerful, an athlete in every sense of the word with his muscular build and infinite stamina. Yet he was also a hugely intelligent footballer, one blessed with exquisite ball skills and a radar-like capacity to see a pass. Arsenal and England striker Ian Wright commented on this shortly after Viera's arrival at the club when he said, 'It's been a while since we've had a midfield player who looks at the front man's run first and then looks at other options. He makes dream passes forward, and he's already put me in several times.'

No surprise, therefore, given Viera's sumptuous talents in the game that, when he finally left Arsenal for Italy and Juventus in 2005, the manager responsible for signing him was Fabio Capello. He, like Sacchi and Wenger, was a massive fan of the 4-4-2 system, seeing Viera at the centre of his own midfield, playing alongside another Brazilian, Emerson. He, like Gilberto Silva, was a more 'invisible' defensive midfielder, renowned for breaking down the opposition's play through his effective tackling and exceptional stamina and energy.

In football once you have a proven formula, then there is no need to change it. Viera subsequently moved on again in 2006, joining Inter Milan where his usual central midfield partner was fellow Frenchman Oliver Dacourt; although the two of them would often be part of a three-man midfield at the San Siro with Roberto Mancini's preference for the 4-3-1-2 formation often requiring a second defensive midfielder, Esteban Cambiasso, to join them in the teams 'engine room'.

Although 4-4-2 can be seen as the 'antidote' to the somewhat more spontaneous and free-flowing football of 4-2-4, it still, like that formation, relies upon that strong spine of needing an exceptional goalkeeper, centre half, central midfielder and striker. The vintage Brazil side of the late 50s and early 60s had it with Gilmar, Bellini, Didi and Vava as did Arsenal with Jens Lehmann, Sol Campbell, Viera and Denis Bergkamp. Sacchi's remarkable Milan side in the 1988/89 season, the one that so comprehensively swept Real Madrid aside with that 5-0 win, had a spine of Galli, Baresi, Rijkaard and Gullit. It provides steel-like strength and presence down the centre of the side, a foundation for the rest of the team; balance and strength throughout with balance being that most vital common denominator that teams which successfully play 4-4-2 must have. Because whilst it isn't the most attractive or fluid of formations, it is one of the strongest, one that, when the balance being right, can be devastatingly effective, as Real Madrid would testify. Every outfield player has at least one teammate who can cover him, but it's cover only. This isn't Total Football. They're not slotting in to provide a seamless change on anything other than an emergency basis. It's football's equivalent of getting a supply teacher in. The wide midfielders are covered by their full-backs and vice versa. The central midfielders have each other and are able to support and cover their forwards when attacking as well as their defence when the opposition is on the ball. Thirty-four goals in 406 appearances for Arsenal suggest that, as far as Viera was concerned, he wasn't only able to support his teammates in attack and provide assists galore, but he could also pop up and score when needed.

The complete player? You have to say he was as close to it as you can get. But, again, who would you have in your midfield? Didi or Patrick Viera?

Given its success and popularity in the modern game as well as its adoption and championing by so many of the world's leading clubs and coaches, can 4-4-2 be regarded as the perfect football formation? After all, like all great discoveries and inventions, it took a while (around a century) to evolve and be realised, but once it had, just about every team in the world, never mind 'just' the great and the good played it in one variation or the other. It's the formation that became the benchmark for the world's leading coaches as well as for those coming into the game. Is it as good as it gets, that effective mix of power, strength and pace one that makes it impossible to ignore, let alone question or even, as has been the case in recent years, criticise as being old-fashioned and tactically backward? Former Barcelona and England striker Gary Lineker, a man who not only became one of England's all-time leading goalscorers as a result of playing in a 4-4-2 formation (and, conversely, struggled at Barcelona when he was played on the left-hand side of an attacking trio in a 4-3-3) was swift to criticise 4-4-2 after England had tumbled out of the 2014 World Cup without winning a game, saying, '...I just think it is too big a task for just two central midfield players and once again we were outnumbered...we end up with flat lines and people getting between us. I think we would have been better – and I said this before the tournament – with three midfield players because you've got to give yourself a chance defensively.'

What's even more surprising is that Lineker then goes on to champion 4-3-3, the very formation that not only saw him struggle at Barcelona but also saw Welsh teammate Mark Hughes shipped out to Bayern Munich, unable to adapt or play in any other system than a 4-4-2.

'Personally, I think Roy [Hodgson] got it wrong. The system that suits this kind of England better, with the lack of experience in it, is probably a 4-3-3.'

So advocating a system that relatively inexperienced players are not so familiar with playing is the solution, and at a World Cup? It should be noted at this point that, with his career focusing on television and lucrative commercial opportunities, Lineker has likely never even considered coaching the game, at any level. You'd like to think that, if he did so, he'd practice what we preached and pick a side and formation that was anything but the 4-4-2 he was so comfortable playing in. Yet now, from the safety of a TV studio, he seems all too ready to criticise successful and respected coaches, such as Roy Hodgson, who have long had it as their formation of choice. Yet Lineker is not alone in his condemnation of 4-4-2. With 4-2-3-1 (see final chapter) set to be 'the' formation of choice as far as the early part of 21st-century football is concerned, its critics have been vocal and numerous, and its effectiveness questioned.

So why is 4-4-2 in the dock? Let's look at its strengths again.

Firstly, it's adaptable with both strength and width in midfield. Think again to that midfield four at Arsenal that comprised Patrick Viera and Gilberto Silva in the middle with the pace, trickery and goal-scoring threat (134 league goals between them during their time at Arsenal) of Freddie Ljungberg and Robert Pires in the wide positions. Are the critics saying a midfield of that calibre would struggle in the modern game, find it difficult to compete against a team with an extra man in midfield? Who's going to tell Patrick Viera that he wouldn't be able to compete in the modern game in the way he did when he was at his peak? Or Frank Rijkaard? Go on, help yourself if you don't think they could. I'm not stopping you.

Secondly, there is its balance in attack. Having two strikers who complement each other in the ways already outlined means that the front line has extra support, that the two forwards selected in the team can compete together without needing to wait for support from the midfield, that, when it comes, it is an addition to the team's attacking armoury rather than the ingredient that it can't work without.

Thirdly, it is a formation that allows for a great deal of in-game flexibility. The two central midfielders can be considered and played as an extra pair of defenders, or the two full-backs can be regarded as an extra pair of attackers. Look at Gareth Bale of Real Madrid and Wales. He started his career as a defender, a left back, but, with his pace and dribbling skills, he was given licence to push forward and attack from that position by Harry Redknapp, his manager at the time. Tottenham's 4-4-2 formation gave Bale the freedom and licence to do that with his defensive position being covered whenever he joined the attack by the side's left-sided midfielder. Simplicity itself. A player moves forward, a player moves back. But the overall shape of the team remains the same. Did Real Madrid make Bale, at the time of writing, the most expensive player in the world because they valued his attributes as a left back? Of course not. He now occupies the left-sided role in a three-pronged attack that includes Cristiano Ronaldo and Karim Benzema. Would he be there if he hadn't been part of this Tottenham side or had a coach who didn't make the very best of that flexibility 4-4-2 gave them? Of course he wouldn't.

4-4-2 can also allow a little variation in its composition. Rather than, for example, the conventional two lines of four (four defenders, four midfielders), one of the central midfielders can drop back to a point just ahead of his back four whilst the other can move forwards to patrol the area of the pitch just behind the two strikers, or 'the hole' as it has become known throughout the game, with the two wide midfielders remaining in their original positions. This stretches the centre of the midfield, giving more obvious and immediate cover in both defence and attack and is known as 'the diamond formation' or 4-4-2 diamond because of the shape the midfield then resembles if seen from above.

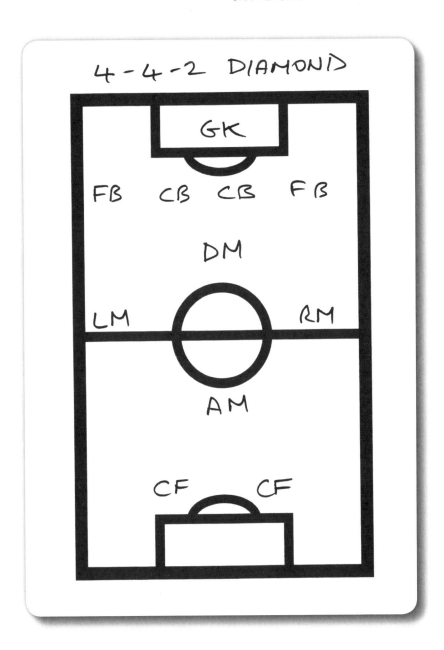

During the 2014 World Cup it was utilised by the Netherlands' coach Louis van Gaal in some matches; Nigel de Jong provided the defensive cover at the rear of the diamond with Wesley Sneijder sat at its tip, tucked in just behind the attacking pair. Van Gaal, who was appointed as coach of Manchester United after the 2014 finals, began his tenure with the English club by experimenting with a 3-5-2 formation, one that he hoped, with the extra man in midfield, would not only help them dominate possession but also ease the pressure on a defence that many see as being weak and ineffective, especially given the solidarity of some of the clubs more conventional back fours in recent years.

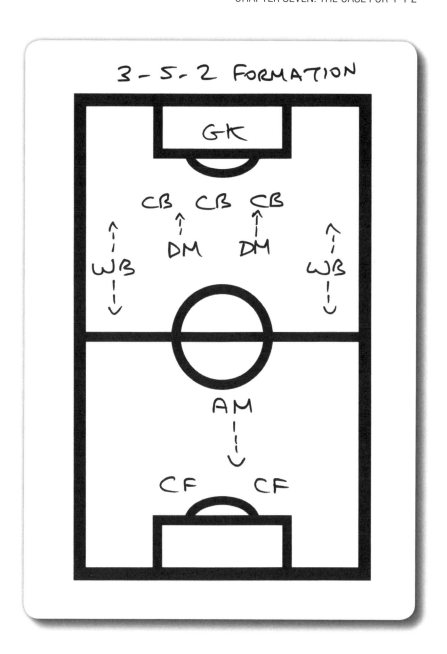

It was effective to a point, with the teams attacking potency suffering as a result. And, whilst reverting to a 4-4-2 formation will see that perceived weak defence of United's be put under more pressure than it previously had, it does allow them, with the formation's flexibility, many more attacking options, not least one that should allow van Gaal to play a midfield diamond, if he chooses, with the likes of Radamel Falcao, Robin van Persie and Wayne Rooney available to slot into any one of those attacking positions.

If there is, or was, such a thing as a 'fashionable' formation to play in the modern game, then those that have five men in midfield, the 4-5-1, 3-5-2 and 4-2-3-1, are the examples for the new age of progressive coaches and tactical thinking to follow. Advocates of same will cite some compelling reasons in favour of having that extra man in midfield. Extra cover for your defence, dominance of play and possession as well as the ability to stifle, by sheer weight of numbers, any attacking potency your opponents might offer with that 'spare' man in the midfield. And yet, as van Gaal discovered at Old Trafford, old habits amongst professional footballers die hard, and, in the English game at least, especially in those divisions below the Premier League, the dearth of technically adept players in favour of those that have been coached to do all of the things that the English games clutches so close to its proud little chest remain dominant. Passion, energy, commitment, blood, sweat and effort. This means that there is no room or scope for tactical sophistication, and, as a consequence, 4-4-2 remains king because it was what every player is brought up to understand and, crucially, what he most easily understands.

It is, therefore, far too early to write off 4-4-2 as easily as some people have been doing, and, as Jonathan Wilson said in an article for *The Guardian* in 2010, '...let players do what comes naturally'. Same goes for coaches. After all, if a side has two formidable centre forwards in its squad, why disrupt that effectiveness by switching to a five-man midfield and either dropping one of those forwards altogether or, as was the case at Norwich City, relegated from England's Premier League in 2014, playing one of your two central strikers in an unfamiliar and, for him, ineffective role in midfield? All because, as a coach, you feel compelled to select a five man midfield in order not to lose the game.

It comes down, yet again, to that subtle difference in footballing philosophies that we have already discussed more than once: Is your priority as a football coach to send out your team to win a match, or is it that you select one with a priority of not losing one? 4-4-2 is, without doubt, a formation that has come about and been developed to win games as illustrated by some of the world's most successful and respected coaches who favour it. For as long as coaches have favoured possession over risk, it has been temporarily supplanted in the hearts and minds of many by the more fashionable modern formations, ones that favour safety in numbers over attacking risk, but they will eventually, not unlike that famous Emperor and his new clothes, be seen for what they are: cautious, sterile and, ultimately, nowhere near as exciting as the cut and thrust of 4-4-2.

Will a team playing with a conventional 4-4-2 system win the 2018 World Cup? Don't bet against it. But don't write it off either.

CHAPTER EIGHT:
TOTAL FOOTBALL

But, wherever you looked in the Dutch side, you saw talent in abundance. Haan, Krol, van Hanegam, Rep – they were frightening, they were Hungary reborn, they were, without a shadow of a doubt going to win this World Cup.

For those of you who remember it, what is your abiding memory of the 1974 World Cup?

Footballing statisticians will point out that it was the first tournament to feature the 'new' FIFA World Cup trophy, the original Jules Rimet trophy having been awarded to Brazil permanently following their success in Mexico four years previously. Or that it was a contest that was, finally, beginning to show that world football was no longer about the establishment. And that is a point worth emphasising. *Fußball-Weltmeisterschaft 1974* was very good for the good of the game globally as Europe's domination began to show its first signs of waning. England had failed to qualify, knocked at the expense of Poland. Former giants of the game, Hungary, were not amongst the finalists either; neither were Austria, Belgium, Portugal, France nor Spain. On the plus side, East Germany qualified for the finals for the first time, as did a team from Oceania (Australia) and Africa (Zaire). It was a stellar shift away from the old and in with the new.

It was also the first tournament to be fully televised in colour. Perfect timing, as the footballing world fell in love with the team made for colour television, the one that was sporting the bright orange shirts rather than the white ones of eventual winners and hosts West Germany. They were the Netherlands, the team that, along with those distinctive orange shirts, also introduced to the watching world the phrase that their style of play would forever become synonymous with.

Total Football.

The Dutch had, up to the 1974 finals, a modest record in international football. At their very first finals in 1934, they'd lost 3-2 to Switzerland in the first round whilst, four years later, they'd also fallen at the first stage, this time losing 3-0 to Czechoslovakia. Two tournaments, two games, two defeats; a very inauspicious start to their hopes and ambitions on football's world stage. So much so in fact, that the Dutch FA declined FIFA's invitations to participate in both the 1950 and 1954 finals, thus missing out on playing in qualifying matches that might at least have given their players a taste of life on a bigger stage and given their FA something to build on, even if they hadn't led to them reaching the final stages of those tournaments. They eventually made their return to the World Cup in 1958 and for each of the next three finals after that, playing a total of 19 qualifying matches over that time but winning only seven, their best chance of qualification coming in 1970 where a 2-0 defeat to Bulgaria eventually proved both terminal to their hopes as well as key to their opponents who eventually won a tight qualifying group two points clear of the Dutch and just one ahead of runners-up Poland. Although they might not have suspected it at the time, these were signs of much better things to come for those two nations as far as the next finals were concerned.

The Dutch national team in 1974

For the Netherlands to succeed at international level they clearly needed an inspirational coach to help them fulfil their ambitions, which, post-1970, would merely have been to qualify for West Germany in 1974. A succession of international teams in Europe had come to the footballing fore due to the influence and vision of their visionary coaches over the previous few decades. Pozzo with the Italians, Sebes with Hungary and Ramsey with England were just three examples. The Dutch now needed to find one of their own. As it was, they got lucky twice, finding not just a coach who would turn them from European minnows into world giants of the game but a player as well – a prodigy of that coach who went on to be more famous in the game than the coach who launched both his club and international career would ever be.

The coach was Rinus Michels. He was born in Amsterdam in 1928, a short walk away from the stadium where local side Ajax played their league games. Unsurprisingly, he soon became a big fan of Ajax; the relationship between the boy and the team was eternally sealed when, on his ninth birthday, he was given a pair of football boots as well as an Ajax shirt. Two years later he became a junior member of the playing staff at Ajax, eventually going on to make his senior debut for the club in 1946, one year after the cessation of hostilities in World War II.

Rinus Michels

His debut could not have gone any better. Michels was drafted into the Ajax side to play in a league game against Den Haag. Ajax won that game 8-3 with five of the goals coming from Michels. Unsurprisingly, Ajax ended that season as divisional champions, going one step better the following season by winning the Dutch national championship, with Michels a prominent and important member of their playing squad. Ironically, at that time, and for a man whose technical awareness and skills as a coach were ultimately recognised on a worldwide scale, he was not thought of as a particularly technically-minded player, but rather one who was more readily characterised for his capabilities as a hard-working and physically imposing striker who was particularly good in the air.

He could almost have been English. Luckily for Ajax and for Dutch football as a whole, his coaching methodology was anything but.

Michels took over as coach of Ajax in 1965 when he was still only 37, winning the Eredivisie (Dutch League title) three times between 1966 and 1968, as well as for a fourth time in 1970. He also guided Ajax to the European Cup Final in 1969 where, after knocking out Nuremberg, Fenerbahce, Benfica and Spartak Trnava, they found AC Milan a little too streetwise and experienced in the final, losing 4-1. But lessons had most definitely been learnt, and, when they reached the final of Europe's most prestigious club football tournament again two years later, meeting Panathinaikos at Wembley, they dispatched the Greek side as easily as they had been seen off themselves by Milan. Michels played his favoured 4-3-3 formation in that final, one that saw Dick van Dijk play as the central striker with fellow forward Sjaak Swart playing just off to his right whilst Pier Keizer offered support from the left-hand side, playing almost as an orthodox winger would in a 4-2-4. Good players all and a system that benefitted the star of the show and his team's best player, the enigmatic Johan Cruyff. Although Cruyff was seen as the right-sided member of the midfield trio, he had, in practice, license to roam the attacking third of the pitch at will. Cruyff was playing in the same sort of false number 9 role that Nándor Hidegkuti had done for Hungary a little over two decades earlier at the same stadium, and, to add even more to the irony, in front of the watching Panathinaikos coach who just happened to be another former Hungarian great, Ferenc Puskás.

Johan Cruyff scoring against Argentina during the 1974 World Cup

As a player, Cruyff was peerless at that time and into the middle of the decade. He didn't look like a footballer at all. He was not particularly tall but was pale and slight of frame, almost gaunt in appearance. But woe betide any footballer who saw him as an easy touch for looks can indeed be deceptive. However he might have looked, Cruyff was devastatingly fit, fast and strong, a player with immense technical ability and the sort of in-game vision which sees moves long before any of his teammates, or the opposition, might have done. Cruyff would make runs or play balls into parts of the pitch that seemed peripheral to where the main action was focused only for his positioning to suddenly become a pivotal moment in the build-up to a goal as he mastered the art of arriving in exactly the right place at the right time. In doing so, he'd inevitably drag a phalanx of markers with him, that or, when in possession, leave a previously attentive opponent for dead. One famous example of this occurred when he was playing for the Netherlands in the 1974 World Cup against Sweden. His feint was, now famously known throughout the world as the 'Cruyff turn', meaning that, even as he looked up in apparent readiness to play a pass, he would drag the ball behind one foot with the instep of the other, turning 180 degrees as he did so, before accelerating away at pace, leaving a dazed and confused defender in his wake. Some might regard such behaviour during a game today as arrogance, the sort of showing-off and gamesmanship that should not be tolerated. Yet Cruyff was not a show-off. To him, conceiving such a play and putting it into action came as naturally as playing a 3-yard cross field pass to another player; his skill on the ball was instinctive and always done for the benefit of the team. Michels had long realised that you could not shackle Cruyff into any given formation or position on the field, choosing instead to hand him his shirt and let him get on with things in whichever way he saw fit.

Which is pretty much how Sebes had treated Hidegkuti in his all-conquering Hungarian side. And with good reason. Why on earth would you have a supremely talented player as part of your team, one who can do just about everything with a football, and then look to restrict their influence by expecting them to observe your tactical master plan? Both Sebes and Michels appreciated that you couldn't, and, as far as such footballers were concerned, you just picked them and let them get on with the game.

But, of course, if you have a player like Hidegkuti in your team, or a Cruyff, one given the freedom to roam at will, then there will also be a need for all of that team's other players to be as flexible to him as he was to the game. They'd need to adapt their own game in order to fit in around his movements. If, therefore, Cruyff popped up in the left wing position, then the left winger needed to move away to take up whatever space Cruyff might have left in the side. Similarly if Cruyff fancied a spell playing as the centre forward, then Van Dijk, or whoever the centre forward was in the Ajax or Netherlands side, similarly, had to switch his role, ensuring, as he did so, that every tactical position in the team remained filled and their overall shape was unaffected. One man could be indulged if he was as special a talent as Cruyff, but, in order for that to work, the rest of the side had to work twice as hard in order to fill in for him from the full-backs and central defenders upwards.

This ability to let players easily switch positions and cover for one another all over the pitch had been the basis of the Hungary team's success, the ethos of their all being able to fill in for and support one another on the field leading to Sebes christening it 'socialist football'. So what the Netherlands were doing, primarily to accommodate Cruyff, was hardly new or original. They were merely copying what the Hungarians had already done. But it couldn't be called 'socialist' football anymore, at least, not in western Europe where the merest hint of the word 'socialist' made people look to the east and what lay on the wrong side of the Berlin Wall. No, it would have to be known as something else; another description had to be made for the way in which both the Ajax players and, in time, the Netherlands' players were so easily able to immerse themselves into any role on the pitch and to have total confidence in their ability to do so.

Total confidence. Total Football. It was, as Ajax and Netherlands defender Barry Hulshoff admitted, '...about making space, coming into space, and organising space-like architecture on the football pitch.' It makes it all sound very complicated, but it isn't really. Hulshoff is likening the team to a technical blueprint, to a well-designed machine (how Herbert Chapman, the football coach who only really wanted to be an engineer[49] would have related to this system and Cruyff) where, if one part needs support, it immediately gets it from another with, as a consequence, that assisting part also receiving some from a third part. All completely independent yet with a common focus. Concise, simple and brilliant, it was, and perhaps remains, football as it should always have been played, a shared joy for 11 individuals playing as one. Simplicity itself. Although as Cruyff has since pointed out, that sort of simple football is, as Hungary and the Netherlands both proved, the most beautiful of all, '...but playing simple football is the hardest thing.'

Ajax put Total Football well and truly on the world map when they reached the European Cup Final again in 1972 where, as luck would have it, their opponents were, once again, Italian giants from Milan, although this time in the guise of Inter rather than AC. Back in 1969, Ajax and Cruyff had been given a footballing lesson by Inter's city rivals, losing 4-1. That had been a team that was still finding its feet, however, still learning the play with Cruyff at the centre of all things. Things were different now. Michels who had by now joined Barcelona had passed the torch on to Ştefan Kovács who had fine tuned it with relish, perfecting the system to such an extent that his side's 2-0 win over Inter in that final was, at times, extremely one sided with the Italian's famed defensive discipline and shape torn to pieces by the marauding Cruyff and his teammates. Inter's demise even led to some Italian newspapers to announce the 'death of Catenaccio' the next day whilst Dutch publication *Algemeen Dagblad* went one further, proclaiming that '...defensive football is destroyed.' Some claim, but then this was some side, and one hell of a style of football that they were playing.

With Ajax dominating both Dutch and European club football and, with it, Cruyff becoming one of the leading players in the world, one who

---

49   *See chapter 4*

eventually joined his previous manager at Barcelona in 1973, there was little, if any doubt, as to who the Dutch FA were going to ask (and, in all likelihood, beg!) to take control of the national team for the 1974 World Cup Finals. It had to be Michels.

Michels took the job and was fortunate in one regard: Many of the players who made up the Dutch squad at the finals played for either his old side or their great domestic rivals, Feyenoord, all of whom he would have been more than familiar with including, from Ajax, midfielders Arie Haan, Piet Keizer and, most notably of all, Johan Neeskens. They were collectively familiar with playing alongside Cruyff as well as what was required from them in order for the team to most effectively perform. But then this was an exceptionally gifted squad anyway, with even the players whose clubs were outside of the Dutch league, such as Ruud Geels and Robbie Resenbrink, swift to adapt and 'plug in' to Michels' playing philosophy. The scene was set for Cruyff and Total Football to take the brand to the world stage in order to see just how effective it could be against some of the leading international sides, including, as it turned out, reigning World Champions and masters of the footballing arts, Brazil. The two sides met in Dortmund on 3 July 1974 with, for the winners, a place in the final as their reward.

It was the match that, as the tournament had progressed, everyone had hoped would come about. Brazil were, after all, the absolute masters of the game – three times winners and, like the Netherlands, beholden to a great individual talent in Pelé. Many had hoped that he might have played in these finals, his fifth had he done so, and, at 33, there seemed little reason why he should not. Pelé, however, had retired from international football three years previously and, with his passing into legend, the Brazilian national side seemed to go into collective mourning. Their progress in West Germany certainly lacked the joy of their football four years previously which was a rather unfair label to attach to them. That 1970 side has often been lauded as the greatest that the world has ever seen, a thrilling mix of sublime skills and technique that married those oh-so-precious European qualities of pace and power to produce a side that was, arguably, better than the one which had won the trophy in 1958. But, disappointing or not, they'd got to within 90 minutes of another final with a brand of football that was slightly more functional and rigid, even, on occasion, a little over physical in approach, than that which had been played by previous sides. It was still, nonetheless, one that most people thought would still have enough about it to ensure that they saw off the Dutch.

West Germany 1974

They were still, after all, Brazil. But then this was the Netherlands, this was Michels, this was Cruyff, Neeskens and Krol. This was Total Football. Brazil's reign as world champions was about to come to an end. Watching the match today, you get the feeling that the Brazilians knew it as they littered the game with hopeful long balls into their opponent's half and a series of niggling fouls, one of which, something that resembled a rugby tackle on Cruyff by Ze Maria, resulted in a series of free kicks to the Dutch side who were making great inroads into a defence that was prone to leaving gaps. It soon became clear, very early on, that there was only ever going to be one winner of this game and that football's torch, held, for so long and so proudly by the Brazilians, was all set to be handed to a new owner. The problem was, at least for most of the footballing world, that the recipients were not going to be the ultimately victorious Dutch side that, eventually and with some ease, saw off a hugely disappointing Brazilian side by two goals to nil.

Total Football had conquered European club football. Now it looked certain to do the same at a World Cup. The Dutch had been glorious throughout, scoring, in their six games leading up to the final, 14 goals whilst conceding only one. Their team and formation, based on the 4-3-3 system favoured by Michels, saw Cruyff at its attacking apex, free to go wherever he wanted with much of the responsibility for covering him going to a player who was almost as prodigiously talented himself, Johan Neeskens, who would, eventually, follow Cruyff to Barcelona.

But, wherever you looked in the Dutch side, you saw talent in abundance. Haan, Krol, van Hanegam, Rep. They were frightening. They were Hungary reborn. They were, without a shadow of a doubt, going to win this World Cup.

Yet where had the world either proclaimed or heard that said about a team before?

Think back, again, to that Hungarian side of the 1950s, the one that, time and time again, provides a ready and obvious reference because, quite simply, so much of what is good about the modern game – players, roles, tactics – originated, one way or the other, from that team, the nation's domestic sides and the legion of talented coaches who worked there. And that included Jimmy Hogan.

They'd been as glorious as the Dutch. As seemingly unbeatable, as revolutionary in style and shape with great players to spare. Not just one or two, but all over the team. The Hungarians had Zoltan Czibor and Jozsef Bozsik; the Dutch had Johnny Rep and Johan Neeskens. Then there was Nándor Hidegkuti and Johan Cruyff, both masters of their arts and players who could play anywhere on the pitch and in any manner they desired, hence, of course, the need for the respective coaches to allow for such an indulgence by ensuring any and all of their other players could slot into place as and when necessary. Yet, for all of that, for all of the similarities between the two sides, for all the majesty of Total Football, it was not foolproof, and it *could* be beaten. Honvéd, if you recall, had been rumbled by Wolverhampton Wanderers, the combination of a soaking wet, if not almost flooded, pitch and the harrying, physical attentions of their players wearing them and their game down. Likewise, in 1954 and the 'miracle of Berne' that had seen West Germany, who had been beaten, if not humiliated, by the Hungarians to the tune of eight goals to three in a group game, reckoned to odds on for a similar thrashing when the two teams met again in the final. Yet, in a game that was played in heavy rain and in similarly heavy conditions, the West German side were able to wear a special stud, developed by Adidas, that gave them a better grip than their opponents. This had initially seemed not to matter as the Hungarians took a two goal lead within the first 10 minutes, goals and early dominance that more than suggested that the Germans were well on their way that second big defeat at the hands of their illustrious opponents.

Except, of course, that turned out not to be what happened at all. Because they'd had found a way to beat them, a way to quietly and nullify the way the Hungarians played. It wasn't pretty and their cause was more than helped by the weather (just as the heavy rain and pitch had suited Wolves against Honvéd), but they did it, they won the game through a combination of dogged defending, tight marking, sheer physical presence and overwhelming superiority in terms of fitness. This was a combination that, when added to the weight of expectation that had been heaped upon the Hungarians' shoulders, was just too much for them. It was a watershed moment in sporting history, the beginning of the end of one footballing dynasty and the dawn of another, one that was certainly less attractive to the eye but which, nevertheless, knew what it took to win football matches and took all steps possible[50] to ensure that they had the best chance of doing so.

Now, 20 years later, the West Germany side found themselves in a similar situation, finalists and underdogs, the team that stood in the way of football's new international darlings and everyone's favourites. The whole world, barring the host nation, wanted the Netherlands to win because of the wonderful football that they played, football the like of which was comparable to Brazil at their best in terms of entertainment and, in terms of style was like the – well, you know what will come next. The Dutch had won their way through to the final on the back of some impressive wins and all-round displays, including three wins against the very best that South America had to offer; for, not only had they beaten Brazil, they'd also seen off Uruguay and Argentina, a side that had travelled to Germany with thoughts of winning the trophy themselves by four goals to nil.

Over and over again the parallels between the Dutch side from 1974 and their Hungarian counterparts from 20 years earlier can be seen. Big wins, lots of goals, enigmatic players, a playmaker with extraordinary talents.

---

50   *The shock at Hungary's unexpected defeat even led to accusations that the German squad may, post-match, have been injected with the stimulant methamphetamine. This came about after a study conducted at the University of Leipzig which, when it was published, was given the name 'Doping in Germany'. Strangely, the finished and published study does not cover the 1954 World Cup.*

And overwhelming favourites to win the final against a West Germany side that had misfired en route to the final. They had, for example, been singularly unimpressive in beating Australia earlier on in the tournament and had even lost one of their group games, that being the historic clash in Hamburg against East Germany. They'd then had the good fortune to enter a final group stage that saw them meet the likes of Sweden and Yugoslavia. The Dutch, meanwhile. had to contend with Brazil and Argentina.

The Netherlands even followed the lead of the Hungarians by scoring an early goal in the final. Back in 1954, Puskás had put Hungary ahead after six minutes. The Netherlands did so in just two minutes here, a goal that summed up their apparent superiority and their football. From kick-off, Cruyff passed the ball back for it to then be passed again, from player to player, at a lazy, walking pace, on 13 occasions before it found Cruyff again (*BBC TV* Commentator David Coleman noting that Cruyff was 'demanding the ball'); the maestro, who had, until that second, been the deepest lying player of the entire Dutch side apart from the goalkeeper, electing to go on a run that left Berti Vogts for dead, ending only when he was fouled by Uli Hoeness. Neeskens converted the penalty and the Dutch were on their way. Eighty seconds of the game had elapsed, and they had not only scored but, at the same time, given the watching millions a textbook lesson in what Total Football was all about. That opening move had seen orange-shirted players heavily infiltrating the Germany right-hand side where, you suspect, Vogts had been singled out as slow and susceptible to pace with, as the move advanced, Cruyff literally playing in the role of sweeper, directed operations from the back before his decisive and deadly run forward.

Stunning stuff. But not enough for them to win the tournament as, again, a West Germany side came back from behind in a final to win. They had done so in 1954, they had even come back from behind on two occasions in the 1966 final to England, just as they had in the quarter-final four years later against the same opponents, 2-0 down and, it seemed, out of the tournament. There is a popular football saying in England: 'Never write off the Germans.' It's one which has been proved, as far as football is concerned, to be correct time and time again. This had been the case in 1954; they'd found a way of beating the Hungarians. Now they'd done the same in 1974, beating the equally fancied Dutch. How? Put it down to sheer tenacity and self-belief, a belief that they were going to win that was unshakable. But, of course, they could not win on that faith alone; they also had to do something which countered the Dutch play. They did this by stretching the game as much as possible, literally taking on the Dutch at their own game. Müller was, therefore, seen operating on the flanks whilst Vogts, a right back, started making runs forward with the ball in the manner of a midfielder. And the Dutch struggled to cope. All too often they had won games as teams struggled to cope with how they were playing; now, in West Germany, it appeared that they were playing a side that disregarded that and focused on what *they* were going to do. Hence those forward runs from Vogts and the likes of Müller and Grabowski popping up all over the pitch. The West Germans were, for one day, and one day only, playing the Dutch at their own game, and it worked. This was the fundamental weakness in the Dutch system that the Germans had discovered – it needs an extraordinary amount of self-discipline to work effectively.

Total Football might look spontaneous. But in reality, it isn't. It demands much of its players, not least for them to have very high technical capabilities, something which wasn't lacking in the Dutch players. Where they and the system did break down was their lack of discipline when things started to go against them, something which is perfectly illustrated in the manner by which the Germans scored their winning goal. The move that started it was an interchange of passes on the Dutch left, inside their own half and, you would think, out of danger. But no.

Hoeness and then Overath have three Dutch players around them, all close but none were committing to a challenge. This meant that the overlapping Bonhof, alone and, it seemed, disregarded by the Dutch, had acres of space in which to make a forward run with the ball. The Dutch system was, therefore, torn apart, with no Dutch players, or most of all, no defenders, where they should be. Even when Bonhof played his pass across the area to the waiting and unmarked Müller, the attentions of another four Dutch players were not enough to prevent him from receiving the ball and, anathema to any coach, scoring at the second attempt.

The Netherlands' Total Football had been countered by a team that had exploited its one major weakness – the need for its players to be on their game and all the time. Concentration cannot drop; discipline must remain high. Lose a little of each, and you and your system is in danger of being picked apart, as Germany had shown. It and the 4-3-3 formation that remains its favourite vehicle is a truly formidable one when it is played well. However, the very fact that it makes such high demands of its players means that it is a formation that is seen more and more rarely in the game today, one that only the biggest sides with the best players can look to play, and one that, if it doesn't go to plan, can lead to heavy and unexpected defeats.

This was perfectly illustrated in February 2015 when Atletico Madrid beat Real Madrid 4-0 in a La Liga game. Fellow La Liga teams had, since the season commenced, looked to benefit from Carlos Ancelotti's preferred 4-3-3 formation by exploiting the space down the Madrid flanks that habitually opens up due to their wide forwards reluctance to track back, in this case, Ronaldo and Gareth Bale. Both players, especially Ronaldo, are indulged by their coach as regards having defensive responsibilities, yet the danger of that is little to no cover for the full-backs, both of whom were tormented by the Atletico wide men. With time and space to continually attack, the Atletico's win came as a triumph of pre-match planning and discipline over indulgence, the indulgence in this case being afforded to two players who, between them, cost Real Madrid something like £170 million.

That's a lot of money to pay for players who'd seemingly rather play for themselves and goal-grabbing glory than play for the team. Two players who, for that reason, are nowhere near as complete as footballers as the true master, Johan Cruyff, was.

4-3-3. Potentially, modern football at its very finest. But not without its flaws.

CHAPTER NINE:
SWEEPERS AND SIX-MAN MIDFIELDS

The problem was, as ridiculous as picking a team that didn't contain any strikers sounded, the reasons for doing so made, as far as some were concerned, complete sense. And that was ruthlessly regardless of all the glorious tradition, history and glamour that surround the number 9 and all the great and good purveyors of that position.

A small footnote to the introduction and development of the 4-2-4 formation, if you recall, was that it was the first to be known by its numerical layout – in other words, four defenders, two midfielders and four attackers became, in the language, just that. 4-2-4.

4-4-2 and 4-3-3 followed. Popular formations within the game that were said as they were seen. Long gone, it seemed, were the days when formations were given a name of their own. The Pyramid, the Danubian School, Metodo, WM, WW. Romantic, even, to a certain degree, a little bit scholarly. Exclusive, maybe even a little secretive. That or, in the name, something given a title to cover up the fact that all it was, was a football formation.

But then the Christmas Tree came along.

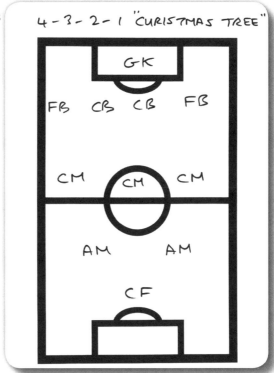

The Christmas Tree formation is the name given to the 4-3-2-1 formation, so titled, as you have probably guessed because, from above, it looks a little like a triangle. A Christmas Tree. Quite why it was never called the Triangle in the first place is beyond this author. Perhaps it has been given its current description because it is so closely linked with former Barcelona and England coach Terry Venables – a formation with a name as comical and irreverent as the public perception of the man most closely linked to it. Yet Venables is not, by any means, the first coach to have played this system, even if we will refer to his use of it with England shortly. Back in 1970, for example, a writer from the English newspaper *The Observer* made reference to it in a report he had written about a game between Crystal Palace and Newcastle, observing that Crystal Palace were '...deployed in a loose 4-3-2-1', and although this appears to have been more by accident than design (the reporter went on to write that it seemed to have happened as the result of '...an extraordinary, almost unprecedented event'[51]) it is, nevertheless, one of the earliest recorded mentions of that specific formation in the British Press.

The triumphant Tottenham team winning the FA Cup with Terry Venables (1st from the left)

---

51   *As written in response to a question in 'The Knowledge' in* The Guardian, *Dec 22 2010.*

One theory, as advocated by Jonathan Wilson in *Inverting The Pyramid,* is that the modern 4-3-2-1 was the tactical creation of Co Adriaanse who, if you recall, we have already come across as a bit of a coaching guru, having reformed and reinvigorated the 3-3-4 formation with FC Porto in 2005. Adriaanse is said to have used 4-3-2-1 at Dutch club Den Haag in the late 1980s. It is with Venables and England, however, where it is most prominently associated. Venables would play the formation and select Alan Shearer as a lone attacker with Peter Beardsley and David Platt tucked in just behind him, then Paul Ince, Paul Gascoigne and Darren Anderton making up the trio behind them in front of a traditional back four. This was the case with the team picked by Venables for the friendly against Denmark in 1994, a side that could have easily switched to a more defensive 4-5-1 (Shearer again the lone attacker with a midfield five of Beardsley, Gascoigne, Ince, Platt and Anderton).

In normal play, however, the 4-3-2-1 sees the middle of those three central midfielders act as the playmaker (Gascoigne) whilst one of the attacking midfielders is given more of a free role. Having this system in place does mean, however, that at least two of the midfielders are going to need to be hugely energetic to cover all the areas of the pitch, from one penalty area to another, which, in Platt and Ince, Venables had. Finally, one of the midfield three also needed to be able to drift to either flank and play as an old-fashioned winger. Here, again, Venables has that option covered with Darren Anderton who was slight, swift and very much able to do just that.

It is not, as can now be seen, a formation where square shapes can be applied into round holes. There is no 'make do and mend' as has been the case with some teams and formations where, in order to make their preferred formation work regardless of whether he has the players to fit into them, a coach will pick the formation first before fitting the players around it. This is what Johan Cruyff famously did with Gary Lineker during his time as coach of Barcelona, playing the centre forward on the right-hand side of his attacking three so he could accommodate Julio Salinas as the lone striker. Was this out of spite, trying to make a point, or, so obsessed with playing 4-3-3, he would do so regardless of where a player's best position on the pitch might be? That is, at least, what Venables did with his 4-3-2-1 formation, he identified it as one he wanted to play then set about playing the best player available in each specific position. It's an approach that seems laughingly obvious but which is not (and Cruyff is not alone in having done this) as common as you might think. Think, after all, how many times have you either said yourself, or heard it from other fans about how they wish the manager would play so-and-so in his 'natural position'?

Another coach who used the 4-3-2-1 formation was AC Milan's Carlo Ancelotti who chose it as the best one to make the best of the attacking talents of Brazilian Kaka, Clarence Seedorf playing alongside him with either Filippo Inzaghi or Alberto Gilardino playing as the main striker. Ancelotti's decision was made with Kaka in mind, and it paid off handsomely, as, during the following 2006/07 season, he became Milan's most important player. For a time he was probably the best player in the world, often dragging, in the manner of Maradona at Napoli, his team through matches on his own in some of their more dogged Champions League games. A notable example is the game against Manchester United in the semi-final, the wonderfully creative make-up of that Milan side completed by the presence of Andrea Pirlo in the midst of the three players behind them. It was, and remains, the most effective and memorable use of the formation to date in football history, one that, not unlike 4-3-3 (not surprising, given the similarities between the two), requires a great deal of flexibility, in terms of position and responsibility, between the more advanced players, not, as it turned out, a problem for Ancelotti's Milan side. He had, after all, Pirlo who was as happy to advance up the pitch to play alongside the striker as Seedorf was to track back and help out with defensive duties.

Andrea Pirlo is another excellent example of a footballer who a coach will select and use as the fulcrum of his team selection, a player who is the focus of much of what his team does on the pitch. In other words, he is another of that rare and special breed: the playmaker.

It's an overused phrase in the modern game, one that is casually applied to any midfield player with a vague appreciation of the game, especially if he just happens to wear the number 10 shirt. The truth, however, is rather different. It is a hugely specialist role for a player who is expected to control the flow of a team's attacking play, the one whose involvement in the build-up is pivotal. He has to possess not only exceptional ability at seeing and playing a pass – of any distance – but also have great vision and be someone who can read a game as it is being played. He needs to know, almost instinctively, what is going to happen and which players are going to be in a certain area of the pitch at any given time. And not only his own, but that of the opposition.

Andrea Pirlo about to do something beautiful with a football

Such abilities are rare in today's game, which is why the role is not only a specialised one but also an overused one. In the case of Pirlo, however, its usage and description of what he does for his team is spot on.

Paradoxically, the more the game quickens up in terms of how vital pace is seen as an attacking weapon of choice now, with games being played at a greater overall tempo as a result, the more important the playmaker's role has become. He can, in an instant, change that tempo, change it because, in the frenetic and physical modern game he always seems to have, or be able to find the time and space on the ball that no other player can.

The great playmakers can, quite literally, take a pass, put their foot on the ball, stop and stand still, surveying the field of play as a general would a battle before, with one incisive pass, completely changing the direction the game might be taking, something TV commentators often allude to when they note that balance or the mood of the match has changed. More often than not, that is down to the playmaker.

Pirlo is what is known as a deep-lying playmaker, someone who operated from a quite deep position on the pitch, usually as one of the two midfielders in a contemporary 4-2-3-1 formation. This puts them in what first appears to be a defensive role, sat just ahead of the back four and cover for same. Yet, in that area of the pitch they are able to find more time and space to have on the ball in order to dictate the moves of the whole team through their passing and reading of the game. Those passing skills will include the unerring ability to hit a 40-yard-plus ball right at the feet of an advancing teammate in what at first might appear to be a long hit-and-hope clearance from defence but which is, in fact, anything but. There is a difference between a ball knocked long and high out of defence and one hit with precision to a teammate, the playmaker being the player who makes that difference. A vital difference, too, as it's one that, all too often, will result in a goal or, at the very least a goal-scoring chance or even a penalty as the player in receipt of the ball advances onto a back four caught out by the scope and audacity of the playmaker's part in proceedings.

These players are revered in Italy in the same way the English worship at the feet of a tough and physical number 9. The Italians refer to deep-lying playmakers as 'regista' (director), and no one has performed that task better, for and in Italy, and, quite probably in world football over the last few years than Pirlo. He started his career as an attacking midfielder until his then coach at Brescia noted that, although Pirlo lacked pace and physical strength, he could read the passing of a game with exceptional clarity. He was, therefore, deployed by Carlo Mazzone into a deeper position on the pitch, one where he could freely utlise these abilities. These included not only the awareness of passes that others couldn't even begin to appreciate, but the technique to be able to play them.

Mazzone had, in an instant, transformed the career of a player who, up until that moment, had been just another professional footballer in Serie A, one of hundreds who occupied the playing level one step down from the superstars. This transformation was noted by Inter Milan who signed him, loaning him back to Brescia for a spell as well as giving him some playing time with Reggina where, again, he impressed in that deep-lying role. This was enough to eventually earn him a move to AC Milan for whom he went on to make over 300 appearances before joining Juventus in 2011, a move and signing that led to Juventus and Italy goalkeeper Gianluigi Buffon commenting, 'God exists! A player of his level and ability...I think it was the signing of the century.'

Pirlo's unique ability and importance came to the fore for Italy during the 2014 World Cup Finals in Brazil. In the game against England he played his part in the opening goal by doing nothing more than selling the English defence an outrageous dummy that saw Daniel Sturridge wrong footed and the English defence looking and running elsewhere, enabling the ball meant for Pirlo to find Claudio Marchisio who, completely unmarked, fired home Italy's opener in their 2-1 win. Marchisio's goal but made by Pirlo, the artist and conductor of the side. Then there is the advanced playmaker, perhaps best positioned just behind an pair of strikers in a 4-3-1-2 or a lone striker in a 4-4-1-1 formation.

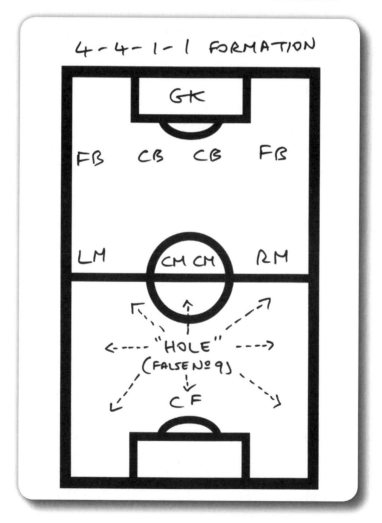

These players don't need to operate as far back in their side's formation as a Pirlo; they have more of a free role and have the appropriate licence to roam at will, not unlike a great cat roaming the Serengeti, forever in search of an opportunity, constantly alert to it. They, therefore, operate in both central attacking positions as well as out wide, either sending in passes (playmakers never 'cross' the ball; it's too arbitrary a phrase. They always pass, stroke, caress or deliver it) to the penalty box for the strikers or cut in themselves, causing some consternation in opposition defences as they do so. They are quick, agile and unpredictable, as well known for scoring goals themselves as they are for sculpting out opportunities for others.

This is far removed from the Pirlo-type role where time, planning and execution is of the essence. These players see time as their foe rather than their friend and want to achieve as much as possible in the shortest time possible using sudden moves, runs, flicks and explosive dribbling. One of the most skilled exponents of this role would have been Diego Maradona, as unpredictable a player as they come, yet one touched with angry genius.

The very nature of their role and the type of player that fills it means that playmakers are more revered in some countries than they are in others. 'Regista' in Italy, or 'Meia atacante' (middle attacker) in Brazil and 'Enganche' in Argentina; in those and other countries, both role and player are revered as sporting gods, much more so than a mere scorer of goals. Where is the art, the beauty in merely putting the ball in the net? The names of the world's great playmakers trip off the tongues from football lovers in countries such as Argentina, Brazil, Italy and Spain like golden syrup from a spoon. Didi, Socrates, Baggio, Hagi, Ronaldinho, Michael Laudrup, Zidane, Messi. Yet, in other countries, they are regarded as an ill-afforded luxury because of their supposed lacking of more important qualities, such as being able to track back, to cover their man, tackle, win balls in the air and run themselves into the ground. These are important qualities, of course, and every team needs a player or two with those in abundance, but at the expense of an artist? No great object of beauty was built without people with shovels, but it wouldn't even have been conceived without an architect. The great sides need both the man with the shovel and the architect, and it is folly to suggest otherwise, that the latter are a luxury. Imagine football without any of the names just listed?

How dull it would be.

Another specialist position within a team, one that merits its own inclusion, is that of the sweeper, or, as they are known in Italy, the 'libero'.

Simplistically, the sweeper can be referred to as someone who provides defensive cover rather than, as just discussed, attacking support. They can also be deep lying, playing just in front of the back four, or, if necessary, just ahead of the goalkeeper. Their presence is apparent in teams that line up in either a 1-3-4-2 formation or 4-1-3-2 (or 5-3-2/ 4-1-4-1); they're akin to a ball-playing centre back who, as the name suggests, 'sweeps up' the ball if the opposition manages to penetrate the defence. As such, and as the formation permutations suggest, his is a more fluid position, and he may not have specific man-marking or zonal responsibilities and will, more often than not, be comfortable on the ball, able to bring it out of defence if required and to pick and find a pass. The sweeper rarely, if ever, lumps the ball 50 yards upfield, especially if it means losing possession; to him, possession is everything. And, for that reason, it is a demanding position, one that requires a very special player to fulfil it. One such player was England captain Bobby Moore. He was a centre half by trade, yet, when you consider the qualities he had as a player, he was so much more than that, something which his former teammate and West Ham (amongst others) Harry Redknapp rightly claims in his book *A Man Walks Onto A Pitch*,[52] saying, '...I don't think any English central defender played the ball out of the back in quite the same way until Bobby came along. Centre halves were all about heading it and kicking it clear...he was the antithesis of the English centre half really. Is he quick? No. Can he head it? No.'

Imagine a playmaker, maybe one of those listed earlier, playing either in, just behind, or in front of his back four. That's the sort of player the sweeper needs to be. Calm, intuitive, disciplined and at ease with the ball at his feet. Moore was that sort of player, one who never ran if he didn't have to, never headed the ball if he didn't have to and didn't tackle if he didn't have to. Although on one occasion when he had to make a tackle, it was as beautiful a sight to behold as any 40-yard pass, goal-bound volley or sweetly hit free kick. The game in question was England versus Brazil in the 1970 World Cup; the man in possession was Jairzinho, running at the England defence at speed and with deadly intent, England stretched as they have been hit on the break with players struggling to get back into possession.

Moore doesn't commit to the tackle. In fact, he does exactly the opposite to what you might expect him or any defender to do, he tracks back ahead of Jairzinho, letting the deadly Brazilian winger advance into the England penalty area. Yet he is alert, eyes fixed on the ball, concentration and focus never wavering, waiting for the perfect moment to make his move, oblivious to the fact that, with every step Jairzinho makes, he is nearer the England goal. Then, swiftly, precisely, it is done. Moore wins the ball cleanly, stopping Jairzinho in his tracks, but that is only the beginning of his defensive concerto. For he now strides away from the scene, ball at his feet, space around him to progress and, after a couple of regal strides, he plays the perfect pass to a teammate

---

52   *Ebury Press (2014), p.75.*

before strolling back to his defensive position. England eventually lost the game 1-0, but the fact that so many of the Brazilian team made for Moore, congratulating, and, in the case of Pelé, embracing him at the final whistle speaks volumes of their respect and admiration for him. He may have been born an Englishman, but he could have played for, and won, 100 caps for any international side in the world. Was he a centre half? No, I agree with Harry Redknapp. He was so much more than that; he was a playmaker who operated in the defensive third of the field and was, for a supposed centre half, one of the first and greatest sweepers to play international football.

The role of sweeper both in the modern game and throughout its history is rarely seen and played. If it is, it makes demands, not just of the player in that position, but of those around him, all of whom will need to be aware of when and where he might be on the pitch at any given time, such is his relative freedom to roam and adapt their own game accordingly. It's, therefore, a specialised position that demands a special player to fulfil it, one like centre half-turned-sweeper Bobby Moore, but also players like Franz Beckenbauer, Franco Baresi and Ronald Koeman, the latter described by many as an 'attacking defender'. A sweeper, in other words, a player who brings the ball out of defence, with ease and confidence and is as comfortable with, if not more so, making a pass or dictating a pattern of play as he is clearing the ball into the top of the stands or taking out a opposing striker. As the modern game continues to evolve, however, with some coaches choosing to play three central defenders at the back in a 3-5-2, the position of sweeper may yet become a more and more popular option again, especially with the current trend in the game of valuing possession and retention of possession above just about anything else.

Franz Beckenbauer playing against Czechoslovakia in 1973

Booby Moore, winning 1:0 against Germany in 1965

3-5-2 is not only an effective way of retaining possession, but it is also a very good formation to have if you want your team to be swiftly able to switch from defence to attack. Room for a sweeper comes in that back row of three, nominally all centre halves. Traditionally, their defensive 'brief' would have been to mark the opposing two forwards with the full-backs looking after the wide midfielders/wingers. In other words, the right back is responsible for the left-sided midfielder/winger, the two centre backs are responsible for the two opposing strikers and the left back looks after the right-sided midfielder/winger. Simple man-marking responsibilities. But wait a minute. If one team is playing five players at the back, that leaves one of the central defenders leftover; he has, literally, no one to pick up, no man-marking responsibilities as such. He is, in effect, a spare man. He could, therefore, operate as a sweeper, have a roaming brief to patrol right along the back four, or even acting as that player who operates just behind it, a final defensive barrier.

Denmark are an example of an international side that played with this system, one that allowed Morten Olsen to sit just ahead of his goalkeeper with the two more conventional centre halves, Soren Busk and Ivan Nielsen, just ahead of him with Frank Arnesen and Jesper Olsen operating as wingbacks. The latter two, in truth, played more like conventional wingers which often left Denmark's defence stretched. But that was the reason that Martin Olsen was there in the first place, to provide that extra cover and insurance along with the two centre backs, together with Jens Jørn Bertelsen who operated as a central defensive midfielder. Morten Olsen's effectiveness in the sweeper role (and that of the position as a whole) was perhaps best demonstrated when Denmark faced West Germany at the 1986 World Cup.

The Danes' first goal in their 2-0 win came when Olsen, who'd just casually strolled over the halfway line with all the intent of a man inspecting the flower beds in his garden, took a pass and, with a swift change of pace, charged, ball at feet, straight into the heart of the West Germany penalty area, being fouled in the process, with Jesper Olsen scoring from the resultant penalty.

The heart and mind of the *libero*, calm and assured in defence but able to switch, in an instant, into a marauding, attacking player from whom numerous chances and goals can be created.

3-5-2 was also preferred and has since been advocated as the best formation for England by their former coach Glenn Hoddle. He famously made the switch to playing three at the back during his time in charge, something which resulted in equal measures of praise and condemnation from those who were more used to seeing a standard 4-4-2 employed by their national side. Their argument was that 4-4-2 was the best and only way for England to play. This, of course, disregards the fact that England weren't utilising that system when they won their sole World

Cup in 1966! Hoddle didn't agree, seeing his faith in both the 3-5-2 system and his players ability to play it. It paid off spectacularly when his England team, with Gareth Southgate playing the sweeper role, got the draw they needed in Italy in a qualifying match for the 1998 World Cup. Hoddle had, ever since taking charge of England, been looking to get his side play unlike any that had gone before. This meant keeping possession and building their attacks from the back, patiently and with purpose rather than a continued barrage of long balls to the front two. It was as good an England performance as there had been in recent years, one that, from a point of view of the tactical acumen and discipline showed, has probably never been replicated since that day in Rome by any England side. Hoddle has never lost his faith or commitment to that type of football, not only having enjoyed a modicum of success with it himself at England but also having seen how successful it had been for both club teams in Italy as well as the Italian national side. He championed 3-5-2 as a very real option for England coach Roy Hodgson in Brazil, citing, again the modern-day thinking of retaining possession as one of its benefits.

Hoddles claim in Brazil was simple. 'We need to pack the midfield more and provide more options when we have the ball whether it's a 4-3-3, a flexible 4-5-1 or even the bold 3-5-2 the Italians have done, which is something I used myself as England manager.' Bold, maybe in England to both players and supporters. Even at the time of writing, over 16 years since Hoddle's time as England coach came to an end, he is still regarded as something of a maverick in that country as a coach for his methods and thinking, just as he was as a player – just 53 international appearances in a decade showing just how much either he, or, more likely, the type of footballer he was, continues to be regarded in that country. As for the 3-5-2 formation, even the introduction of it by one of the world's foremost and respected coaches to one of the world's biggest and most successful club teams resulted in failure when the

Dutch Louis van Gaal attempted to implement it at Manchester United soon after he took over at Old Trafford in the summer of 2014. One of most vocal and foremost critics, ex-Manchester United and England full-back Paul Parker, a former manager of Chelmsford City, Welling United and Folkestone Invicta said, '...his insistence on 3-5-2 and playing at a slower tempo is a complete rejection of the identity Sir Alex Ferguson so carefully and brilliantly constructed at Old Trafford. The club has lost touch with its core identity this season...but Manchester United do not have that under Van Gaal. Perhaps the most famous identity in British football has been obscured. They don't play with urgency, there are no flying wide wingers, they are not a team I would say I want to watch very much. There is no thrill with United at the moment.

'The Premier League has never been about 3-5-2. When I first played in the First Division with QPR in 1987-88 we played a 3-5-2 but that was for strategic defensive reasons and flooding the midfield. It was a slow, deliberate approach. But Manchester United have always been about high tempo. When you think of the club's most successful sides, teams that have won titles and achieved at the highest level, they have played at a high tempo. The way they play at the moment is foreign to United fans.

'You can't go away to QPR and play with three at the back – it is a surrender. It says you want to contain and are happy with a draw. It is not a positive approach. Teams who win the league play at pace – the tempo is quick, with players of high technical ability keeping the ball under control. United have moved away from that model and have even added a long-ball element to their play. You wouldn't think you'd play long ball in a 3-5-2, but they have been doing so increasingly.'[53]

---

53   *From Yahoo Sport/www.yahoo.com, January 15th 2015.*

Parker's apparent dislike of 3-5-2 is unusual when you consider that, as part of England's 1990 World Cup squad, he was part of a line-up that included three central defenders, a sweeper and wingbacks (he was one of them). This system was, according to the stories circulating out of the England camp at the time, one demanded by the England players after a disappointing 1-1 draw in their opening fixture against the Republic of Ireland. England had certainly lined up with their own tried and over tested 4-4-2 formation for that game, one that had seen Robson withdraw mercurial winger Chris Waddle, a rarity amongst England players in that his career included a successful period spent playing abroad, in his case, for Olympique de Marseille, with the aggressive, shaven-headed figure of Steve Bull. The latter was very much the characteristic old-fashioned number 9 who had spent his entire long career, bar just the one game, playing outside the top flight of English football.

Had English football regressed so much that Robson felt the need to bring on a lower league bruiser for someone who'd won three consecutive Ligue One titles in France and who would, in time, play in a European Cup Final? It seemed that way. Waddle was, like so many of his contemporaries, a player who was far more valued and respected on the European continent than he had ever been in his home country. In 2003, former Arsenal, Barcelona and France legend Thierry Henry named Waddle in his all-time footballing 11. Praise indeed. Henry might also have been recalling the removal of Waddle for Bull in that match when he went on to comment, 'The FA sit on their backsides and do nothing tournament after tournament after tournament. Why don't they listen? Why don't they look at other countries and ask 'how do they keep producing talent?' We coach talent out of players. We lack so many ideas and it is so frustrating. The amount of money in our league is frightening and all we do is waste it on rubbish ideas. We kid ourselves thinking we have a chance if we keep the tempo up. We can only play one way and it is poor. You can't go on playing football and hoping to win trophies playing a hundred miles an hour and putting teams under pressure for 90 minutes. You've got to be able to play slow, slow, quick and we can't do it.'[54]

England, under both Robson and Hoddle showed signs of moving forward with that choice of 3-5-2, with Mark Wright playing as the sweeper under Robson. It worked. The predictable football played against the Republic of Ireland – long balls, plenty of running and effort – was replaced with the more considered football that 3-5-2 demanded in their next game against the Netherlands. That ended in a 0-0 draw with England dominating the match. Same team, different approach, one that saw them lose on penalties to West Germany in a thrilling semi-final. No England team has been as successful since. Is it a coincidence that it all went right for them because they, finally, changed their approach, confident enough to play a new system as well as having a coach who believed his players could rise up to the challenge? Most England fans would like to think not, which begs the question as to why, short of a couple of brief dalliances under Venables and Hoddle (both coaches who were never really trusted or liked by the English footballing establishment) England have never tried 3-5-2 again? Why, for all its success in 1990 and the part he played in that team, someone like Parker ('...three at the back? It is a surrender.') is so against it now especially at a team like Manchester United, one that has access to the best players, the best coaches and the best facilities in the world? They are a team which surely, just as Juventus have shown, could dominate both their domestic and European rivals for years if they played and perfected that formation, such is its proven flexibility and manner in which it can encourage both midfield dominance and possession of the ball, not least through having that 'spare' man at the back to orchestrate things.

---

54   *In conversation with the BBC.*

Yet Paul Parker is not the only critic of 3-5-2. Another former Manchester United and England full-back, Gary Neville, has also commented on Louis van Gaal's attempts to play it at Manchester United from the start of the 2014/15 season, his thoughts on the matter being as scathing as Parkers:

'I'm not a fan of 3-5-2 because centre-backs are the free men and they become the safe option. They play out the back but the tempo too slow. Far too often they are keeping possession and passing backwards.'[55]

Neville is uncomfortable with 3-5-2 because it encourages teams and players to retain possession at the expense of going forward. But what is the point of the latter if possession is easily lost, a particular fault with 4-4-2 if, as often is the case, there is a gap between a midfield that sits deep and an advanced front pairing. Similarly, his negative attitude towards a sweeper-based system and five-man midfield comes at a time when the winners of the 2010 World Cup as well as the 2008 and 2012 European Football Championships had been Spain, the footballing nation whose coaches and players value one thing above all else: possession. So who is right? Parker and Neville with their apparent championing of tactics and formations that are based on discipline and midfield rigidity? Or 3-5-2 and Spain?

Spain were anything but rigid in their approach to the 2008 European Championships. For their first two games against Russia and Sweden, coach Luis Aragones lined them up in a more or less conventional 4-4-2 formation with one of the 'conventional' forwards, David Villa, reaping the rewards of that striker-centric formation with three goals in the two games. For their final group game, however, and, despite the fact they'd already qualified for the knock-out stages, Aragones switched to a

---

55   *From the Manchester Evening News, January 15th 2015.*

4-2-3-1 formation against Greece, choosing to match his opponents' numbers in midfield and, with technically superior players, win the battle for possession that would be key to both the match and the result.

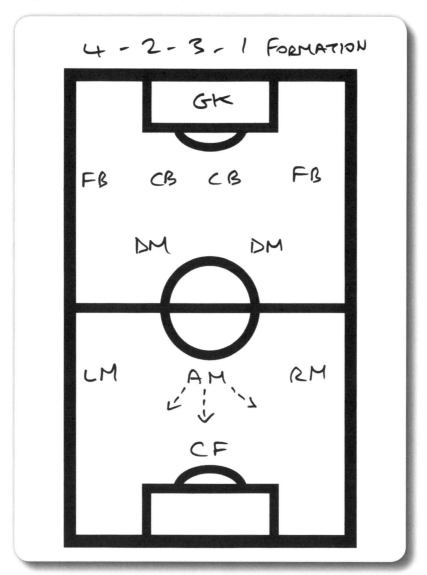

MAPPING **THE PITCH**

This turned out to be exactly what happened, as, with both Xabi Alonso and Cesc Fabregas making their first starts in the role of deep-lying playmaker and false number 9, respectively, Spain threw off the potentially damaging effect of Greece, taking an early lead to win with second-half goals from Ruben de la Red, the central midfielder whose role it was to shadow and mind the more creative Alonso. Lone striker Daniel Guiza was another player making his first appearance at the tournament.

That win and the introduction of both new players and a line-up to go with it emphasised the flexibility of the Spanish system and its coaching philosophy in general. For Aragones, the game against Greece demanded changes in both formation and personnel in order to best combat their opponents. Greece were a team that would seek to dominate the midfield both in terms of sheer physicality as well as numbers, looking to score a goal on the break. It had served them well at the previous European Championships in 2004 when, against all the odds (and then some), they had won the tournament. They'd done that by playing a strict man-marking system, focusing on stopping other teams from playing, stifling both space and flair by using a flat four in midfield charged with constantly pressing their opponents so that they never got the chance to settle, to make possession work for them. It was, for the most part, stupefyingly dull. But it worked. Aragones knew that if he matched their numbers in the midfield area – and with technically gifted players in abundance – the Spaniards would come out on top, especially with both Alonso and Fàbregas having both grown accustomed to playing in and surviving a similarly congested and physical midfield environment in domestic English football. Both players subsequently shone with Alonso being named man of the match.

Great coaches are never afraid to change formations and personnel, even for just one match. Aragones knew that if he had kept to the 4-4-2 formation in the game against Greece, his midfield would have been smothered out of the game with few or any chances being made for his two strikers. Bringing in Alonso and Fabregas completely changed the picture. Aragones then switched things around again for Spain's quarter- and semi-final clashes, returning to the modified 4-4-2 formation he'd employed in the first two games before, in the final against Germany, changing again, this time playing a 4-1-4-1 with Marcos Senna positioned in between defence and attack. He was, therefore, in the perfect position to receive passes from the Spanish back four which he could then bring out of defence with the option of laying the ball off to either one of a sparkling midfield four which comprised of Andres Iniesta, Xavi, Fabregas and David Silva.

A midfield that was so good and so effective it began to change the way that people thought about the midfield in football as a whole and its influence on what formations teams played. Except their collective thinking was not about midfield players, shape or formations at all, at least, not in the first instance. It was about centre forwards and whether, in the modern game, there was, in fact, any room for them at all. Footballing heresy? Perhaps. The problem was, as ridiculous as picking a team that didn't contain any strikers sounded,[56] the reasons for doing so made, as far as some were concerned, complete sense. And that was ruthlessly regardless of all the glorious tradition, history and glamour that surround the number 9 and all the great and good purveyors of that position.

The centre forward is dead. Long live the trequisata?

---

56 *From 1-1-8 to 4-6-0 in a little under 150 years – have footballs formations been steadily going backwards in order for the game to move forwards?*

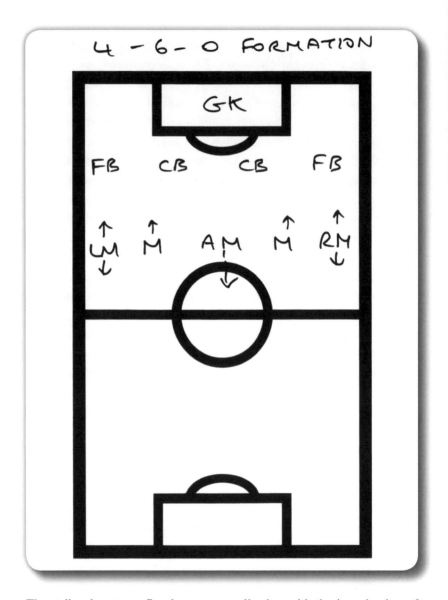

The striker-less team first became a realisation with the introduction of the 4-6-0 formation, the natural evolution of 4-2-3-1 which saw the last lonely striker exchanged for an advanced playmaker, someone with the ability to make goals as well as score them, a deadly hybrid of midfielder and striker. The position and responsibilities are not new ones, neither are the names of some of the players who have perfected the art. This includes some of the greatest names in the game's history: Hidegkuti, Cruyff, Maradona and Messi. And, whilst the implementation of 4-6-0 may still be relatively new, the concept most certainly isn't. As long ago as 2002, Carlos Alberto Parreira, the man who had led Brazil to victory in the 1994 World Cup (playing a 4-2-2-2 formation) caused shockwaves to reverberate around the room as, during a coaching conference he was taking part in, dared to suggest that the footballing formation of the future may well turn out to be one with no traditional striker but one that featured four midfielders with two lying deep just behind a line of four, the latter sited on the pitch in the same place as the middle four might have been in a 4-4-2. In other words, four right at the back, two just ahead of them and four across the middle. With no one in attack at all. Difficult to conceive but, as it turned out, difficult also for opposing teams to know quite how to react to it. With no central attackers, defenders suddenly have no one to mark. So what do they do? Stay back anyway and, in doing so, risk playing the opposition onside every time they attack or, in an effort to mark the front four players of that midfield six, leave space behind themselves for the opposition to take advantage of. It is, as the saying goes, a whole new ball game.

One of the first teams to adopt the tactic was Sir Alex Ferguson's Manchester United team during the 2007/08 season, one that not only saw them win the English Premier League title but also the Champions League where they defeated another English team, the London-based Chelsea in the final. For that game, Ferguson's team selection consisted of a traditional back four with two covering midfielders just ahead of them: Michael Carrick defensively minded with his partner, Paul Scholes, operating alongside him in the role of deep-lying playmaker. Then, ahead of them was a line of four players in the conventional central midfield positions, except, of course, three[57] of them – Cristiano Ronaldo, Carlos Tevez and Wayne Rooney – were, traditionally, anything but conventional midfield players.

It was a tactical masterstroke by Ferguson and worked perfectly, one that gave Ronaldo, Rooney and Tevez time and space in order to collect passes from (because they were playing so deep) the relatively protected Scholes or Carrick. Once in possession, they would push, ball at their feet, into the attacking third of the pitch. If, for example, Rooney was that man in possession, Ronaldo and Tevez would time their runs as to be just behind and on either side of him with, as already mentioned, the Chelsea defence uncertain as to whether they should sit back and let them advance onto their positions or push forward themselves, leaving, as they did, that all too vulnerable space behind them. In terms of entertainment value, 4-6-0 sounds a non-starter, a game plan based more on possession and numerical superiority in the key areas of the pitch above everything else. Yet, when it is played as it was with Manchester United in that game, it can be anything but tedious to watch.

That is, of course, unless you pick the formation with simply avoiding defeat in mind. Or, worse than that, almost accepting defeat pre-match but wanting to make sure the damage done to your side in the process is as light as possible.

This would have at the forefront of Scotland coach Craig Levein's mind when he selected his starting line-up for a European Championship qualifying game against the Czech Republic in Prague in 2010, an approach that led to his side 'only' losing 1-0 with the coach saying after the game that the result showed that his tactical plan had worked. This

---

57   *The fourth member of that illustrious quartet, Owen Hargreaves, played as a first line of defence, a 'destroyer' charged with breaking up any attacking play from Chelsea at the earliest possible opportunity.*

comment led *Daily Telegraph* correspondent Ewing Grahame to declare that if that was his conclusion after a game and Scotland performance that was '...so negative, the BBC should have shown it in black and white' then it was '...a sure case of the operation being a success but the patient dying.'[58] Levein justified his actions by pointing out that the teams his Scotland side were playing were so much stronger and more technically adept than his was that he really had no other choice than to take the safety first approach.[59] He further added that it was all very well wanting him to play offensive football in a 4-4-2 or 4-3-3 formation but that then the end result of that would be that his side would be more vulnerable and, as a result, concede lots of goals. And it is a fair point, even if the approach is hardly going to endear him, or any coach that has that approach, to either the media or the fans. What does he do in such a situation, attempt to appease the fans by picking an attacking line-up and going for the goals and a win from kick-off, and, in doing so, run the very real risk of suffering a heavy defeat? Or does he maximise his resources and look to stop the opposition from playing in the hope that they might get a point or even a win from a counterattack? If his job and livelihood is on the line, then it's going to be the latter every time.

4-6-0 clearly has an image problem. When modern-day football supporters are contemplating a match or their team's line-up, the most important number in their formation is the last one, the one that indicates how many attacking players the coach is fielding. Four, as in 4-2-4, is a seldomly seen treat, but it worked wonders for Brazil, signifying, as it did, two strikers and two old-fashioned wingers. A preferred shape today is that potentially risky 4-3-3. One striker with support on either side of him, fast, aggressive and with attacking intent; think of Manchester

---

58   *Daily Telegraph / Ewing Graham, October 10th 2010.*
59   *Levein was only repeating what the Scotland selection committee had done back in 1872 – adapting his side to cope with the opposition's strengths rather than trying to play in the same way and lose.*

City, for example, with Sergio Aguero leading the line with David Silva and Samir Nasri on either side of him in an attacking trio. It was an exciting prospect for Manchester City fans but a daunting one to both their opponents and their supporters. Even 4-4-2, for all of its supposed predictability, still presented the prospect of the attacking duo up front, one that always got the pulse racing, certainly in English football when, in the 1970s, 80s and 90s, it reigned supreme. And little wonder, considering some of the famous goalscoring partnerships that prevailed at that time. Mick Jones and Allan Clarke for Leeds United; Kevin Keegan and John Toshack for Liverpool; Ted MacDougall and Phil Boyer for Norwich City in the 1970s; Alan Sunderland and Frank Stapleton for Arsenal; Kenny Dalglish and Ian Rush for Liverpool and Brian McClair with Mark Hughes at Manchester United in the 1980s, footballing names that are so irrecoverably linked together that you can't think of one player in any of those teams without immediately recalling the other.

Not many people, for example, even in England, will be able to recall too many of the members of the Blackburn Rovers side that defied convention to win the Premier League title at the end of the 1994/95 season (Mark Atkins and Ian Pearce, anyone?), but most will remember their striking partnership that season, the 'SAS' of Shearer and Sutton; Alan Shearer and Chris Sutton who scored 49 league goals between them that campaign: over 60% of their total goals scored. No Shearer and Sutton? Then no Premier League title. Recent as that title success was, it still came at a time when the goalscoring responsibilities in a side were primarily those of the two strikers; there was no need or expectation for the goals to be shared around the squad. And that season was no different, after Shearer and Sutton, the next highest goalscorer in the Blackburn side that season was the aforementioned Mark Atkins, a midfielder, who scored just six.

No one at Blackburn would have been questioning 4-4-2 or calling it an outdated formation that season.

No one in Spain was complaining either when they won the 2008 European Championships with a team that, for four out of their six games played a 4-4-2 formation as well. Yet, by the time they added the 2012 European Championships to their run of tournament successes, they were playing 4-6-0 as well.

And therein is the great strength of 4-6-0 as a football formation, the reason why two teams with completely different objectives resorted to playing it. Scotland as a means of looking to avoid defeat and to be as difficult to break down as possible and Spain as a means of winning games and as creating as many chances as possible. The two game plans should be mutually exclusive, like a 4-2-4 and a 5-4-1. Yet they aren't. Because both Craig Levein and Vicente del Bosque both understood that the key to either avoiding defeat or winning was one and the same.

Winning possession. Because in the modern game, possession isn't just everything. It is the only thing.

Possession is god.

The Spanish side that won the 2012 European Championships were obsessed about keeping possession. So much, in fact, that, if they won a corner they would hardly ever use it as an opportunity to launch the ball, as convention has always dictated, into the opposition penalty area. Why? Because by doing that, there is a more than even chance they will lose possession. The result of taking a corner, unless it leads to a goal, is losing possession. For Spain that wasn't good enough; the risk involved was unacceptable. It's why, if they were in the attacking third of the pitch, their players would rather knock the ball back to the halfway line or even farther in order to retain possession, rather than chance losing it with an inaccurate shot or wayward pass. It's why Spain have often been accused of wanting to take too many touches, of wanting to walk the ball into the goal. Like corners, long shots are, again, opportunities of losing possession, just are shots from in and around the penalty area if there is a good chance an opposing defender will block the shot or the goalkeeper might have it covered. It's because they don't want to lose possession. For Spain, neither attack or defence is the best means of defence. Retaining possession is. It's one of the oldest coaching clichés there is, and they are not only playing it, they are living it. If you've got the ball, the other team can't score.

Which is why Craig Levein and Vicente del Bosque both valued 4-6-0 so much.

It works. Spain only conceded one goal throughout the 2012 European Championships. Six games played, one goal conceded. Trophy-winning form by any standards. They scored four without reply in one of the group games against the Republic of Ireland whose players spent almost all of the match chasing shadows. It was the same in the final, a game that saw them play without one recognised striker, where a frustrated and ragged Italian side, unable to impose their own slow and deliberate tempo onto a team that refused to give them sight of it, were passed into submission, losing 4-0. The normally peerless Pirlo was rendered impotent. For, as good as he undoubtedly is, if Pirlo can't get the ball, then he and his teammates are nothing more than passengers who, on this occasion, were the victims of a master class in possession football.

So, if 4-6-0 is so good, then why isn't everyone playing that system?

It's probably because, for now anyway, they're all busy playing 4-2-3-1 which, for many nations at the 2014 World Cup, was the formation of choice. It's one that first came to prominence in Spain in the 1990s from whence its influence grew to such an extent that, apart from both domestic and international teams throughout Europe using it (even in

England, the previously undisputed world champion of 4-4-2), it has also grown in popularity in the rest of the world with, at the 2014 World Cup in Brazil, nearly half the competing nations using it as their default formation. This included favourites Brazil and perennial underachievers England as well as, amongst others, Australia, Belgium, Croatia, Ghana and Switzerland. The Brazilian take on it featured defensive midfield duo Luiz Gustavo and Paulinho operating just behind a very offensively minded attacking trio of Neymar, Oscar and Hulk. It's a very appealing one. Strength and stability in Paulinho as well as flamboyance and skill to the extreme in the hugely talented Neymar. No wonder Brazil were favourites to win the trophy. They had, for them, a decent spine running throughout the team, one that consisted of Júlio César in goal; captain and £50 million man David Luiz in the centre of their defence; Paulinho providing the midfield steel and support; with, in attack, Neymar and, playing as the lone striker, the enigmatic Fred, the top scorer at the previous year's FIFA Confederations Cup.

They looked as good as the formation suggests it can be, one that marries that defensive stability with a lot of attacking options. And not only from the striker but the playmaker operating just behind him as well as the two wider players operating just to each side of him who would, for all intents and purposes, be playing as old-fashioned wingers. So not that far removed from the much loved 4-2-4 in many ways.

As with 4-6-0, the great strength of 4-2-3-1 as far as coaches are concerned is that it gives their sides the chance to impose themselves on the midfield, that most vital part of the pitch in today's game. In addition to that, the fact that it also gives sides the opportunity to play as many as four advanced players also means it has great attacking flexibility. Thus, also like 4-6-0, it is deceptive. 4-6-0 naturally looks very negative and can be exactly what necessity demands of it. Remember Levein and his 'don't lose at all costs' Scotland side in the Czech Republic?

But that is exactly why it and 4-2-3-1 are so favoured today, because of that enormous flexibility and the ability it gives sides to dominate the midfield. Dominate and dictating their terms, either from a defensive (Scotland) or offensive (Spain) plan.

Coaches and managers will, over and over again, talk about how flexible they want players to be, championing new signings to the hilt for being able to 'play in several positions'. The phrase for players with the ability to do this in football was almost as negative in its connotations as 4-6-0 and 4-2-3-1 appear to be, he was known as the 'utility' player. Useful, even decent in a number of positions across the pitch, but hardly a class act individually and not someone who would merit his place in the side every week, unless there were a lot of injuries or suspensions. He is the perfect player to have on the bench as he could slot in anywhere across the back four or midfield, even, at a push, in attack. Ideal for a 4-4-2 certainly, and every club had a player or two that fitted that description. Changes in tactics and formations now mean that the utility player is seen as a lot more valuable a commodity than he has ever been. Take Phil Jones at Manchester United, for example. A £17 million signing in 2011, his value determined not so much by what he had already achieved in the game (just 35 league appearances for Blackburn prior to his being signed) but for what he could do for his new club and the variety of positions he could play. This is something recognised by the English FA who, on their website, champion Jones as '...a combative and adaptable player who can play at centre-half, right-back or in central midfield', going on to say that he is tipped by some as a 'future England Captain'.[60] The once maligned utility player, clearly, has come a long way in recent years, thanks primarily to the demands of a modern game which expects its players to be as flexible as the formations they are part of.

---

60   *www.theFA.com*

Is football now really all about possession and the players who practice that art to the limits? Arrigo Sacchi, that doyen of 4-4-2 in the 1990s thinks so, even if he sees the current trend for 4-2-3-1 as something which panders to the egos of the three attacking players benefitting favourably from the two midfield holders behind them. He sees that formation as an excuse for the attacking trip to be relinquished from their duties elsewhere on the pitch, regarding those teammates as minders charged with doing a job that should be the responsibility of the whole team. He is an advocate of Total Football, or, if not that, at least a team where the players can all perform more than one role, for instance, a centre forward who can also play as an attacking midfielder or a winger who can slot into a central attacking role. Wayne Rooney has already proved his worth at Manchester United in that aspect. He is a player who was long seen as the typical centre forward. Strong, physical and uncompromising, a player who existed to feed off the chances created for him by his teammates and score goals, period. Not so, according to Louis van Gaal who has championed Rooney as a multifunctional player capable of playing in more than just the one role. Interviewed by *The Guardian* newspaper, Van Gaal said, 'Not so many players can easily switch positions but Rooney can, he is multi-functional. He does not like switching positions within a game; I moved him from midfield to striker once and he was not so good, but he can definitely play in more than one position. I have come across such exceptional players before. Edgar Davids was an extreme left-winger and I made him a midfielder. Michael Reiziger was a No.10 who became a full-back and Frank Rijkaard was a No.6 who played as a centre-half in my winning team at Ajax. I always look at the qualities of the player and decide where he can perform better for himself.'

This is, should you have forgotten, coming from a coach who received a lot of criticism from the Manchester United spectators for 'daring' to continue with his perceived experimentation 3-5-2 onto their team in January 2015. Fans who, during Manchester United's game at QPR repeatedly chanted for the return of the 4-4-2 formation, even though their side won comfortably and displayed more than enough attacking intent with players like Mata, Rooney, Di Maria and Falcao all starting. Feasible in a 5-3-2 but not so much of an option in a 4-4-2 when any two of the aforementioned quartet would have to play in midfield, something which would put a lot of pressure on the other two midfielders to act as both cover for their more adventurous teammates as well as for their own defence. That occurs at great risk to that all important value that rides above all else in modern football, that of having and retaining possession, something which can only be truly mastered if every player in the team is comfortable on the ball and in any part of the pitch.

So yes, Planet Football in the year 2015 is, increasingly, all about possession as these midfield-rich (both in terms of numbers and the players' technical abilities) modern formations illustrate. But those formations need adaptable and flexible players in order to be able to work. Why else would Louis van Gaal want to play Wayne Rooney in midfield? He has been one of the great traditional centre forwards in the game for over a decade, his performances for England in the 2004 European Championships, where he scored four goals, showcasing him as an extraordinary goalscoring talent, a player who might well have gone on to be one of the greatest in the world. And he may well have done. Sadly for English football, he has not. But why is this, why has he underachieved? The answer is a simple one, but it is, nonetheless, telling. He is not versatile enough as a player to be considered of such an accolade.

That is not a criticism of Rooney in any way. His game and potential has been stifled by the limitations of the formation that he has, for much of his career, played in. And that's as one of the two central strikers in a strict 4-4-2 line-up, the one which, more than any other, limits players by pigeonholing them into one role, one position and one duty; formations by numbers. In 4-4-2 no one can hear you dream; if you are right-sided midfielder then a right-sided midfielder you will forever be and, ridiculous as it sounds, one of the consequences of that will be players who can't even kick with their left feet, something which leads pundits and their fellow pros to inevitably pass comments along the lines of '...he only uses it for standing on.' Shouldn't we find it unusual that an international footballer playing in the Champions League and for his country is so fundamentally flawed in technique that he is not even able to kick the ball proficiently with his left foot?

Apparently not.

When Neymar was just 13, he was given special coaching focused almost exclusively on making him learn to kick and control the ball with his left foot as well as he could with his right. Yet, at those aforementioned 2004 European Championships, England were forced to play the right-sided Paul Scholes on the left of the England midfield four as the nation which boasts the most cash-rich, watched and prestigious domestic league on the planet didn't have a naturally sided left-footed player good enough to slot into that position.

The modern game demands slightly more versatility than merely having left-footed players good enough to play for your national team. Total versatility is seen as an increasingly important quality with players not only asked, but expected to play in different positions in differing formations constantly, sometimes on a match-by-match basis. The concept of Total Football, as first practiced by the Hungarians in the 1950s, something which was briefly and gloriously resurrected by the Dutch in the 1970s has now been supplanted by the concept of the total player. This is one who is able to master more than one role and position on the pitch and who could, if required, more than competently play in the position of left back one week and advanced playmaker the next. A fanciful notion? Not really. Remember, John Charles was good enough to play for Juventus as either a centre half or a centre forward. He was one of the game's early pioneers in that instance, a prototype 'total footballer', one described by Harry Redknapp as '...always the best in the penalty area, and at either end. There wasn't a better player in the team to defend a corner, and not a better player to attack one either. Yet he went to Italy, where the game was more technical and tactical and fitted straight in.'[61]

John Charles (far right) during the group stage match against Mexico during the 1958 World Cup

In *Pep Confidential*, his compelling story about his first season with Bayern Munich, Pep Guardiola states how, in an ideal footballing world, he would build up a squad of players for any team that he coached. He would want no more than 20 in his first team squad – a welcome change in these days where some squads are 50-plus strong in terms of player

---

61   Redknapp, Harry. 2014. A Man Walks Onto a Pitch. *Ebury.*

numbers. Each of those players would be able to fulfil two or three different positions on the pitch each; in other words, it wouldn't just be one player like Charles who 'fitted straight in', it would be every one of them. And with players able to fit into any role, the football formation, as we have known it for the last 150 years or so will become a relic, surpassed and even improved on by players who can fit into any role at any time with the freedom to do just that.

Football's future will be formation-less. Even the modern team shapes, the aforementioned 4-6-0 and 4-2-3-1 formations are debatable as far as their matching a precise shape is concerned as the movement of the players in both is so flexible. As the former Croatian coach Slaven Bilic has already stated, 'Systems are dying. It's about the movement of 10 players now.' And he's right. Football is moving on. Again. Just as it always has and always will, led, unquestionably by a small band of visionary coaches, men like Jack Hunter, Jimmy Hogan, Vittorio Pozzo, Hugo Meisl and Gustavo Sebes.

Plus Pep Guardiola and Slaven Bilic.

But what about the land that claims it gave football to the world?

As far as English players and the England team are concerned, former Liverpool, Real Madrid and England striker Michael Owen thinks there is little to no chance of English football surrendering its long-held belief in structure, shape and discipline for something resembling football's shapeless new world. And for the simple reason that he is convinced that English clubs and players can't and will never be able to do so. And he's probably right. The onus on young English players, right from the age that clubs first start to sign them (and that can be as young as 8 upwards) is for them to be strong, muscular and athletic with enough stamina to chase around the pitch for 90 minutes.

Take a look, if you get the chance, at any game in England featuring young players and listen to the demands of both coaches and, all too often, watching parents. Cries of 'get rid of it' and 'get it forward' run rife as the players are not so much encouraged as ordered to get rid of the ball almost as soon as they get it in the first place. Slowing the game down, putting their foot on the ball, passing it around in the sort of little intricate triangles that Barcelona practice is unheard of and would, in all likelihood, lead to accusations that they weren't 'up for it' and that their 'commitment' was lacking.

What chance have the national team in England got if the nation's youth are being encouraged to play a game that doesn't look that much different to the mob football they might have been playing a couple of centuries earlier?

Football may well be changing. It's a pity that mentalities sometimes do not.

———————————

ACKNOWLEDGEMENTS

It has been both a pleasure and a privilege to write this book, one that has seen me discover so much more about the game and some of the very early coaching and tactical visionaries from its most formative days.

I hope that I have done the men, players and teams that have helped contribute so much to the game some justice. This book is not, and was never intended to be, a formal or definitive work on the subject and the game's history; it is intended as a reverential nod of respect to those discussed, and if, in doing so, it invites the reader to delve deeper and find out more about some of the coaches, players and teams mentioned, I will be delighted.

My thanks and gratitude for all of their help and support throughout must go to Manuel Morschel of Meyer and Meyer Sport and to my editor and good friend, David Lane.

Thanks also to Jonathan Wilson, author of the wonderful exploration of football formations *Inverting The Pyramid (Orion, 2008)* and to Simon Briggs for his informative and highly entertaining account of the English national side's travails in *Don't Mention The Score (Quercus, 2008)*.

Both titles come very highly recommended.

Finally, my thanks to those close friends who have always been willing to lend a hand and support me with my work – opinions, support and feedback always there and always welcomed from Russell Saunders, Jeremy Goss, Mick Dennis, Nigel Nudds, Paul McVeigh, Rob Butler, Chris Goreham, Chris Rushby and all at Jarrold Books, and Paul King.

And to my wife Sarah for putting up with me, my writing and my ridiculous obsession with football.

Edward Couzens-Lake

CREDITS

Cover:	Martin Herrmann
Copyediting:	Elizabeth Evans
Layout and typesetting:	Andreas Reuel

PHOTO CREDITS

Cover: upper left & bottom right; ©picture-alliance/dpa
upper right & bottom left; ©Edward Couzens-Lake

Inside: ©Wikipedia CC BY-SA 4.0; p. 32, 42, 45, 58, 63, 77, 89, 96, 100
©picture-alliance/dpa; p. 83, 84, 129, 132, 134, 167, 173, 185, 198, 201, 228, 246, 247, 249, 254, 267, 275, 276, 298
©imago-sportfotodienst; p. 63, 100, 143, 229, 264

Graphics: ©Thinkstock/iStock/pjirawat; p. 20, 22, 97, 115, 177, 183, 223, 239, 241, 263, 270, 283, 286

Chapter lead-in: ©Thinkstock/iStock/JeepPhoto; p. 6, 14, 24, 56, 74, 102, 128, 172, 222, 244, 262, 302

Author photo: ©Sarah Povey